Web Menus with Beauty and Brains

Web Menus with Beauty and Brains

Wendy Peck

Hungry Minds™

Best-Selling Books • Digital Downloads • e-Books • Answer Networks • e-Newsletters • Branded Web Sites • e-Learning

New York, NY ✦ Cleveland, OH ✦ Indianapolis, IN

Web Menus with Beauty and Brains

Published by
Hungry Minds, Inc.
909 Third Avenue
New York, NY 10022
www.hungryminds.com

Library of Congress Control Number: 2001092920

ISBN: 0-7645-3643-5

Printed in the United States of America

10 9 8 7 6 5 4 3 2 1

1O/TQ/RR/QR/IN

Distributed in the United States by Hungry Minds, Inc.

Distributed by CDG Books Canada Inc. for Canada; by Transworld Publishers Limited in the United Kingdom; by IDG Norge Books for Norway; by IDG Sweden Books for Sweden; by IDG Books Australia Publishing Corporation Pty. Ltd. for Australia and New Zealand; by TransQuest Publishers Pte Ltd. for Singapore, Malaysia, Thailand, Indonesia, and Hong Kong; by Gotop Information Inc. for Taiwan; by ICG Muse, Inc. for Japan; by Intersoft for South Africa; by Eyrolles for France; by International Thomson Publishing for Germany, Austria, and Switzerland; by Distribuidora Cuspide for Argentina; by LR International for Brazil; by Galileo Libros for Chile; by Ediciones ZETA S.C.R. Ltda. for Peru; by WS Computer Publishing Corporation, Inc., for the Philippines; by Contemporanea de Ediciones for Venezuela; by Express Computer Distributors for the Caribbean and West Indies; by Micronesia Media Distributor, Inc. for Micronesia; by Chips Computadoras S.A. de C.V. for Mexico; by Editorial Norma de Panama S.A. for Panama; by American Bookshops for Finland.

For general information on Hungry Minds' products and services please contact our Customer Care department within the U.S. at 800-762-2974, outside the U.S. at 317-572-3993 or fax 317-572-4002.

For sales inquiries and reseller information, including discounts, premium and bulk quantity sales, and foreign-language translations, please contact our Customer Care department at 800-434-3422, fax 317-572-4002 or write to Hungry Minds, Inc., Attn: Customer Care Department, 10475 Crosspoint Boulevard, Indianapolis, IN 46256.

For information on licensing foreign or domestic rights, please contact our Sub-Rights Customer Care department at 212-884-5000.

For information on using Hungry Minds' products and services in the classroom or for ordering examination copies, please contact our Educational Sales department at 800-434-2086 or fax 317-572-4005.

For press review copies, author interviews, or other publicity information, please contact our Public Relations department at 317-572-3168 or fax 317-572-4168.

For authorization to photocopy items for corporate, personal, or educational use, please contact Copyright Clearance Center, 222 Rosewood Drive, Danvers, MA 01923, or fax 978-750-4470.

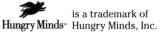 is a trademark of Hungry Minds, Inc.

About the Author

Wendy Peck is the author of *Dreamweaver 4 Weekend Crash Course*, a professional Web designer, and a columnist for Webreference.com. She has been in the commercial graphic design business since 1989, moving from print to the Web in 1998. She has been in business in one way or another since she was 15 years old and started teaching adult classes when she was 18. In addition to her design business, she is also a professional trainer for business and marketing, graphics, desktop publishing, and communication.

Credits

Acquisitions Editor
Michael Roney

Project Editor
Katharine Dvorak

Technical Editor
Kyle Bowen

Copy Editor
Jerelind Charles

Editorial Manager
Rev Mengle

**Senior Vice President,
Technical Publishing**
Richard Swadley

Publishing Director
Barry Pruett

Project Coordinator
Dale White

Graphics and Production Specialists
Beth Brooks, Sean Decker, Jill Piscitelli

Quality Control Technician
Charles Spencer

Senior Permissions Editor
Carmen Krikorian

Media Development Specialist
Angela Denny

Cover Design
Michael Trent

Proofreading and Indexing
Vickie Broyles,
TECHBOOKS Production Services

Cover Image
©FPG/Getty Images

This book is dedicated to my mom, Isabel MacLean.

I fought valiantly, but you persevered and forced me to speak and write correctly . . . no doubt, the best battle I could ever lose.

Preface

*M*enu, *interface, site architecture, navigation* are confusing terms that are constantly floating through the Web design world. You can find many excellent books that describe site goals, user preferences, and how to keep visitors clicking through your Web pages. But when you close these books, you may have more understanding, but you still may not be certain where to start. This book can help you make the leap so that you can get started — the interface book with instructions.

I admire much that has been published about interface design, but I have often felt that one step was missing — taking the theory to the computer to create an effective menu system. This book is designed to fill in that missing piece and to not only give you the tools to plan effective navigation for your visitors, but also to move to the construction phase and complete the graphics and code for your menus.

I have been a professional graphics designer for over ten years and a Web designer for nearly five. The common thread that I have faced through all of the design work I have done, whether for print, video, or for the Web, has been quite simply, communication. No product of any type is effective unless you can reach your reader, watcher, or visitor in a way that that he or she can understand easily. Language style, layout, color, and graphic presentation are important, but on the Web, the primary concern is how your visitor will navigate the site. In print, readers can refer to a table of contents and an index to help. For video, the person watching most likely knows how to move the video forward or back and how to make it play and stop. The Web, however, is a completely new challenge.

When you design a Web site, you must guide visitors to the information that they seek without asking for much thought from them. Often a person reading a book does not have several other books waiting if he or she cannot find the information he seeks immediately. A Web site visitor, however, does have many other choices. If you cannot lead the visitor on a smooth path to the "meat" of your site with a few easy mouse clicks, he or she will try elsewhere.

The good news is that designing your site to accommodate the needs of your visitors is relatively easy when you plan well and use the right tools. More good news is that the planning is really quite simple, mostly common sense, and the tools are probably already in your toolbox. In this book, I take you through the planning process in steps and provide exercises that help you to determine your site goals and visitor needs. Perhaps designing an effective menu system to match your site's "mood" is where you need help. I delve into the various types of menus you can use and give you the tools to choose the most appropriate style. I also provide step-by-step instructions to build many different menus.

No matter whether you use Adobe Photoshop, Macromedia Fireworks, or JASC Paint Shop Pro as your graphics program or Macromedia Dreamweaver, Adobe GoLive, or hand coding to produce your code, specific instructions are covered in this book . But what about Flash? Yes, I have included a special section on Macromedia Flash, because most graphic or coding techniques do not apply to Flash.

I planned to accomplish one more goal with this book — taking the mystery out of *interface* and *navigation*. Although theory is wonderful, and some sites require full teams to design an appropriate architecture, most Web sites require nothing more sophisticated than a well-thought-out menu. That is what this book is about. I do not attempt to bring you to the Zen mountaintop of interface design. My role with the following chapters is to teach you how to create a menu so that your visitors can find their way easily through your site, period. A simple task that involves a lot of work. So roll up those sleeves — with this book you get a little dirty.

Acknowledgments

What a project! What a team! Michael Roney, my acquisitions editor, is the one person most responsible for my move from prolific article writer to book author. As always, thanks, and sorry to make you work so hard on the schedule.

Katharine Dvorak was my project editor and one of the most professional, understanding people that I have ever worked with. Thank you so much, Katie. I was running too fast to spend the time to let you know how glad I was to have you leading this project. That doesn't mean I didn't think it often. Kyle Bowen, my technical editor, made sure that I didn't transpose steps three and five, and only told the technological truth. Thanks Kyle. And thank you to Jerelind Charles, my copy editor, who made sure that every last word was perfect before we put our pencils down.

As always, family comes in front and center when I work on any major project. My kids, Shawnda, Danille, and Brian have mastered the perfect balance between being my best supporters and making sure that I don't get the idea that I have become anything more than just plain "Mom." My sisters, Debbie and Heather MacLean, always contribute. This time Heather spread four gallons of paint on my house when I seemed to have time for nothing but typing. Debbie continued her decades-old role as "you can do it" cheerleader. My mom, Isabel MacLean, is the world's best resource for obscure grammar and has always been an evangelist for correct word use. I didn't appreciate the constant training when I was growing up, but I am certainly thankful today.

Where would I be without my friends? Val, Elsie, and Marion have been there through countless projects, always waiting with a calm voice when they pick up the phone to me wailing, "I'm in trouble . . . again." Rob, you make my life wonderful in so many ways.

I will write another book. Without the rich support I have, personally and professionally, I doubt that I could say that with total confidence. I am a lucky woman.

Contents at a Glance

Contents

Chapter 17: Preparing Graphics for Slicing and Rollovers 205

Chapter 18: Optimizing and Slicing Graphics for Menus 215

Chapter 19: Creating Tables that Stay Put in Any Browser 233

PART IV: Lights, Camera, Action!
Time to Create the Show   273

Putting the Brains into Menu-Based Interfaces

What Is a Menu?

So, what exactly is a menu? You may think that a menu is a few buttons placed across the top or down the left side of a Web page. You aren't wrong with that definition, but we are going to step through a much deeper description of menus in this chapter. To understand how to create a great menu system for your site, first you must understand exactly what I mean when I say *menu*, and learn to view a Web page in a new way — as a functional whole.

In this chapter, I define menu terms that are used throughout this book, and show you several examples of effective menus. I also risk ruining your surfing forevermore, as I show you how to look at every Web site as a learning experience.

The Big Picture

Without a menu, you do not have a Web site. You may have a Web page, but visitors are stopped dead in their tracks without a menu. Some designers err by creating beautiful pages and adding the menu items as a necessary evil. Other designers focus so hard on the menu areas of the page, that they neglect to offer content that is easy to use. Both errors can destroy the success of a site.

This book is about menus, but I am going to wander to a slightly wider topic for this section. In order to truly understand a menu's role, I first want to make sure that you understand where they fit into the total package for an effective Web site.

Web design is not like any other type of design. In no other medium do you have as much to juggle to produce a quality product. You want to create attractive pages, but you also have to make sure visitors can get from one page to another. You must make sure that your page displays well on many different monitors and computers and is one that search engines can find. One Web page is a small part of a much larger network of pages. In order to create a successful site, you must understand all of the layers of that network, from your page, to your site, to the Web.

Even a good page must be found

Imagine you are surfing the Web. You are looking for more information about a news story or product that you have curiosity about. The first step for most people is to enter a keyword or two into a search engine and then choose the page that looks most promising—a simple process for anyone who has been on the Web for a while.

But what is your guide to which page offers the best chance for success? I use two clues. The first, of course, is the title and description that appears with the listing, and the second is the actual address of the site. This is the first step in understanding the big picture. You must be aware of how your listings will appear in the search engines, and design your site to deliver information that your most promising visitors will find.

Tip   You can find volumes of information on the Web about submitting your Web pages to search engines, such as www.spider-food.net, which is an excellent starting point.

What do the search engines have to do with design? A page must be designed so that the engines can find it. Although you can market your page in other ways, the search engines are still vitally important for attracting traffic. Having said all that, do not get completely focused on designing your site for search engines. Getting the visitors to your page is important, but if you have nothing to offer them after they arrive, the success is wasted. Keep in mind that you first have to have a great site and then bring people to it. Understanding how search engines work helps you to make choices that work for both content and attracting visitors.

Content truly is king

Menus are important, but the best menu system won't disguise fluff for content. I am sure you have been to sites that look great and seem to offer great promise, but after several minutes of clicking, you realize that nothing is there.

Web surfers are fussy creatures. Consumers may accept no nutritional value in fast food, or pay outrageous prices for things they do not need because they are convinced that these objects will make their lives better, but let the same people move to the Web, and they want value. Free is best, but at the very least, you must deliver value, because they *are* checking. People are naturally more suspicious of the Web than they are of retail, or even mail order sales. You are playing to a tough crowd on the Web.

With this book you learn to make menus that guide your visitors instinctively to the content of your site, but make sure that you are leading them to something of value—products, information, entertainment, you name it—or your site won't succeed. Many sites fail to deliver quality to visitors, not because they have nothing to offer, but because they have not stopped and truly analyzed whether they are attracting the right customers for their products. The Web is huge, and the potential to attract thousands of the wrong people to your site is very real. However, with planning and direction, you can also find thousands, perhaps even millions of customers who are truly seeking your product. That's success!

Cross-Reference Chapter 2 and Chapter 3 help you to determine what your visitor is looking for and where your products fit into those needs.

"Web" and "art" are not interchangeable words

You may notice a very hard-line approach to Web design in this book. I do not believe that most sites on the Web are an "artistic" product. The best Web site designers work their artistic hearts out to create effective pages, and while each designer has a distinctive style, and the results are often beautiful, a Web site is not an artistic expression from them. Web designers are doing a job—finding the best way to put people and products together. On weekends and evenings, many of these designers may don a smock and open the paints, pick up the charcoal, or fire up the pottery wheel to express their inner art, but the good ones leave that personal desire behind when they are creating Web pages.

Note I can hear a few of you saying, "But I am not selling anything, so this premise does not apply." Not true. Every page on the Web sells something, whether it is information about the high school reunion, or diamond rings. Again, Chapters 2 and 3 help you to step through the process to determine your product and visitor's needs.

Web design has been through a "look at what I can do" phase on the Web. I am quite relieved, personally, that this phase is grinding to a halt. My connection speed is usually 24K, not because I am uninformed or lacking in any way, but because I live in a rural area of Canada. Although Canada has a solid reputation for developing excellent telecommunications structure, the best connections are not always available here. I have been locked out of many sites where designers, whom I must assume are testing pages with fast connections, have paid no attention to page size. Trust me, I am not the only one. Millions of people in North America are still surfing the Web with modem connections. Did you know that many people in the world pay for every minute of surfing time? Local telephone is not free worldwide.

Download time counts. Easy navigation counts. Content that is delivered quickly and simply counts. If you can deliver these features, and still make a page look good, perhaps even exciting, then you can call yourself a successful Web designer.

Using the whole Web

This book is about creating great menus. But menus do not come from thin air. Excellent navigation is the result of gathering great amounts of relevant information and considering every aspect of site goals and visitor expectation. It can be said that a menu is the public presentation of how well you have done your homework and is a wonderful measure of your planning focus. The rewards for keeping your focus where it counts are great. You must look beyond your site boundaries, however, to find the full potential for your site. If you have a site that delivers directed content to your visitors and moves them through your site with effective menus, your popularity can soar. Although the search engines are important traffic generators, links to other sites are extremely important and can help to increase your search engine placement. The number of links to your site is one of the criteria a search engine spider seeks.

The power of the larger network should not be underestimated as you plan and build your site. When you ponder whether to expand your site goals to include another area, consider whether that area is already well-supported by another site and consider working out a reciprocal link, or even an affiliate or true partnership arrangement with the owner of the desired site.

Caution   While the number of links or partnerships you form may be important, always keep your site goals in mind when you are building your network. Sharing a related site with your visitors can help to build goodwill and turn your customers into regular visitors — the ones you want. Placing unrelated links or partnerships on your site can lead to confusion for the visitor and undermine your careful strategy work.

Exploiting the network nature of the Web can help to increase your earnings for a commercial site or help to offset your hosting costs for a personal site. Featuring affiliate links to products that are interesting to your readers can net surprising results. Links to books and music sites are the links most surfers today recognize, but many specialized opportunities are available, too. Imagine that you create a site featuring home maintenance tips and add affiliate links for either specific tools or to a respected tool supplier. Always watch for the opportunities.

You can profit in the opposite direction as well. If you are selling a product, would other sites be willing to feature an affiliate link as a compliment to their products or information? Affiliate tracking scripts are not complicated and can be free or purchased for a reasonable fee.

Spend some time thinking through the full potential of your site during the planning process. You may not have a need for affiliate links or advertisements now, but you may if your traffic increases. I always ask clients if ads are a possibility now or in the future and try to work an ad spot into the design. An affiliate area on key pages also should be reserved from the beginning of the design process. Planning your pages, especially for basic layout or menus, is easy in the beginning, and gets much harder as each step progresses.

Although you will design your site one page at a time, keeping the site picture, your direct network picture, and the full extent of the Web in mind as you plan your goals and page look is important.

Identifying and Building a Great Site

Theory is wonderful, but what makes a great site? Here I take you on a trip through several Web sites that I admire for one reason or another. I have a certain style, and my likes and dislikes play a part in the sites I select for any discussion. That does not mean a site must look like the ones I choose to be good sites. The look can be totally different, yet the navigation and site goals can be exceptional. Pay attention not so much to the site I have chosen, but what my justification is for deeming it to be a great site or having great features. There are times when I think a menu is brilliant, but other areas of the site may have problems.

Yahoo!

I am going to start with one of the most successful and best known Web sites in existence: Yahoo! (www.yahoo.com). Although Yahoo! is not often associated with great design, the site is well worth study because it does so much so well.

Yahoo! is fast — screaming fast, even on my horse-and-carriage connection. The entire entry page, complete with images, is less than 50K. And what do you get for that 50K? In the top 150 pixels (approximate), you can search the Web, check your e-mail, start a chat session, create or check a personal calendar, create customized options, get help, and book a vacation. In the remaining entry screen, even with only an 800 x 600 pixel display, you have nearly 80 choices for products or information. I don't have the patience to count the links on the rest of the page.

Yahoo! may not be the prettiest site on the Web, but few sites can claim to be in the same league for efficiently moving millions of people to their goals. Study this site! I have never created a site that looks anything like Yahoo!, but I have certainly used it many times for ideas when I was setting the structure for content-heavy sites.

Elle

The next example is far away from the Yahoo! look, but also does what it does very well. *Elle* is a women's fashion magazine, and www.elle.com is its associated Web site that presents clean, easy to navigate pages, with no doubt of the fashion personality on any page.

An amazing amount of information is tucked behind this site's simple menus. *Elle* has used a different method than Yahoo! for moving people through the site. The designer has added one more click for the visitor — you must first choose the major category you want to pursue before you get the menu for that section. Although you always want to reduce the number of clicks required for your visitors to reach their final destination, breaking a site into major sections is an effective way to keep a site simple and allow more freedom with graphics and images to secure the correct mood.

Elle captures the high fashion mood exceptionally well in this site, working with top-quality photos and unusual text color. It often does not take much to create the right feeling. The final product page is a highly versatile layout, allowing many different products and additions to the pages.

Kinkos

With the next site, we move into the business services world, and the Kinkos Web site does it well (www.kinkos.com). I like the mood that is presented by combining a very corporate and conservative framework in the menus of the Kinkos site and a more energetic mood with the images. This combination is excellent for a company that offers business products on demand and is known for quick delivery.

Belladonna Design

I have seen some sparse sites in my travels around the Web, and I was quite proud of my tiny four page site (http://wpeck.com). But my site is bloated compared to Belladonna Designs (www.belladonnadesign.com). Okay, so maybe small is not always good, but this site says everything it has to say. The entry page is shown in Figure 1-1, and while many designer sites have a splash page, few carry the menu as you can see here. There is no doubt that the mood for this site is artistic.

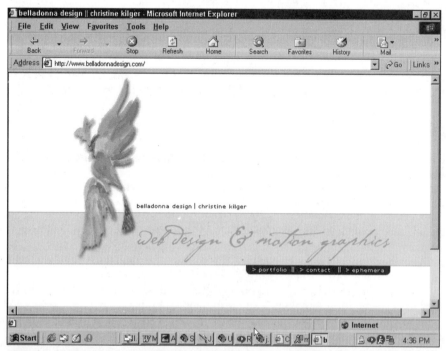

Figure 1-1: The Belladonnadesigns.com entry page, complete with the full menu for the site

The real magic in the site comes after you click through to the portfolio (if you want homework, visit the sites in the portfolio where terrific designs are featured) and then click to the contact, where you realize that the site has given the information that many clients need to contact the company. (See Figure 1-2.) The only other page in the site features the designer's recommended books.

I wanted to feature a designer's site in this section of the book. But as I wandered through the maze of sites, I was beginning to wonder if I would come up with one that struck me as excellent design, did not force me to wait several minutes for a Macromedia Flash presentation, and didn't do anything else to annoy me. Belladonnadesign.com is like a breath of fresh air. I wonder if clients feel the same? You may find a message in my experience for your site.

The rest is up to you

No designers in any medium have had more opportunity to study excellent examples of their craft than Web designers. I try to do some casual surfing at least once a week and always pay attention to the site layout and navigation, even when I am shopping for information or a product. I will admit that most pages you do visit are not worth noting, but each session usually produces at least one or two notable sites. If something on a page grabs my attention or if the overall appearance is remarkable in any way, I have learned to stop and observe what or why I wanted to pay closer attention.

Figure 1-2: The portfolio page for belladonnadesigns.com. This page is the heart of the site.

This type of learning is priceless. You are learning continually, and your design level increases automatically. You also keep abreast of new trends and can watch what is falling away. The Web may be a practical place, but trends do appear. Constant observation, combined with always watching industry news is enough to keep you at the forefront of the Web. Don't forget that your skills should grow weekly, too. You cannot afford to rest on your laurels for even a month.

A Menu Is Not a Table of Contents

The first instinct for a new designer is often to think of a menu as a table of contents or an index. But the comparison to book or magazine terminology does not hold. (See Figure 1-3.) If you are reading a paper copy of any kind, you always return to the index or table of contents to find the next place you want to go. Web sites should not work in that way. An ideally constructed site has routes from everywhere to everywhere else, usually by dividing the site into major categories, such as many of the previous samples did.

When a book or magazine is created, the table of contents or index is usually created at the end of the project. In Web design, your menu system should be set before the site is started. I always create a site map (see Chapter 5) before the menu is developed, because the structure of the site determines many of the menu characteristics.

The comparison between print publication and Web sites breaks down further after you consider the way each medium is used. With a magazine or book, it is conceivable that a reader can read every word of content without seeing the table of contents or index. He or she can physically turn the pages and "discover" what is on the next page. Web sites cannot be navigated in that way. Without a menu system, your visitors are stopped dead in their tracks. The only option open would be to try to guess the name of pages that are part of the site, which of course would be an impossible task.

So, while you have similarities to finding your way in a book or a Web site, if you need a comparison, thinking of the structure of a Web site more along the lines of architecture, as in a house or office building, is better. You of course have an entry, but beyond the entry, you can choose many routes to connect rooms or areas of the house. You probably have no reason to make sure that the mudroom of a house is attached to the master bedroom, but you may have very good reasons to ensure that the mud and laundry rooms are connected. This architectural plan is a much more accurate model than using a print publication as you plan your Web site.

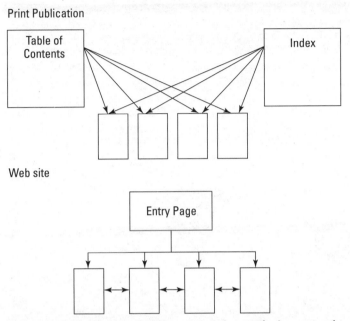

Figure 1-3: The flow from menu to page in a Web site cannot be compared to the table of contents and index in relation to pages in a print publication.

Defining Menu Types

Any book-length discussion about a subject requires a definition of terms. The following sections discuss the terms I define in order to discuss navigation with clients. As far as I know, we have no standard for defining menu terms yet (heck, we aren't even close to standardized browsers).

Note   All samples in the following sections are taken from the W. Atlee Burpee Company site (www.burpee.com). I recommend that you visit the site to see how the navigation that you see in this section works. This site is one of my favorite sample sites for excellent navigation. Figure 1-4 features a secondary page on the Burpee site.

Figure 1-4: Burpee.com's full-page view

Housekeeping menus

Housekeeping menus refers to the business end of a site, such as contact pages, company information, shopping cart, wish lists, FAQs, and other help pages. These menus almost always appear on every page and should be an integral part of the site design. For many sites, housekeeping menus can be kept quite low-key, but available when the visitor looks for them. On some sites, housekeeping items are a critical element of the site and contain many menu items. Commerce sites featuring high-ticket products must provide exceptional company information to build the visitor confidence level. Housekeeping menus should be highly visible for this type of site. On the Burpee site, housekeeping menus appear in the top right corner of every page and are highlighted in Figure 1-5.

Figure 1-5: The two housekeeping menus shown here appear near the top of every page on the Burpee Web site.

Category menus

Category menus comprise the main division for most sites. Perhaps the site is divided by product type, such as babies, toddlers, and teens, or by interest group, such as teachers, students, and parents for an educational site. This type of menu directs visitors into their focus area as quickly as possible, but should not contain too many choices. I try to work with a maximum of six or seven categories, but prefer not to exceed four or five. Designing an attractive layout is easier if you have fewer category menu items, and I believe that it is easier for the visitor as well. Note how clear the Burpee main menu is, as shown in Figure 1-6. If the category menu is placed vertically, I also want the full menu "above the fold," or completely on the initial screen.

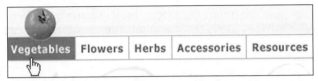

Figure 1-6: The main menu, or category menu, is large and clear, while marking where the visitor is in the site with images above the menu items. This marking image also provides the mouseover action.

Sub-category menus

If you cannot take your visitor to the end goal in two clicks, the second level should provide its own menu — a *sub-category* menu. This menu is most effective if you have absolute consistency with the sub-category look and placement throughout the site. I usually treat the second level page as an entry page on its own. Here you can highlight products using teaser menus (defined later in this section) or provide specific sub-category information in addition to providing the sub-category menu. Figure 1-7 features one of the sub-category menus for the Burpee site.

Subcategories: **Vegetables • Fruit**

Figure 1-7: After you click into a category, you are presented with a sub-category menu. This menu appears right below the category menu to keep the visitor on track. If every category were listed in the main category menu, the listings would be tiny and crowded. The designer has created an effective way to keep visitors focused.

Content or interior menus

After you direct your visitor into a category, and perhaps sub-category, often many further divisions make sense. Content or interior menus can be fully integrated into the graphics for the section or presented simply as a text menu at the top of the section page.

Ideally, a content or interior menu should be the "end-of-the-line" for most sites — the next click should bring visitors to detailed information, as does the menu shown in Figure 1-8 from the Burpee site. Organization is wonderful, and clicking a link takes less time than scrolling through a long page for the desired information. For information-rich sites or large product lines, you may need another level. However, let the warning bells ring loudly whenever you require your visitor to click more than three times before they hit the information they require. Not only do you risk losing them because the route is too long, but you also risk making it hard for them to identify where they are in the site and confusing when they want to visit another section.

Figure 1-8: Reaching the final category page brings you an interior menu specific to that category. This menu is generated dynamically by the content.

Teaser menus

A *teaser* is a tiny bit of copy that is designed to entice the visitor to learn more. Often, this menu is used to list articles, giving the visitor a glimpse of the topic with a descriptive title or a lead-in sentence. A teaser menu also can be used to describe where each link leads and is often located in the content area of the entry page, or on an interior page when an extra level of navigation is required. The Burpee site uses both text and images in teaser menus, as shown in Figure 1-9.

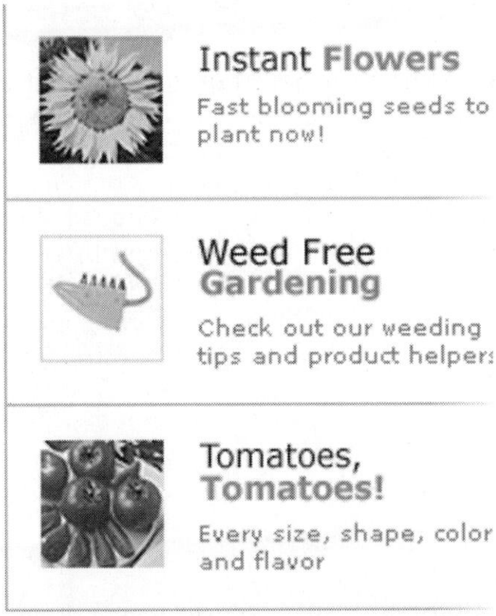

Instant Flowers

Fast blooming seeds to
plant now!

**Weed Free
Gardening**

Check out our weeding
tips and product helpers

**Tomatoes,
Tomatoes!**

Every size, shape, color
and flavor

Figure 1-9: Teaser menus are distributed
throughout the site. This one appears at the
right side of the screen on the main page
of the site.

Text menus

Most designers include a *text* menu that lists the category menu items as well as
housekeeping items. This menu is usually placed at the bottom of the page and is
small and unobtrusive. Text menus help people who cannot see the graphics on a
site, because of a disability or browsing with images turned off. Text menus are con-
venient for all visitors because they see this menu at the end of a page where they
are most likely to require a link. The Burpee site text menu, as shown in Figure 1-10,
appears at the bottom of every page.

Text menus can also be used as part of the main or secondary menu types
described earlier in this section.

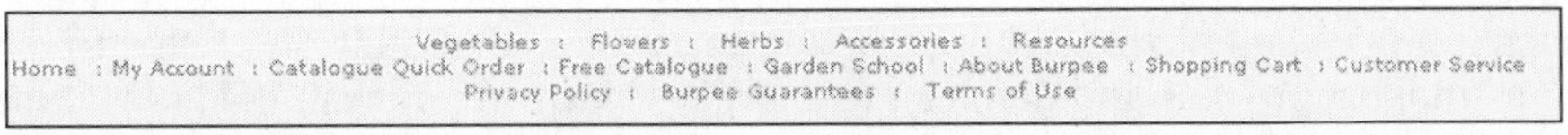

Vegetables : Flowers : Herbs : Accessories : Resources
Home : My Account : Catalogue Quick Order : Free Catalogue : Garden School : About Burpee : Shopping Cart : Customer Service
Privacy Policy : Burpee Guarantees : Terms of Use

Figure 1-10: Text menus at the bottom of a page help to keep visitors moving
through the site.

Marker menus

The *marker* menu refers to an icon or text that lists the page numbers that are available. Most search and return type of sites use this system as both a page marker and to allow quick navigation between return pages. Check out the example in Figure 1-11. I am not sure how many designers class these markers as official menu items, but because they help your visitors move through the site, I choose to consider markers as menus.

Figure 1-11: This small menu provides a map for the visitor and provides links to click to a different level if required. Sites featuring large product lines should provide this convenience for their visitors.

Figure 1-12 features another marker menu that tells visitors what page of their search results they are viewing. With high numbers of page returns, I prefer to see a reference for each page with a clickable link (dynamically generated). In this case though, the categories and sub-categories take the visitor to a search that rarely returns more than a few pages so that the clickable previous and next arrows are very effective.

> ⋅⋰⋅ BACK Page 2 of 7 MORE ⋅⋰⋅

Figure 1-12: Another form of marker menu

I want to repeat that the terms defined in this section are my terms. These terms may not necessarily even be logical for you, but creating a set of menu divisions in your mind and naming them is important. Not only will you have much more intelligent conversations with your clients, but the various menu types will begin to take on a personality of their own in your mind.

Effective navigation is the most important part of any site and creating it can be like completing a giant puzzle. Working with clearly defined menu types helps to direct your thinking process and defines menu areas clearly in your mind. I know it makes the initial design phase of a new project much easier for me. Another little trick is to assign "tasks" to menus in much the same way as you would assign jobs to various team members. After you start thinking that "this menu will handle that job," you are well on your way to creating a navigation system that works for your visitors.

Menus Do Not Start with Design

My guess is now that you have focused on some great sites and have gone through the menu naming process by getting to know the menu types, you are anxious to get started. I understand, but I must ask you to hold on for a little while.

With menus, finding a starting point is hard. Menus can seem quite simple until you decide to start the process, fire up the graphics program, create a new document, your optimism is high . . . but then . . . nothing. Nothing works. You go from design to menu to color to content, but nothing seems to gel. Just when you think you have it just right, you think of one more detail you must include. Where have you gone wrong?

You skipped the most important steps in the process. To put it in terms of this book, you have skipped ahead to Chapter 7, which describes how to create a rough comp.

Is it possible to create a menu without doing all of the background work? Yes, and sometimes you even get lucky and create an effective menu. But how much confidence would you have in an architect who went out and started throwing boards together, skipping the steps of creating a drawing and checking to make sure that all of the principles of keeping a building upright were in place? I would rather someone else hire that architect—I want one who does the background work.

Web design is much like architecture. The planning is the biggest part of the job. After a detailed drawing is created for a building, the construction can proceed quickly with a focus on quality construction—not design or whether the building can stand up against a stiff breeze. Web menu design is the same. If you create a solid plan, incorporating all the essential elements into the structure, creating the menu will be a simple matter of selecting the correct mood and technique.

Chapters 2 through 6 help you to put a solid structure in place for your site menus. Although explaining the techniques takes many words, after you have worked through it, the process is not difficult nor terribly time consuming. But the amount of time you save in the long run can be very dramatic.

✦　　✦　　✦

Setting Site Direction and Assessing Available Tools

Don't skip this chapter, please. You may see that there are many words, and maybe decide that because you want to learn to "make" menus, you can slide on by and get to the work. But this chapter — and Chapter 3 — are essential to everything else you will do with Web menus.

After a client contacts me, a common early question is, "What type of menu will you create?" My answer is always that I have no idea . . . yet. Choosing the format or look of a menu falls in the middle of a site creation project. I cannot design an effective navigation system for customers I do not know, or a product I do not yet understand. Professional designers don't fire up their graphics programs without doing their homework. You may not aspire to be a professional, but personal sites also benefit from first establishing goals and identifying potential visitors.

If creating a great site is not motivation enough to do the homework, what if I told you that by doing a bit of work beforehand, you can save a lot of time and frustration? A well-planned site rarely needs to be stripped down and rebuilt. Your goals or visitors may evolve over time, and change will be required. But how many of you have built a complete site and then scrapped it? I thought so. Read on . . . and you won't have to do that again.

Identifying Your "Real" Product

Every Web site has a product. You decided to find a host, perhaps buy a domain name, and put the work into building your pages for a reason. That reason is your product. Perhaps you just had a child and want to share his or her growth with family and friends. At the other end of the scale, you may have a completely new concept for the Web, venture capital secured, and are poised to become the next great Internet success story. No matter what the size or scope of a project, the route to a successful site is exactly the same.

The first task you face is identifying what you are "selling" on your Web site. This "selling" does not always mean that products and dollars will change hands. In fact, ignoring tangible items is best while you determine your site's product. You may think you are selling a toaster, but the actual appliance has little to do with what your Web site is selling. You may think that you are not selling anything if you have a high school reunion site, but you *are* selling, exactly as if you were selling tangible products.

So, Rule Number One is that when you create a Web site, you *are* selling. And your first task is to figure out exactly *what* you are selling. Trust me for a few minutes if you think that you are not selling. This concept becomes clear by the end of this chapter.

Solutions not products

If you have done any marketing or selling research, you should be familiar with the concept that successful selling offers solutions, not products. Grasping this concept for any selling is important, but it is also the critical success factor for any Web site. Your visitors arrive, look around, perhaps click a few times, and make decisions without contact. If you do not know why they are there, or what you have to offer, how can you ensure that they will find it? You can't. You may get lucky and stumble into success, but I demand more certainty than luck if I go to the work and expense to create a site.

Note   Although this book is touching on basic marketing and selling, I recommend this area for continual study for anyone who has a Web site. A firm understanding of marketing principles can help you with your site structure, menus, and copy. Learning how a sale works is the basis for everything you do on a commercial site. Remember, you are not there to fill in missing pieces on a Web page.

Take a look at an example. Suppose you are selling cameras in a retail setting. Rob, a potential customer, tells you that he is looking for a digital camera. Your instinct may be to ask, "What kind of camera?" but that is a poor sales tactic. Asking, "What are you planning to do with this camera?" is much better. For a productive answer to come from the first question, you must assume that Rob is an expert in the field, has researched current models, and has spent the time to figure out exactly why he wants a digital camera. If you have any retail experience, you know this profile does not describe the average customer.

However, ask Rob what he plans to do with the product, and he can usually answer without pause. He knows whether he wants to take photos during an upcoming tropical vacation, take family pictures, or take product shots for a Web site. You may find out that his friends have digital cameras, and that he thinks digital cameras look like fun. Perhaps he spends too much on photo processing, and thinks a digital camera will save money, plus give him more creative freedom. Rob's answer draws a map, and with your product knowledge, you can quickly guide him to the best camera for him.

Rob is not buying a camera; he has a problem. And you are not selling a camera, but rather custom photos, or entertainment, or cost-savings, or photographic freedom. If you can solve Rob's problem, you will make the sale. Rule Number One is that you must know what you are selling. Not only will you be able to list the features of the camera, but he will feel that you understand his needs and be comfortable with the purchase.

How does this work on the Web?

The same principle applies to Web products. You must understand what your visitor is seeking, but instead of a personal interaction with your customer, you have a menu. Think about this idea for a minute. Menu items provide the questions you would ask a customer in a retail setting. Questions such as, are visitors looking for cost-savings or entertainment, today's news or archived information? Instead of asking a customer the appropriate question to determine the next step, you will be providing menu links.

Visualizing your Web site as a store, library, or information center may help, and then imagining what someone entering that physical location would do. What would someone new want to know? How is that different for a regular visitor? After they have been to one place, what is the next logical information they will seek? Well-designed public places have natural traffic flow, based on how customers are expected to proceed through the building. As a Web designer, you must use site structure to create a natural traffic flow, instead of aisles or departments in a physical location. Menus are your tools to direct traffic, replacing sales staff to assist visitors.

Determining your product

Assuming that you have a Web site, or are planning one, think back to when you decided you would create the site. I'm guessing that you had a good idea what your product was going to be at that stage. "I am going to create a Web site to . . . (fill in your own words)." Do you recognize that statement?

Your reasons for creating a Web site form the base for your site planning. Did you decide to build your site because you determined that information or widgets of a special type are not available on the Web? Do you think you can do a better job than competitors because of your skill, experience, passion for the subject, or contacts?

What are your plans for your site? Do you plan to earn a profit, build your status as an expert, provide a place for others to share? Why are you doing what you are doing? You must establish what your niche is in the larger market to succeed and understand the exact nature of your product.

The most important question is, "What makes my product special?" It may be your geographic location, or that you offer a highly specialized product, such as the definitive source for margarita glasses. Perhaps competing sites provide information about a subject, but you also offer several interactive features, such as classified ads, message boards, and/or chat facilities for your visitors.

I include an exercise at the end of this chapter that will help you to determine exactly what your Web site product is and how to identify the perfect customer for you. The next two sections help you to narrow your marketing, navigation, and design focus, and work hand in hand with your product knowledge to provide the direction you need to understand what your site must deliver.

Identifying the Right Customers

Our focus is on the World Wide Web, right? That means that the entire world is a potential customer base for us. An exciting concept, isn't it? Unfortunately, it is dead wrong and is probably why so many retired links and dying sites are in every corner of the Web. A few rags to riches stories always surface, but that is not the average story, even on the Web. My guess is that your chances are better to win a lottery than they are to "luck into" a runaway success on the Internet.

Creating a successful site on the Internet is identical to building a successful business off-line. Knowing your niche and understanding your product is critical, as I touched on earlier in this chapter. Identifying your ideal customer is equally important. Every well-defined product has a matching perfect customer base. If the two concepts are present, and a need exists, success follows.

Finding your customer "bubble"

I want to convince you to give up most of the world in your search for the ideal customer. But isn't the chance to succeed greater with millions of potential customers? Not at all. In fact, trying to attract and serve millions of unrelated clients is an impossible marketing challenge, and more to our purposes here, a nightmare for creating site structure, design, and menus.

Whatever your product, whether it is one-of-a-kind fine art selling for thousands of dollars, or Sewing for New Moms tutorials offered at no charge, specific groups are your best potential customers. In the art and tutorial example, it is unlikely that the best customers for one are the same for the other.

A couple with a new baby may appreciate fine art, but in most cases, young families are not in a financial position to acquire fine art. In fact, even if the family with a new baby falls into a high-income tax bracket, the family focus for major purchases is not likely to be art.

Of course you have exceptions. Some devoted art fans will do without other pleasures and save to buy art, no matter what their income. A few couples, no doubt, celebrate the birth of a child by buying a fine art piece. However, the customers who fall outside your main group will not make your site a success. The secret for any Web site is to identify the common characteristics of people for whom your product is a perfect solution. I call this group your customer "bubble," and refer to this group many times throughout this book. (See Figure 2-1.) The customers in your bubble are the mainstay of your traffic, and if you are wise, you will focus on this group at every stage of the planning, construction, and marketing of your site.

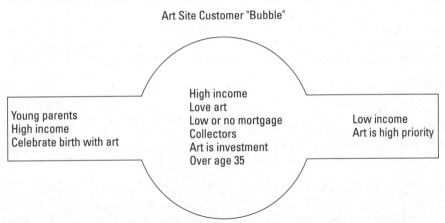

Art Site Customer "Bubble"

Young parents
High income
Celebrate birth with art

High income
Love art
Low or no mortgage
Collectors
Art is investment
Over age 35

Low income
Art is high priority

Figure 2-1: The "bubble" in this diagram represents the main customer group for a fictitious art site. The highest number of qualified visitors fall into a pattern for any product. Although the customers at the right and left of the diagram provide some traffic or sales, the numbers do not warrant specific targeting for these groups.

Using your bubble

The exercise at the end of this chapter guides you to identify your customer bubble. Before you complete the exercise, however, first taking a look at how you put your knowledge to work may help. Identifying your customer bubble enables you to form a solid image of your most important visitor and helps you make faster, better decisions in your planning and design.

This exercise may be difficult, as we all strive to be non-judgmental and inclusive. I've had many people in my classes squirm about dismissing an economic or educational group as poor candidates for a product. Identifying your ideal customer does not place a "value" on any group over another. You are simply determining who is most likely to benefit from your product.

For example, suppose you identify that the customer bubble for a Blues Festival site is between the ages of 40 and 55, with a high-level of music knowledge and interest, mid to high income, well-educated, professional or self-employed, with a general interest in the arts. These few characteristics provide a map for you.

In this case, although music is often associated with youth, this group is older. This factor can mean that your visitors do not possess computer savvy, although several other characteristics can raise the expected level (see the next section in this chapter). A higher income level may support advertising and makes secondary income opportunities worth investigating. The interest in music and art provides good clues for enticing a visitor to remain on your site for a longer time, perhaps by offering in-depth biographies of performers, or of the various music styles. An appreciation of the arts provides instant clues to the look of the site. Unusual color combinations may be perfect, and a controlled "corporate look" is guaranteed to be wrong.

The age of your projected visitors may mean that they have less time to wander through your site. Added to that, when you are serving professionals or self-employed people, you must make access exceptionally simple, logical, and direct. This group generally has very little patience (personal observation from years of teaching primarily business owners and professionals).

After you work through the process of identifying your bubble group and creating a site that is focused for this group a few times, the wide range of choices available to us as Web developers narrows almost instantly to a manageable selection. I've done this exercise countless times. As soon as I have my bubble identified, I can see the menu structure and general graphic direction forming almost automatically.

You have one more step to add though before you have a firm understanding of your potential visitor.

Calculating Your Visitor's Equipment and Computer Savvy

Because your Web work must be viewed on many computers, your comprehension of customer computer knowledge and equipment is important. I try to design sites for a low common denominator in both expertise and equipment, even when I suspect that most visitors will have solid expertise and good computers with current browsers. This premise is an excellent general policy, and one you will hear many times throughout this book, but you can err by being too safe as well. Newer technology can go well beyond novelty purpose, and raising the minimum standard that you design for can enable you to add exceptional features that are ideal for your site purpose and visitors.

But how do you know? Identifying your customer bubble helps. Age, education, and profession can help to narrow down an average for you. As a gross generalization, people younger than 35 may have good computer knowledge and often have current equipment. People over 35 may have excellent computer skills, but the average certainly drops as you move up the age scale. If your client bubble includes people over 60, there is a good chance that many of your potential clients are very new to computers, and that their equipment may not be current.

Age is not a perfect gauge for computer skills or equipment, however. Many older people have used computers at work for years and have exceptional skills and equipment. I am 44 and had no computer exposure through my entire education. However, I became interested in computers soon after I left school and have been earning my living with a computer since 1989. In my case, age is irrelevant, but my profession gives excellent clues to my high computer knowledge, and likely possession of current computer equipment. Don't place me right into the top-level yet, though. I live in a rural area of northern Canada and connect most days at 24K, and that is not likely to change in the next two years.

As Web developers, you probably have very current equipment, fast connections, and the latest browsers. This advanced technology can be dangerous to your site's success if you fail to acknowledge that you are not an average Internet or computer user. You must examine every aspect of your customer group to make sure that you are providing a site that will serve your best customers.

Age, income, education, profession, and location are all factors that can help you determine what demands your site must meet. As soon as your site is running, you can track your traffic and make adjustments. Unfortunately, this is a terrible time to discover that 20 percent of your users arrived with browsers that cannot display much of the interactivity on your site. You certainly don't want to find out that your bubble group is actually 40 percent Mac users (graphic or education bubbles can reach this level), not the standard accepted 10 percent when you have a site that does not display well on the Macintosh platform.

I always come back to the lowest common standards that you can live with. If you do want to add a feature that requires current browsers, try to work that feature in as an add-on. Follow your site log (many hosts provide traffic logs) to see what your visitors are using before you implement the questionable function. You can also be careful to ensure that features requiring recent browsers also degrade without serious function loss.

Exercise: Who Are You?

The time has come to nail down exactly what your product is, identify your best potential visitor, and try to determine what computer skill and equipment they will bring to your site.

On the CD-ROM   The worksheet that follows also appears in an expanded version in the Chapter 2 folder on the CD-ROM included with this book.

1. If you are selling tangible items (that is, books or furniture), list your products in groups. Next to the listing, state what the product group is used for. If your site also offers services, list each service as a separate product.

2. If you are selling an intangible product, such as providing information about a community group or medical condition, list each type of information you can provide, and any services, such as message boards, as separate products.

3. What problems are your products solving for your customers? Answer this question for each product that you listed in Question 1.

4. Put yourself in your customer's shoes. What benefit can you see for customers who use your product?

5. What makes your product special? Depending on your product, you may have one answer for all products, or a separate answer for each product.

6. What would your customers or potential customers lose if you were to close your site or fail to start it?

7. List as many characteristics as possible about your customers or potential customers.

8. Using your answers from Question 7, establish which customer characteristics are common enough to be included in your customer "bubble." List these and using the results, write one sentence that describes your ideal customer.

9. Using your "bubble" results from Question 8, make your best guess as to your customer's computer savvy and equipment. If you currently have a site, use your site log results to help.

10. Considering your answer to Question 9, what is the lowest standard browser version you must consider when creating a site? Do any of your customers have special needs (that is, disabilities or slow connections)?

11. List any problems that you must overcome to reach your customers through a Web site (in other words, customer needs are ideally suited to a service or design element that is not supported by their computer equipment or savvy). List ideas to resolve each problem.

✦   ✦   ✦

Why Are Your Visitors Here?

If you have not yet read Chapter 2, you should. Chapters 2 and 3 work together to provide the tools that you need to create an effective menu for any Web site. In this chapter, I look at what your visitors may be seeking when they visit your site and discuss what makes them want to have your product in their hands. Isn't that what it is all about?

You have to lose something to be successful with the next steps, though. You have to prepare to give up control of what you think your site should be. You may have to decide that the bell or whistle that tickled your interest in Web design in the first place has to go. Relinquishing control is not always easy to do, but if you do not set aside your personal needs, you are in danger of creating a site that chases your best customers away. If you do have to make sacrifices, you will realize the power that comes from a visitor-driven site and will do so without pain.

Shocking, but Your Visitors Are Here for Selfish Reasons

Web design is a lot of work and demands high skill development, but let's face it, Web design is also a lot of fun. You work hard to keep up with the latest developments and fall behind quickly if you do not. You want to show off your skill, darn it. If you are a professional or professional in training or are an amateur with a passion or cause you want to share with the world, I have a valuable piece of advice for you. Create a personal site where you can play and develop your skills. After you have a place to apply what you learn, you won't be as tempted to include it inappropriately for commercial or general interest sites.

Even today, while it seems as if we have advanced far with the Web, most "cool" techniques have no place on a commercial or general interest site. Sorry, but that is the reality. I make my living with Web design and like you, I am always trying new techniques. But other than cascading style sheets (CSS), liquid design, and better image optimization, most sites I work on now use shockingly similar code to the sites I created in 1997. In fact, most of the commercially practical change in Web sites has been in dynamic content or pages created on the fly from database content. The upsurge in wireless communication with bandwidth restrictions and tiny screens is actually lowering the standards for safe design.

 See Chapter 9 for a discussion of cascading style sheets (CSS). Chapter 18 focuses on image optimization, and Chapter 20 covers liquid design.

I have good news, however. You can make your mark in the Web development world more easily by learning to build great navigation rather than by learning the latest cool JavaScript or animation trick. The reason is simple: Sites that are easy to navigate have the best chance for success. A visitor who says, "Hey, cool, but where the heck do I go?" has not advanced your site goals. A visitor who gets to what they want without thinking tells friends and colleagues and comes back. That's success. Visitors are selfish — they want the goods, and they want it now. They are not there to be wowed by your skill. In fact, if you do it exactly right, most visitors won't even realize that they have seen a site constructed with skill. They simply know they found what they were seeking.

Big lessons from a search for a small bear

The best way to illustrate what I mean is to send you surfing, not for Web techniques, but for a product or non-Web related information. Give yourself an hour and pay attention to what you find. This search is one of the more enlightening exercises you can do.

I recently conducted a search for a specific Ty Beanie Baby. I never shop for toys or collectibles of any type, so I knew nothing. I was on a mission for a special gift. Beanie Baby sites must take the prize as the largest collection of amateur sites on the Web, but that did not surprise or bother me, even for sites that were truly commercial. What made me crazy and cost me far more time than I will ever admit, is that the sites that were slow were slow for all the wrong reasons: marquees, animation, and bad code (of course I looked). A slow loading page to show me bear images is almost acceptable. Slow loading so that the designer could show a cool trick sent me away. Almost none of the sites had a search function, shipping information seemed to be classed as a state secret, and I never did find out the real difference between a Beanie *Baby* and a Beanie *Buddie*. (Don't laugh — the Beanie Baby I was after is retired, and those little guys can carry high price tags. I wanted confidence in my purchase.)

Somebody lost a sale that day. I finally gave up and decided to check eBay.com (www.ebay.com), the well-known auction Web site. I had no idea if I could find what I was looking for, but I knew I could get around. I found my bear on eBay at less than half the cost I was expecting to pay and have to admit to having some fun with the auction (you have to be very good to win a Beanie Baby auction). If you analyze the result of my search, you can see how the one site that understood my needs won the sale.

I may never want another Beanie Baby, but if I do, I will head straight to eBay. If I am ever talking to anyone looking for a Beanie, I will recommend eBay. More important, that was the first time I bid on anything. Because eBay made it so easy, I discovered the fun part of buying through a Web auction. I will be back. Add one more win for eBay: I just mentioned what a great source eBay is for collectibles in a book. The theme of this entire chapter can be defined by my bear search. Read it, understand it, and take it to heart, and you are halfway to creating great Web sites.

Is it all about speed?

I think I am a pretty normal surfer. Deliver or lose. I wanted a bear, and I wanted it fast. I am sure that I visited sites owned by very nice people with admirable knowledge and excellent ethics. Unfortunately, I had no way to tell. Yet, my "fast" bear search on eBay probably cost me several hours by the time I won an auction, far more time than I would have spent at the sites I abandoned. Why am I so happy?

I am happy for the same reason that people who go to a trendy restaurant, discover a long wait for a table, and are invited into the bar to wait, are happy. Sure they have to wait for their food, but a nice restaurant is not solving the problem of hunger for its customers; the restaurant is solving the problem that people like to get away and relax in a nice surrounding over good food with friends or family. Entertainment. Going to the bar while they wait starts that process, so they are happy.

Now take this concept to the Web. Why was I happy at eBay and unhappy at the sites that probably would have been faster in the long run for my purchase? eBay not only solved my problem, it also provided entertainment for me. I admit, as soon as I started looking for the bear, the world I stepped into was fascinating. I was quite willing to spend time learning more about Ty, the company, and the bear collecting culture. I was just not interested in spending time waiting for pages, or being lost as to how to make a purchase. Keeping visitors happy is not always about speed. In fact, for as little patience as surfers have, they are often easily distracted to related information.

You may have heard the term *sticky pages*. This term refers to keeping a visitor on a site and is the ideal for any Web site. Some people try to accomplish holding visitors by creating frames or pop-up schemes that hold people hostage. That is the worst thing you can do. I compare covert techniques such as this as equivalent to having a security guard at a store refuse to let you leave because you have not spent enough time or money. No business would dream of that tactic — and it has no place in the Web world either.

What Are Your Visitors Seeking?

Before you can deliver what your visitor is seeking, you must know who your visitors are. You must also understand your product fully. The two concepts add up to what your customer is seeking. After you know what they are seeking, your menu system starts to build itself. I use a residential real estate site as an example.

Cross-Reference See Chapter 2 for more information and an exercise on how to determine your product and who your customers are.

Although people selling a home are a crucial part of any real estate business, I am going to ignore that market in the interest of brevity and proceed as if home buyers were the only target customer.

A lot of marketing experience isn't necessary to realize that listings with photos is a must for this Web site. Most of you may automatically assume that the details of the home and listed price are also critical. But stretch a little to understand your visitors' problems. They have to find the house they want to buy, but they also need financing information (how to qualify and apply, as well as rates), they will soon have to move, and they may need to purchase major appliances or seek the services of renovation/decorating experts. The potential homebuyer likely wants information about local schools, medical services, community amenities, shopping, and recreational facilities in the neighborhood in which they are thinking of buying a home. In addition, if the local area is booming, visitors may be coming from outside the immediate area and may require information that is common knowledge locally, such as yearly weather patterns or how to obtain a state driver's license and register vehicles.

Take the time to discover what your visitors' immediate needs may be and stretch that to additional information that may be of great interest because they are in the market for one of your products. That information provides the map to build a site that serves your visitors' needs and keeps them clicking through your pages. You may also uncover many secondary income opportunities. In our real estate example, affiliate partnerships can be set up with lenders, home inspectors, professional movers, waste removal services, moving supply retailers, renovators, and decorators, for example.

If you take the time and trouble to establish what your visitors are seeking, you establish yourself as the desired source for a product. The real estate company that provides a complete source for information that their potential customers may need put forth the image that they truly understand visitor needs. That concept is a powerful selling tool. When customers believe you understand what they need, how they feel, and what is important, they have confidence in you and want to buy from you.

That is just one short example, but the process is the same for any Web site. You are not quite ready to start with the menu yet, though. First you must consult your visitors to ensure that you are building a site that suits their needs.

Hedging Your Bets in the Guessing Game

The examples I use are generally easy to understand and feature common knowledge products. Of course, most of you may recognize that your products do not fall into neatly defined categories with easily determined secondary information and income categories. I have a few suggestions to help you come up with ideas and sort many possibilities for the answers.

Ask your current visitors

If you have an operating site with some traffic, you can ask your current visitors. Creating a short survey from a free Common Gateway Interface (CGI) script is not difficult. To increase your return rate, consider offering a bonus, perhaps a discount on a product or special information, as a reward for filling out the survey. Make sure that the questions are carefully chosen to provide the answers you require. For example, location is a standard question on a survey, but if you have no interest in where your visitors live, don't waste the question. If you can keep a survey between four and six questions, you will get more responses and more thoughtful answers. Make the questions multiple choice, if possible, or short answers. Always provide a text entry section at the end of the survey to allow respondents to list needs or comments you have not considered.

On the CD-ROM You find listings for CGI script sources on the CD-ROM included in the back of this book.

If you do not have a current site, but do have (or your client has) an existing off-line business, you can conduct a short, formal survey at the business location, or make it a point to ask customers for information that can help you build your site. Make the questions specific, but always allow a chance for free comment. If you are creating a site for a group or cause, ask the group members to gather as much information as they can. Again, make your questions specific with the opportunity for random comments.

Check the competition

Naturally, you should be aware of your competition. But have you put your competitors under a microscope? You can see many patterns of required site features and opportunities by visiting competing sites and actually listing what they offer. To use the information, go back to your original site goals, your knowledge of your customers and your product, and compare. Where are you similar to each competitor and where do you differ? What extra services or products do you offer? What features do competitors offer that you have decided to skip? For competing products or services, does anything separate you from your competitors? How have they organized their sites? Can you see where visitors can stumble?

Tip   Blindly copying errors from a competing site is easy . . . make sure you always check your goals before you adopt features from the competition.

Writing down relevant information about competitors — rather than just visiting the sites — can be compared to trying to find a building with verbal directions or with a map. Although you may have a good idea what you are looking for or the direction you are going, if you make one wrong turn, you are lost without a map. Much of what separates a great site from a mediocre one is not always obvious. Doing a con-centrated study of existing competing and similar sites can uncover many ideas and can make your site stronger.

Beware of the sample of one

I get a lot of mail as the result of my graphics column at WebReference.com (`www.webreference.com`). Readers generously offer suggestions for how the site could be improved by adding a program to the list of featured programs, offering suggestions to increase my audience, or with a specific request for a topic. However, if I tried to do everything that was suggested, I would now feature about 35 programs that would appear in 14 different formats. The articles would be trans-lated into several languages and I would have to publish an article every day rather than biweekly. I consider every suggestion, comparing it to my well-established site goals. Some suggestions instantly stand out as good ones; others do not fit into the plan. If I get several pieces of mail requesting the same thing, I go back to the plan and often make a small change. One e-mail message on a topic makes me wonder. Ten similar suggestions are worthy of longer thought.

Ideas are plentiful. Focus is the route to a successful site. I want to encourage you to watch for new ideas constantly, from colleagues, customers, by checking com-petitors, and even talking to friends and family. However, measure everything you hear against your site goals, your visitor needs, and your product. Without that solid base, you will be spinning out of control, never knowing where to go next and not knowing if you have just tossed the best idea to come along.

Exercise: Who Are Your Visitors and What Do They Want?

Now that you have a few ideas that will help identify what your visitor may be seek-ing, you should start the final phase of the planning process and start writing. To get you started, following is an exercise to help you define customer needs. It may not feel like you are creating a menu, but as sure as the foundation is part of house construction, this step is one of the most important aspects of building your Web menu.

On the CD-ROM The worksheet that follows also appears in an expanded version in the Chapter 3 folder on the CD-ROM included with this book.

1. What is your product? (Complete the exercise in Chapter 2 or copy your results for this information.)

2. What are the characteristics of your best customers? (Complete the exercise in Chapter 2 or copy your results for this information.)

3. What is the primary motivator for a customer to visit your site?

4. Using your answer from Question 3, what secondary information can your visitors be seeking because they have the primary reason to visit your site? List as many potential answers as possible — we worry about how any feature can be delivered later.

5. Using your answer from Question 4, how can you tap into your visitors' desires for more information or related products (in other words, an educational section on the site or an interactive feature).

6. List at least three methods to tap into your potential customer group and discover what they are seeking.

7. List your competition by assigning a direct competition or indirect competition label to each one as appropriate.

8. List the menu items and site features for each of the competitors you listed in Question 7. Next to each list, state whether you will include this feature on your site and why.

9. List features or information that you can include that are not featured on competing sites.

10. Using the information about what your customer is seeking and considering your site goals, as well as the equipment and expertise your customers are likely to possess, sketch out your main menu categories. (This is a preliminary exercise to help you make the leap from theory to practice.)

✦   ✦   ✦

Understanding Browsers, Intranets, and Wireless

One of the toughest tasks any Web developer faces is creating pages that display for the end user, regardless of the visitor's browser, monitor, and platform. Print designers require a lot of knowledge to successfully deliver printable files to the printer or service bureau, but the end product remains the same after it is printed, no matter where it goes. Video producers face a little more variation in how their product is displayed, but industry standards help.

The Web is still the Wild West of the design world with very few standards and far more exceptions than rules. In this chapter, I offer some direction and resources to try to make sense of this crazy part of the Web development world.

Internet and Browsers: Ignore at Your Peril

Putting your first Web page together makes the process look so easy. That many people believe anyone can build a Web site in an evening is not surprising. But those of us who have been in the industry for a while understand that working with browser standards, or more accurately, a lack of standards, makes Web design a never-ending learning process. As fast as you learn all the tricks for one set of browsers, new versions are added, creating a new set of rules.

Caution   Don't ignore the issues that follow! You will waste your time developing graphic or programming skills unless you become, and remain, fully aware of how your work appears as a final product.

Touring the major browsers

Designing a page that works in every browser, on every platform, is completely accessible for those who use aids to browse, and still looks the way we expect a Web page to look is almost impossible. You always have a tradeoff between features and compatibility, especially if you want to add interactivity to your site or have a customer base that demands a "cool" factor for their favorite sites.

But the task is not impossible. When you understand the issues to watch out for, you can make informed choices that work for your visitor base. Unfortunately in this section of the book, I only have the space to alert you to the important topics, not list the solutions for every possible problem. (By the time the book is printed, my list would be out of date, even if I were arrogant enough to pretend that I had discovered the answer to every single problem on every single browser.) However, for menus, knowing what to watch for is vitally important as a broken menu stops your visitors in their tracks.

Tip   Webreview.com features an excellent guide for browser compatibility at `www.webreview.com/browsers/browsers.shtml`. This guide provides a general listing and won't make you an instant expert, but it is a great place to start.

Netscape Navigator and Internet Explorer

Netscape Navigator (NS) and Internet Explorer (IE) are, by far, the most popular browsers. Any site must display in each of these browsers, and menus should work as expected. How can there be much difference? Take a look at Figure 4-1. Tables are the most widely used page layout method for HTML pages, yet the differences between how NS and IE display tables is significant.

If you are serious about Web design, both NS and IE must be installed on your computer. If you are deadly serious, you should have several versions of each program for testing and have a route to test on a PC if you are working on a Macintosh and vice versa. NS is fairly consistent across both platforms, but IE displays wildly inconsistent results on a PC and Macintosh.

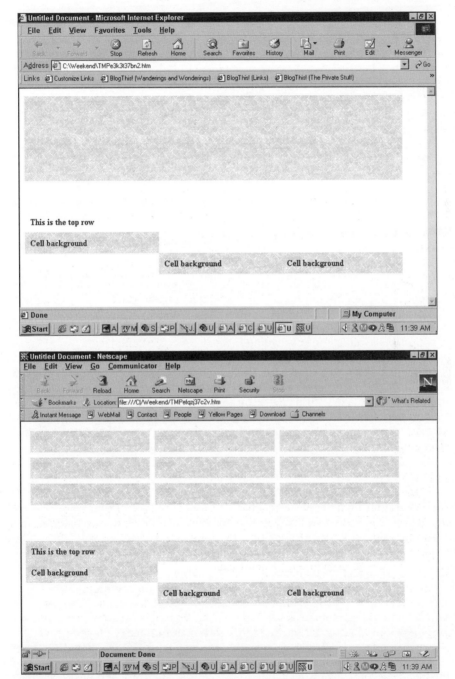

Figure 4-1: Identical code displayed in Internet Explorer 5.0 (top) and Netscape Navigator 4.5 (bottom).

America Online

While the "big two" Web browsers are crucial and cannot be ignored, you also have other vitally important browsers to consider. America Online (AOL) currently features a form of Internet Explorer, but it is not exactly the same as the stand-alone version. If your site expects to serve the general public in the United States, you cannot afford to ignore the millions of users who are connecting to the Web through AOL. If you do not have AOL access, find a friend who can test pages for you. I use AOL as my connection to the Web for travel, as it provides me with Internet access on the road almost anywhere I travel. You can also use any browser after you are connected to AOL, but more importantly, using AOL gives me a test to see how millions of people may see my pages.

Tip   AOL has a special information section for Web developers who want to design pages that display well on AOL (http://webmaster.info.aol.com).

WebTV

WebTV is a Microsoft-owned Internet connection for people without computers — Web pages are displayed on any TV screen. If you offer a commercial product that is geared for the general population, especially if your product is not a computer-based product, you must be aware of how WebTV displays your Web pages. Small graphic text can be difficult or impossible to read (trouble for menus) and only limited support is available for Cascading Style Sheets (CSS) and Flash.

Not all developers need to make their pages completely compatible with WebTV, but I believe it is best to understand the issues that affect this browser. Often, a few tiny changes can make your pages useable on WebTV, even if you do not expect a large number of visitors to use it. How serious is the WebTV market? Does the fact that a Microsoft WebTV Plus Recliner by La-Z-Boy was released in early 2001 give you a clue?

Tip   A good resource for developers who need to know how to make their pages is available to WebTV users. Visit http://developer.webtv.net for the parameters you must use for your pages. You can also download a program that enables you to see your pages as they are seen on WebTV.

Opera

Opera is a Norwegian-based browser that is making some serious gains in the browser market. Opera claims to be the world's fastest browser and proudly adheres to the W3C (World Wide Web Consortium) standards, an organization devoted to providing standards for the Internet. Experienced computer users tend to be Opera fans, and recent partnerships with major industry players, such as IBM, are making this the browser to watch. Designing for Opera compatibility does not require many adjustments for most pages, so it is a worthwhile exercise, especially because Opera is now available for Macintosh platform and has recently been offered in a free, advertising-based form for Windows users, as shown in Figure 4-2.

Opera is also wireless compatible and supports both the wireless application proto-col (WAP) and the wireless markup language (WML) — one of the first browsers to extend that support. This browser cannot be ignored, especially if your market includes people with sophisticated computer or Web skills.

Tip   Learn more about Opera or download a free (Windows only) or paid version at www.opera.com.

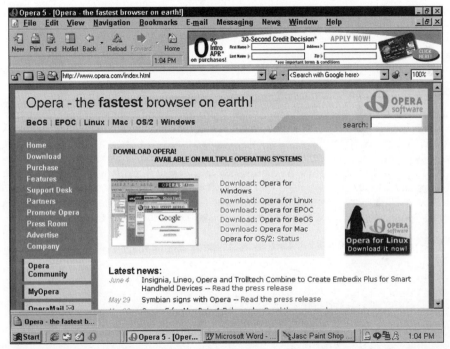

Figure 4-2: Free Windows version of Opera, showing the entry page for the Opera site. The paid version of Opera does not have ads.

Although this section does not provide a complete listing of all of the browsers people are using, if you are aware of how your pages will display in the browsers I cover, you certainly have considered the majority of visitors. Remember: You may well have to compromise. As I mentioned at the beginning of this book, you are always making choices for browser compatibility. The secret is to know what you are working with and to make your choices with knowledge, based on your site goals and your customer base. Follow up on the links I provide for further research. Knowing too much about browser compatibility is impossible.

Working with monitor resolution

Do not mix up monitor resolution with monitor size. A 15" monitor can be set to 1024 x 768 pixel display (making the text hard to read) or a 21" monitor can be set to 640 x 480 pixel display (you can read text across the room). What makes the difference to a Web page is the display resolution, ranging from 640 to over 1500 pixels wide. Very simply, this number indicates the number of pixels that are available across the screen.

As designers, you must be aware of the settings that your visitors will be using or at least decide on a standard. If you design your page for 800 pixel width (only the width matters for most Web pages) and visitors arrive with their browser set to 640 pixels wide display, they will have to scroll to see the far right pixels. Most designers won't tolerate a horizontal scroll for their lowest resolution visitors. Figure 4-3 illustrates the differences between a monitor with 800-pixel resolution and 1024-pixel resolution.

On the other hand, if you keep all of your content within a 640-pixel boundary, visitors with higher resolution settings will see your page filling only a tiny portion of the screen. Again, compromise comes into play for Web design. Most of the designers I know design for 800-pixel wide display (approximately half of all monitors are set to 800 by 600 pixels) but use what is called *liquid design* so that content will stretch to fit higher resolution monitors. As a concession to a still notable number who are using 640-pixel wide display, we do try to keep all essential content to the left and center of the page. That way, even though visitors with lower settings have to scroll to see the entire page, they are not missing out on essential elements of the page.

Cross-Reference   See Chapter 20 for a full discussion of liquid design and more about monitor resolution.

Understanding accessibility

In Web design, *accessibility* refers to gearing Web pages toward those who are unable to use the Web in the way that most do. For example, blind users can obviously not use any visual clues on a site, but they can still have the benefit of the information when a designer keeps accessibility issues in mind.

Accessibility is a growing issue as more and more businesses and government services move some or all of their services to the Web. If you are working for the government, or hoping to work with government agencies, you often must be able to create fully accessible sites. For more information, check Bobby, an accessibility information center and page tester at `www.cast.org/bobby`. You should also visit `www.w3.org`, a site with information on current Web standards and a section on accessibility.

Tip   Macromedia recently released an extension for Dreamweaver that checks accessibility for an entire site. You can download the extension from `http://macromedia.com`.

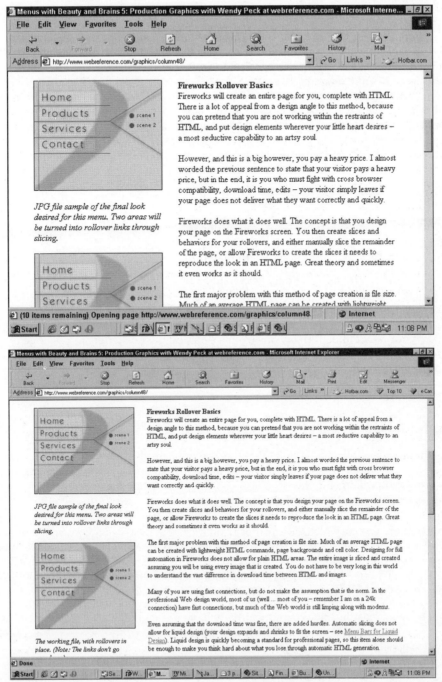

Figure 4-3: The screen shots shown here are of the same page, on the same monitor, but with different resolution settings. The top image shows the resolution set to 800 pixels wide. The bottom image is set to 1024 pixels wide. Note how the text lines are longer with the higher resolution, and more information fits on the screen.

Designing Web Pages for the Widest Audience

Unless you are certain that your visitors are using especially current or outdated equipment, a fairly safe combination is as follows: Create your site for both Netscape and Internet Explorer Version 4 and above and be aware of what happens to your pages in AOL, WebTV, and Opera. Design your pages to look best at 800-pixel wide display but make sure that it also looks good at 1024-wide pixel display. Use liquid design when you can. Keep your page download time as fast as possible. The difference of a few bytes doesn't matter if a digital subscriber line (DSL) is powering the connection, but page download time does matter for any visitors with dial-up connections. (See Chapter 18 for a full discussion of image optimization.)

These specifics deliver your pages as you intend them to be seen to the largest number of surfers today. But don't take my word for it. If your tracking results show that 30 percent of your clients are arriving with AOL, make sure that your page is perfect for them.

Not every Web site must be fully accessible, but adding the pieces, such as Alt tags for images, is easy for developers. Small additions or changes that do not affect the appearance or function of your site can make a huge difference to people with disabilities. Again, follow up on the links to become familiar with accessibility and make your development decisions from a position of knowledge. Knowledge in areas such as compatibility and accessibility separates a professional from an amateur designer.

Where Does Your Work Go? You Must Know!

In Chapters 2 and 3, I focus on understanding your product and your customers, as well as the equipment they use to visit your site. If you have worked through that process, you will have a better chance to determine which browser compatibility issues are important to you. This process helps you decide on the correct resolution to use as your design base and which functions can add to your visitor experience.

In order to fully service the visitors who come to your page, you must determine the most likely browsers, operating system (OS), monitor resolution, and accessibility requirements. How do you know? As with determining the computer equipment and savvy your visitors possess, you should always keep abreast of news in the Internet world. Intuition does develop if you are always aware of the latest news. If you have an existing site, you may already have a tracker that provides the information you require. Many Web site hosting companies offer this service as part of their Web site hosting package.

If a host-based visitor and traffic tracker is not available to you, many free and reasonably priced trackers are available that you can place on your pages. I have used WebTracker, which features an invisible tracker. WebTracker is available at `www.fxweb.com/tracker`. You can find many others, however. If you are using a free tracker, placing it at the bottom of a page that has a fair amount of content is best. Connecting to a free service can be slow, and if not placed well, can slow your page display down.

It is important that you do track your visitors or for a new site, have a reasonable idea of what your visitors will be using. If your customer base is an experienced computer group, as in an advanced tutorial site, assuming that they will be using reasonably current equipment (and not WebTV as a browser) is fairly safe in most cases. Opera is a solid possibility, however. Experienced computer users will likely be viewing your pages at a resolution of 800 pixels wide or above, but may still have a modem connection to the Web. To some extent, until you have the traffic tracking from a running site, you are guessing.

Intranets: Not Just the Web with Manners

More and more companies are providing a Web site for their employees to use as a communication and development tool. Known as an *intranet*, these internal sites are proving to be an effective and cost-efficient way to unify and inform highly special-ized visitor groups. While an intranet site works very much like any Web site, they are often much different in customer requirements.

The visitor group for an intranet site is always well defined as the site is only for employees or even a specific group of employees. Visitors or potential visitors are easier to track — at times you can possibly reach each and every visitor for feed-back. In many cases, you know exactly what browser the visitors to the site are using as equipment and software may be consistent throughout the company.

Do you sense a "but" coming? Those who work on intranet sites certainly should suspect that I have a few more things to say. While intranet design can be a dream assignment, it is not without many exceptions to the ideal I describe in the previous sidebar "Designing Web Pages for the Widest Audience." Designing for a specific group can be tough, too. The expectations for an intranet are necessarily high, and your customers can be demanding. They are likely depending on your work to get at least a portion of their work done.

Establishing visitor's capability

A dream intranet site serves only people with the latest equipment and browsers. That is the exception, however, as few companies replace equipment across the organization at one time. In addition, not every department has the same need for current computers or computing power. In most cases, you face similar variations that are present in the general population.

Your route to establish what that capability is should be easier and more accurate, however. For smaller companies, you may be provided with a list of the systems in use. Larger companies most often have people who are responsible for keeping the company computer systems working and updated, and they can provide the information you require.

When working with the general public, it is hard to instigate a change that brings your visitor's capability up. For the most part, developers must deliver a lower-end product until the market catches up. When building an intranet site, you may be able to have the lowest level raised by working with the technology department. You need solid, practical reasons to suggest upgrading browsers, monitors, and so on, but if you can present a plan for a more efficient final product if the lowest level capability can be raised, you should expect some cooperation.

As you analyze what you are working with and the development compromises that are required, always keep in mind that you may have some control over how the end product is viewed. Simply having everyone in the company using the same browser to use the intranet site can make a big difference in development freedom and can offer significant savings to the company. Designing for cross-compatibility is expensive, as it takes more time and skill. I repeat, though, you must be able to justify why a change would benefit the company — and that your job would be easier and your profit margin better is not one reason that is likely to motivate change.

Dealing with a vocal customer base

Intranet customers are sometimes dragged kicking and screaming to your site. Not everyone thinks that moving part of his or her job to an intranet base is a good idea. Even when the idea is well supported for every employee, you have another idea as to how the final product should work. Establishing customer needs can be very easy, very difficult, or both.

With an intranet, you can usually count on some guidance coming directly from users or from management for each group of users. That is a refreshing change from trying to pull intelligent decisions on visitor needs from well-thought-out thin air. While the benefit is that you can hear exactly what your customers want from their intranet, the problem is also that you hear exactly what your customers want from their intranet. It is not unusual for management — your real client, the one who authorizes payment of your paycheck or invoice — to want a different product than your other very real customers — the people who use your site.

Ironically, if you ignore end user suggestions and needs in favor of the direction in your contract, it will most likely be your fault if the site is not used, underused, or used incorrectly. Finding common ground between all groups involved in the project is in your best interest. Do not ever make the mistake that your customer discovery and service is simple with an intranet site.

The best way to bridge any gaps and deliver a strong, efficient, and effective intranet site is to speak with knowledge about the subject. If you are an intranet developer, you may have smugly sailed by Chapter 2, thinking you could skip that part of site design and establishing menus. Not so. If anything, you must work through the identification twice, once for end users and once for the company goals, and then find the perfect common ground.

I want to end this section on a positive note. Through years of establishing client goals and needs, I assure you that the corporate balancing act (which can also be present in Web design) is outweighed by the great gift of direct, or semi-direct contact with the end user. Few problems cannot be solved after they are identified, and intranet development provides the means to more closely identify real issues.

Wireless: When Going Forward Brings Us Back

Wireless technology is the next great wave for the Internet — the next natural step. As we become dependent on the Internet and e-mail for information and communication, being tied to a static computer is too restrictive. For years many, myself included, have carried laptops and sought data ports while on the road to keep up. A good solution, but awkward.

Enter the personal digital assistant (PDA) as the hope for the future. We are not quite "there" yet, but significant leaps in technology are made every year, and advancements such as Nokia's fast 3G wireless service are making a truly portable communication device seem like an achievable goal. It is too early for a mass defection of Web developers to the wireless side of the industry, but wireless technology is an area that a wise person will keep an eye on, especially if you make your living designing for the Web.

But that is in the future. Today, the industry is bound by tiny screens (that will remain — that is the point), one-color displays, and at best, one pixel or black images. Fast data transfer is essential. The menu system is vitally important because you can only see a tiny bit of information at a time. Wireless terminology reflects the limitation with users moving between cards as in a deck of cards rather than pages.

More and more, Web developers will be asked to create WAP pages as part of a traditional site. The number of wireless users is expected to double in the next two years. The good news is that the technology from a design perspective is not difficult. The bad news is that designing for these miniature screens takes us back to before the beginning of time in Web design. You cannot even use tables when designing for the wireless market.

Cross-Reference Chapter 14 focuses on creating a menu for wireless use if you are interested in keeping abreast of this exciting industry that is still in its infancy.

Exercise: Creating an Oddity Tracker

I hope I have made you sit up and take notice of the minefield that Web development can be if you do not keep your eyes wide open. However, contrary to my introduction to this topic, I really did not want to scare you. If you keep learning and make sure that you stay up-to-date with at least the current browser requirements, it is not really so hard.

However, it is hard to keep track of all that you learn. I am going to pass on a tip that I sincerely wish I had known when I was first started in Web design. Many of the tiny glitches, most not even documented, that you run into as you work through site after site only occur occasionally. Knowing that you have run into a problem before is no comfort if you cannot remember the tiny code fix that corrected it. Sometimes that code oddity is as benign as an extra space in your code. (I know, I know, spaces in code have no effect, but tell that to a table cell that will not align until you remove it.)

As a solution, I eventually became wise enough to track everything I discovered. I jot it down in a tiny freeware program called TreePad (a notebook would do just as well). However, I know that you are more likely to pay attention to what I say if I can add an official-sounding label to this tip, such as *The Oddity Tracker*. Whether you need to be tricked or not, get it down. When you find that a table cell does this or that on a Macintosh with Internet Explorer, write it down. There is one fix where you must place a <br> tag to remove a line space in a sliced layout. Perhaps your brain is better than mine, but I still have a hard time with the logic on that one. It feels really good when I can consult my notes and confirm that the fix is multi-browser and platform tested.

If you would like to create an HTML page, word processing document, or just a simple notebook that sits beside your computer, the results will be the same. I am featuring TreePad, as it is a handy tool for any research and planning. I often send a copy of the program and strategy notes to clients in this form.

Note   TreePad is only available for the PC.

To create an Oddity Tracker in TreePad, follow these steps:

1. Go to www.treepad.com and download the freeware version of TreePad (less than 400K) and install.

2. Open the program.

3. Choose File ➪ New to create a new document and then choose File ➪ Save As to save the file with the name **Oddity**, in the desired location. The filename appears at the top of the window and the top of the screen. The name at the top of the screen is the document root.

4. Click the name Oddity at the top of the screen to highlight. You are now going to add a node, which is similar to a folder.

5. Choose Edit ➪ Insert Node ➪ Child (or right-click to bring up a context menu). The words "New Subject" appear and are highlighted. Type **Internet Explorer**. This is now the main node for IE.

6. With the Internet Explorer node highlighted, repeat Step 5 to insert a node but label the new node **v3.x**, representing all IE version 3 browsers. Always place a new node under the selected node.

7. To create a new node under the main node, select Oddity and repeat Step 5 to create a new node, labeling it **Netscape Navigator**.

8. Continue adding nodes in the same way until you have a node for Internet Explorer, with child nodes for versions 3.x, 4.x, and 5.x., as well as Netscape Navigator v3.x, 4.x, and 6. I have also included one for Table Backgrounds (important for liquid design). You may want to add one for media, JavaScript, or any other subject that will help you to find the topic later.

9. To enter your notes, select the node where you want to place information. For this example, select the Table background node, under Internet Explorer. In the right screen, type **Use <TD> tag only for placing background in a row. Background will not print.** (See Figure 4-4.)

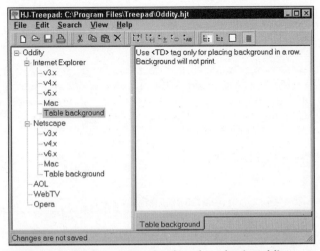

Figure 4-4: Node structure in place for a basic Oddity Tracker in TreePad. Only the text for the highlighted node shows in the window on the right.

The beauty of this system is that you can keep many references and many folders in one file and collapse or expand the nodes as you require. TreePad also has an excellent search function.

You find more exciting topics in this book than browser oddities and capabilities. However, without fully accepting the responsibility to understand how your pages are seen, you risk wasting your time. Your work deserves to be seen at its best — make sure that is how 100 percent of your visitors will see it.

✦   ✦   ✦

Putting the "Map" into a Site Map

Many designers, myself included, use the term *site map* to describe the tool used to set and illustrate the structure of a site. Others refer to this stage as setting or building the site architecture. I believe that words are powerful and even with my experience, the idea of creating the "architecture" for a site intimidates me. However, drawing a map is not a scary concept. So, for this book, *site map* refers to the document described in this chapter.

Caution If you do not have a solid understanding of your customer, product, and site goals, I recommend that you start with Chapter 2 and Chapter 3 of this book before you delve any further into trying to develop a site map.

What Is a Site Map?

I love the word *map* in association with a Web site. A trip through a Web site is similar to a trip in a car. You can go in a straight line to your destination, or take many side trips, but each segment of the trip must be connected. You can't make a leap 50 miles to the east in a car without following connected roads. You often have many choices for how you will get from point A to point B, but you must have a road. Anyone who has traveled also knows that it is much easier to find the right route when there are many road signs to point the way — even with a map, signs along the road help to confirm the direction, and correct slight errors. The site map you will build in this chapter is the equivalent to the map you would use to plan a road trip.

Defining structure with a site map

The most useful site map is created before any work is done on the appearance of your site. Using the information you establish about your customer needs and site goals, you create a site map describing the site structure. As you move to the design phase, the site map provides the information that you need to create an easy-to-use menu system.

You can create a site map with a computer program, as I did in Figure 5-1. If you are presenting a site map to a client, it should be presented in a professional form—after all, you have been hired to make their site look good. Impressions count. However, if you are creating a site for your own use, a site map created with a pen and paper will do the job equally well. The format you choose doesn't matter as long as you can clearly see how the pages link and re-link to each other. You may not have perfection in linking at this stage, but having the major routes established is important. You will often connect pages with unplanned links as the project moves along.

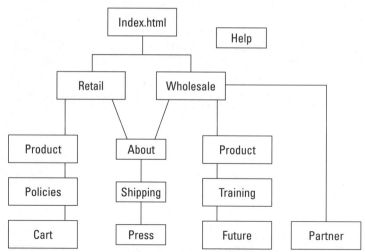

Figure 5-1: A site map created by hand or with a computer graphics program provides the direction for a site. This example shows a division from the entry page into two customer groups. Help is shown as not connected, but the link to this page will appear on every page as an icon. Connecting this page to every other page on the map would create too many lines and cause confusion, so I have left it floating.

Generating a site map with an HTML editor

The term *site map* is also used to describe a graphic representation of the links in an HTML editing program, such as Macromedia Dreamweaver or Adobe GoLive. This function only comes into play after the site is built however, as the program simply collects existing structural information and presents it in graphic form. I use this feature to create a site map several times through a project in order to check that the structure is working well and to spot any problem areas. Figure 5-2 shows a Dreamweaver-generated site map for a small site.

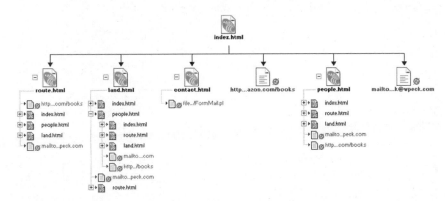

Figure 5-2: Site map created in Dreamweaver, representing the existing structure of a site and indicating all links. Entries with a + (plus sign) can be expanded to show more links.

Navigating an existing site with a site map

Finally, the most visible form of site map appears on all large sites to help visitors understand the site structure and reach a particular page quickly. Site maps are usually available from any page on the site, and as a surfer, are a valuable tool to me. Figure 5-3 illustrates a portion of the Multinational Insurance Arrangement Web site map, which is an example of an excellent site map.

Planning the Basic Route

Now that you know the various forms that site maps can take, you can focus on the most important function, the one that you use to create a site. Creating a meaningful site map can save many hours. After you move to producing menus, especially if using graphics, even a small structural change can require starting over.

> **Note**
>
> If you are working with clients, having them approve a site map can save many headaches later in the project. My standard contract clearly states that any menu changes after the site map is approved will result in extra charges, therefore preventing the frustration of redoing work with no compensation. Without the site map, structure becomes intertwined with design and it is very hard to find a place for "can't go back now" approval.

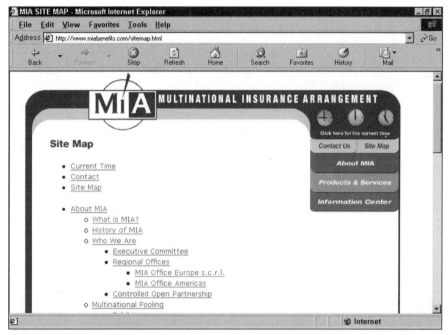

Figure 5-3: Excerpt from the Multinational Insurance Arrangement site map page (`www.miabenefits.com/sitemap.html`). Note how the links are grouped into logical categories to make it easier for a visitor to reach the desired page.

When you are sitting with a blank piece of paper or a blank screen in front of you, creating a map that will form the entire structure of your project can be intimidating. Breaking the project into pieces is a great way to get the initial direction.

Finding the direction for your map

Review your site goals and why you have determined your visitors will arrive at your site. Gather the obvious first. You may have originally decided to create the site in order to offer a particular feature. If your research supports the idea, start with how this feature can be the highlight.

You may notice that I use the terms *menu* and *map* in much the same way, calling on the term that is most appropriate for the discussion. In reality, the individual entries on a site map correspond exactly to menu items.

I find that menus fall naturally into a pattern. Although there are exceptions with very simple or extremely focused sites, for most of the maps you create, menus will fall into one of several categories. You should have a fairly accurate idea of the content you want to present. Creating the site map is really no more than deciding what content fits into each category.

Determining major divisions

If you have two distinct customer groups, your structure may be well suited to a division upon entry as in the site map sample shown in Figure 5-1 earlier in this chapter. This is a good example of your first step. If as you progress you find that your menus are becoming very large or confusing, start over and see if there is a way to divide them.

Divisions that come to mind are retail/wholesale for an e-commerce site, patient/provider in a health setting, student/teacher/parent for an educational site or men/women/children for a clothing site. Where should the division appear? Your entry page can be used to direct visitors immediately to separate categories if they will recognize instantly where they should be. At times, division comes only after education gives visitors the information they need to select the correct place. Your site map should reflect where the choice is made.

Distributing content into menu types

As soon as you have major content areas determined, or you have only one, divide your content into menu areas. Keep in mind that the following menu types are just a guide.

Cross-Reference

See Chapter 1 for definitions and samples of menu types.

Categories

Categories is your main menu area and will appear on every page. Don't waste a single category — it is the backbone of your site. I recommend that you keep this section to no more than five or six items, because it will be an important part of your design and the tool for your visitors to hop around your site easily. Too many options can be confusing.

Housekeeping

Housekeeping menus appear on every page and are usually designed to fade to the background unless the visitor has a question about the company or policies. Like the categories menu, housekeeping menus should be chosen with great care. If a visitor says, "I wonder how (or who, or why)," they should be able to get the answer here. Four is the maximum number of items that I like to use for a house-keeping menu.

Secondary menus

This is the place to make your visitors happy. A secondary menu should take your visitors to the "meat" of your content and is generally reached through a major category menu item. If you have any major divisions as described in the previous section, your visitor's click on a secondary menu item is click number three. Your site success drops dramatically with each click a visitor must make to reach their goal. Secondary menus often contain many links.

Teaser menus

Teaser menus are your little sales force. Demos, slide shows, special products, sale items, new items — all perfect as teaser menu items. Special help sections can also be designed as a teaser menu item with a brief description of the content included with the link. Teaser menus are the most flexible and are valuable as a design tool as well as navigation. You can add teaser menus to balance and expand content areas or as visual relief on content heavy pages. On your map, do not connect teaser menus to the main map. You may want to design an icon to represent each teaser menu, and use that symbol to represent where teaser menus appear.

Text menus

Each page should have at least one plain text menu that repeats any graphic menus on the page. The most common place for this menu is at the bottom of every page. Although, ideally, you have all category and housekeeping menu items repeated in this menu, you also have to make decisions as to whether some secondary menu items should be included. Teaser menu items are usually excluded, unless they are the same as other menu type links. Some visitors cannot see graphics or choose to surf with graphics disabled. Providing a text menu means that they can still navigate your site. As a surfer, I like to have the links right at my fingertips after I reach the bottom of a page and am ready to move on.

Working out your linking pattern

After you know what type of menu items are directing your content, you must determine how the various pages will be linked. Category and housekeeping menus appear on every page, so these menus can be reached from anywhere on the site. Teaser menus can be placed on any page. Secondary menu items can be tricky, however. In a standard example, each category leads to a secondary menu. The links in the secondary menu for one category are not available through the secondary menu for another category. At times, they should be.

There is no rule that prevents the same links from appearing in every secondary menu. That is one solution. You can also create a teaser menu item for the same link and place it on a page in a different category. This is a good solution when you do not require the link on every secondary menu. Do not just keep adding links to secondary menus to make sure you "have all the bases covered." Every additional link in a menu adds thinking time for visitors — not a way to keep them on your site. The best menus have everything at hand when the visitors look for it, but are seen and understood instantly with not much more than a glance. A secondary menu with 25 items does not provide that ideal.

Getting your map on paper

Show time! You've done your homework and are ready to get your site rolling. Many developers find that sketching initial ideas on paper is the most efficient way to work. When you start with a computer program, by its very nature, you must assign a structure to your page (I mean the graphic page — you already have the structure for your site), which may not enable the thought process to work as freely as it does with a pencil or pen.

I always start with paper when I am building a map. I find it is easier to plan when I am working roughly with the layout of a page, as you can see in Figure 5-4. This figure was the initial working draft for Diamonds.com (http://diamonds.com), a large diamond and jewelry commerce site. The work I produce at this stage is not shared with clients, but does help me shape my ideas. The final site has three menu areas, but at this stage, there are only two. Notice how the help reference appears in three places. On the final site, this feature is a distinctive yellow icon that appears in many different places on the various pages.

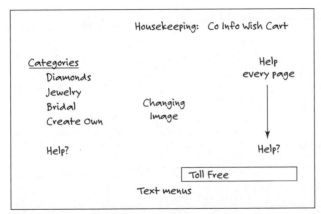

Figure 5-4: Initial draft for a site map. There is no correct form for this stage of your map development. I prefer to visualize menu areas as if they are on a page, but you may prefer to create your menu areas without thinking of where they will appear on the page. I used this sample as the start point for the final map, complete with linking patterns that were created in a graphics program.

Exercise: Creating a Map by Hand

Create a hand drawn map for your site. Make sure that you have your site goals and customer needs firmly in your mind, or better yet, in writing (such as in the worksheets from Chapter 2 and Chapter 3). Sketch out a map in the form of a Web page as shown in Figure 5-4, or in lists, or both. What your page looks like does not matter, but make sure that you have the following clearly identified:

✦ Major divisions

✦ Category menus

✦ Housekeeping menus

✦ Secondary menus

✦ Teaser menus

✦ Items included in text menus

✦ Elements appearing on every page

You may find that you must start over several times. This is a natural part of the process and truly valuable. The reasons that you decide to proceed in a different way often provide clues to creating a site that is valuable to visitors.

Creating a Site Map in Graphics Programs

You may want to skip the hand drawn version of a site map and create your map directly in a graphics program. Or, you may require a professional version of the site map you create by hand. The draft I created in Figure 5-4 was a simple sketch that I expanded to a full site map for my client. An excerpt of that map is shown in Figure 5-5.

The full map is available on the CD-ROM included with this book. Look for `map.pdf` in the Chapter 5 folder.

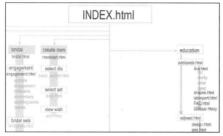

Figure 5-5: An excerpt from a client-quality site map for Diamonds.com, created in an illustration program.

Choosing a tool for computer-generated site maps

Any program that will allow side-by-side placement of objects, plus create lines and text can be used to create a professional site map, including a word processing program or presentation software, such as Microsoft PowerPoint. The tool is not important. However, Web developers usually have software programs that are much better suited to the task than office programs.

My preference is always to use a vector-based program, such as Macromedia Fireworks (hybrid vector and raster), CorelDraw from Corel Corporation, Adobe Illustrator, or Macromedia Freehand to create site maps. The vector format lends itself well to moving objects and text around on the page. However, if you do not have one of these programs mentioned, a raster program, such as Adobe Photoshop or JASC Software's Paint Shop Pro can do the job.

General tips for creating site maps in graphic programs

You can use different methods to create a map depending on which program you use, but you have some general guidelines to follow for creating any map:

✦ The style of the map does not matter. I tend to use boxes to represent pages, but that is a personal choice mainly because it gives me an extra color-coding element if needed. A plain text map is every bit as valuable as a pretty one — your personal style is appropriate for the map.

✦ Use file names for map items if the names are representative of the content. If the file names are meaningless, assign a page name, and list the file name with the page name. On large sites, confusing similar pages is very easy if the file name is not always part of the map.

✦ If a map is to be viewed on a monitor, try to keep the size to one screen, where possible. The true value of a site map is that each file is seen in relation to the entire site. If the information will not fit on one screen, find a logical division for the site sections.

✦ Show connections between pages where possible but avoid a maze of lines twisting through your map. Many connections can be assumed, such as the category and housekeeping menus if they appear on every page.

✦ Save your map document in the native format for the program you are using, with layers intact. You will often make changes in a site map, and native formats offer the easiest editing.

✦ To export for Web use, the GIF format is usually best for site maps.

The following suggestions apply only to a site map that will be printed. Creating a site map that is to be viewed only on a monitor is no different from creating any other graphic for the Web.

✦ Work in inches or centimeters. If your site map is going to be produced on paper, pixels will be difficult for map placement and sizing.

✦ Try to keep your map on one page or plan to physically connect your map with tape or glue. The value of a site map is that you can see each element in relation to the entire site — you lose this perspective if you have a map on several pages.

✦ Use the appropriate resolution.

✦ Save your map as the native format for the program you are using. This option will always give you the maximum flexibility for changes. You can always export a Web ready version of the map from your file if necessary.

Caution   Many of the maps I do are never seen on paper by the client, but rather transferred and evaluated via the Web. However, if you are creating a map that is to be printed, you will require a higher resolution for your document (pure illustration programs, such as CorelDraw, Illustrator, and Freehand are not dependent on pre-set resolution). I recommend setting the resolution to a minimum of 150 to 200 dots per inch (dpi) and 200 to 250 dpi if you are printing the map on a high-quality desktop printer.

Making your map

Following are instructions for building a map in Fireworks, Photoshop, and Paint Shop Pro.

Note   I use an illustration program to create most of my site maps. However, this book focuses on specific graphics programs that are used heavily in Web production, and at this point, that list does not include a pure vector program.

Creating a site map in Fireworks

Fireworks works like a vector program as you build a site map, but becomes a raster program after you save the document, by saving the files in PNG (portable network graphics) format. However, when you reopen the file, all layers and objects remain, which allows vector editing. Make sure that you always save the document, not just export to a pure raster format.

To build a site map in Fireworks, follow these steps:

1. Create a new document by choosing File ➪ New. The New Document window opens.

   For monitor viewing only: If you are creating a site map for monitor display only, set the width to 730 pixels, and the height to 450 pixels (recommended setting to display your map in one screen on most monitors). Set Resolution to 72 pixels per inch (ppi).

   For a site map to be printed: Set the width to 7 inches and the height to 8 to 10 inches. This setting is the actual printed size of your document. Set the resolution to 150 to 200 ppi for most desktop printers, or to 200 to 250 ppi for higher quality printers.

2. Activate the text tool and click at the center of the page close to the top to open the Text Editor. Set the font to a plain, easy to read font, such as Arial or Helvetica, 16 pts, and black fill (a site map is a utility document and legibility outweighs style). Type **index.html** to represent the entry page for your site. Click OK.

3. If you are using boxes to represent pages, create the first rectangle around the text. Set outline color to black and fill to none by using the color wells at the bottom of the toolbox. Click and drag to draw a rectangle around the text, allowing plenty of space at the left and right of the text.

4. Your map will be easier and faster to create, as well as look better if you duplicate your rectangles rather than creating new ones. Click the rectangle to select and drag it to the left and down. *Before releasing the mouse button,* press the Alt key to place a duplicate. Figure 5-6 shows the duplicate ready to be placed. Repeat to create as many boxes as you have pages. Arrange the rectangles in the order you require.

Tip   If you will be creating several sizes of rectangles for your map, create one rectangle in each required size and then repeat Step 4 to create the number of rectangles in each size you require.

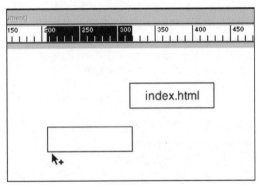

Figure 5-6: Duplicating a rectangle in Fireworks for a site map

5. Activate the Text tool and type file or page names in each rectangle (or in the location you require to complete the map if you are not using boxes). Center the text in the rectangles.

6. Activate the line tool. Click and drag to draw connecting lines between the rectangles (or text if not using boxes) to illustrate links.

7. Save the file and print (if applicable). To export a file that was designed at 72 ppi, simply export to the desired format. If you have designed your map at higher resolution for printing, choose File ⇨ Export Preview. The Export Preview window opens. Click the File tab near the top of the window. In the Scale section, specify 730 pixels for the W (width) value. The H value should automatically adjust to hold the proportion. Select Export to complete the export process.

Creating a site map in Photoshop or Paint Shop Pro

Creating a site map is so similar in Photoshop and Paint Shop Pro that I feature both in one exercise. The vector capabilities in these raster programs make short work of building a site map.

To create a site map in Paint Shop Pro (PSP) or Photoshop (PS), follow these steps:

1. Create a new document by choosing File ➪ New. The New Document window opens.

    For monitor viewing only: If you are creating a site map for monitor display only, set the width to 730 pixels, and the height to 450 pixels (recommended setting to display your map in one screen on most monitors). Set Resolution to 72 ppi.

    For a site map to be printed: Set the width to 7 inches and the height to 8 to 10 inches. This setting is the actual printed size of your document. Set the resolution to 150 to 200 ppi for most desktop printers or to 200 to 250 ppi for higher quality printers.

2. If you are using boxes to represent pages, create the first rectangle near the top center of the page. Select the Rectangle tool (PS) or Preset Shapes tool and choose Rectangle in the Tool Options window (PSP). Set outline color to black and 1px and fill to white using the Layer Styles window (PS) or the Tool Options window (PSP). Click and drag to draw a rectangle of the desired size.

To duplicate the vector rectangles, you have many ways, but I find copy and paste to be the quickest method. Although you can create a new layer for each new rectangle, I prefer to place several vector objects on one layer, usually all the entries for one section.

3. Select the rectangle with the Path Component Selection Tool (in PS) or the Object Selector (in PSP). Choose Edit ➪ Copy (Ctrl + C in Windows; Command + C for Mac). Make sure that the rectangle layer is active and (PS) choose Edit ➪ Paste (Ctrl + V in Windows; Command + V for Mac). (PSP) Choose Edit ➪ Paste ➪ New Vector Selection (Ctrl + G) and click to place the new rectangle. Position the new rectangles as desired.

4. Activate the text tool and click in the first rectangle to place the cursor (PS) or open the Text Editor (PSP). Set the font to a plain, easy to read font, such as Arial or Helvetica, 16 pts, and black fill. Type **index.html** to represent the entry page for your site. Click the Accept button (PS) or OK (PSP). Repeat for each page you require.

Tip

If you are placing pages on a site map in a vertical row, you can use one text entry for all pages in that section. Simply set the leading to the desired level to adjust the spacing between the text. If you are also using boxes with the text, create the text first and place the boxes around the text.

5. Activate the Line tool (PS) or Draw tool with Point to Point Line option set in the Tool Options window (PSP). Click and drag to draw connecting lines between the rectangles (or text if not using boxes) to illustrate links. Add arrowheads if desired through the toolbar (PS) or the Line Style ⇨ Custom option in the Tool Options window (PSP).

6. Save the file and print (if applicable). To export a file that was designed at 72 ppi, simply export to the desired format (usually GIF) by using File ⇨ Save for Web (PS) or File ⇨ Export ⇨ GIF Optimizer (PSP). If you have designed your map at higher resolution for printing, you must adjust the size as you export the document.

   Photoshop: Choose File ⇨ Save for Web. Click the Image Size tab in the lower right corner of the Save for Web window. Set the width to 800 and the height should scale automatically. Click OK to save.

   Paint Shop Pro: You have to resize the document before exporting to create a Web document. Choose Image ⇨ Resize and select Pixel size in the Resize window. Enter 800 in the width field and the height should adjust automatically. Now export to the desired format, usually GIF, by using File ⇨ Export ⇨ GIF Optimizer.

Although the instructions through this chapter have been general, they should give you some direction to create your own site map. Unfortunately, no exact instruction is possible for site maps or many menu topics, as each site has a unique structure. Don't be afraid to start over if your original direction does not work as you progress. Every time I try to shortcut, I end up with the long route back to correcting the map. Tossing some work now is much better than investing many hours and ending up losing the graphic and design work. If your map is not right, your site will not be right.

✦　　✦　　✦

Choosing the Right Look

Is there any tougher job in the world than deciding where to start with the design of a new site? You always have a few guidelines whether you are working on your own site or creating one for a client. Maybe you know that you must put forth a somber and professional tone, as would be appropriate for a funeral home. Perhaps you must use the same logo and font that appears in print material for the same company. But even with a good start, designing a new site is a scary, clear screen that starts the process.

Eventually you probably get to a design result that makes you relatively happy — after all, you are interested enough in Web design to be reading this book. In this chapter I am going to help you shorten the process, narrow down your options, and hopefully have the designs hopping onto your page. Okay, maybe that isn't quite realistic, but by taking a logical route to your design, the time between blank, white screen to effective design can be dramatically shortened.

But what does site design have to do with menus? Just everything! Take a look at any six Web pages you choose and I guarantee that the menu system forms the most important element of the design. If it does not, you have found sites that are not well integrated. Web design is not "graphic art moved to the Web." Web design is taking the required elements and working them into an effective design. Swallow hard before reading on if you come from an art background — a menu can get by without your brilliant design, but your brilliant design is useless without a clear and functional menu. So when I talk about site design, for the most part, I am talking about menus and the "stuff" that goes around the menu.

Pick Your Mood and Run with It

You have moods. You behave differently in different situations. I doubt that you talk in the same tone to your bank manager as you do with your friends when you get together on the weekend. If your business is audited, I have no doubt you use different body language than you do when you are discussing a purchase with your partner. We all have many pieces to our personalities. Web sites need a personality, too, but it must be well defined to be effective. People can change according to the company—Web sites can't.

That doesn't mean you can't have a site that is playful and professional or serious and friendly. What it means is that you can't change the personality of your site. If you do not already have a good understanding of your product and where it fits with competitors, your customers, or potential customers, finding the correct mood and look for site will be tough.

 Cross-Reference   Chapter 2 helps you identify your product and industry niche, and Chapter 3 discusses how to predict or identify potential visitors.

What is mood in graphics?

Mood can best be described for a Web page as the emotion that a color combination and set of graphic images draws from a visitor. A bright site, alive with red, black, and yellow can be seen as energetic, powerful, exciting, or professional, depending on the proportion of each color and the balance of the page. In Figure 6-1, the same colors and the same elements are used to create three looks. The font is even in the same family. However, the mood in each is very different. The top example has a solid, business-like mood. The second image is much more playful, even though it could be appropriate for a professional site. The final example is more artsy, with a slight futuristic mood. Although the color and design elements are quite similar, these three images would not work well on the same page, simply because the mood does not match.

Fonts alone can set the mood of a page. In Figure 6-2, the two samples are identical, but the first sample features a classic font, carefully kerned (characters adjusted for perfect spacing), with a subtle drop shadow for a rich look. The second sample displays the same word but this time in a novelty font with an embossed effect.

HOME
HOME
HOME

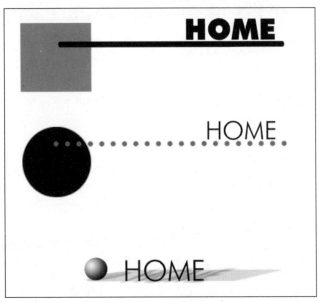

Figure 6-1: Three images with identical colors, fonts from the same family, and similar design elements. Each projects a different mood.

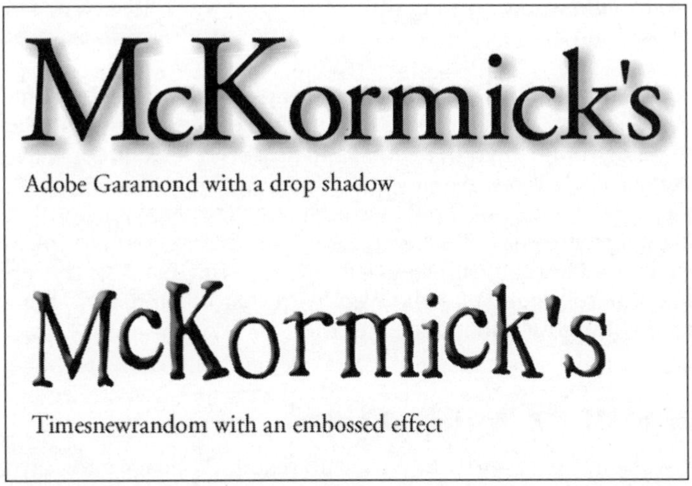

McKormick's
Adobe Garamond with a drop shadow
McKormick's
Timesnewrandom with an embossed effect

Figure 6-2: The same word with font and effect change projects a totally different mood.

Where does color fit in?

Color, of course, is one of the most important elements in setting mood on a Web page. Color should be the most comfortable design element for us, as we are immersed in color from the first day of our lives. We may know what our favorite color is, but do we understand why? You may choose a certain outfit on a certain day, and often it is because the color is appropriate, but we do not always stop to figure out why.

When you design a Web page, however, you are faced with using color in a logical way. You may have instructions from your client that a blue site is desired. They have told you nothing. There are too many shades of blue. There are too many contrasting levels of blue to have the word *blue* mean anything. Add black to blue and the page changes. Take the same page and use brown instead of black, and the entire mood shifts.

Generally, colors such as red, orange, and yellow are exciting and vibrant. Cooler colors are more relaxing, such as cool blues and greens. But put lime green and royal blue together in dramatic quantities and the result is not relaxing. Likewise, line drawings in orange, red, and yellow on a light background could produce a very relaxing mood.

Unfortunately, I do not have color magic for you. Color is another subject that fills books larger than this one. If you have had formal design training, the color skills you develop for another medium transfer well to the Web. If you have not had design training and struggle when working with color, go to your library, or bookstore, and immerse yourself in the subject as much as you can.

An excellent series of articles about color for Web design is at WebDesignClinic.com (`www.webdesignclinic.com/ezine/color.html`). One of the best ways to educate yourself about color, mood, layout, menus, and any other design topics is to view hundreds, maybe even thousands, of well-done sites. Cool Home Pages (`www.coolhomepages.com`) is one of the Web's largest collections of beautiful Web sites. Although the Cool Home Page sites are impressive, they do tend to the artistic side and are usually quite graphics heavy—in other words, many of the sites do not follow current commercial needs for the Web. With that in mind, however, the site is a valuable source for education and inspiration.

How do your visitors want to feel?

I start this process working backwards from the end result. Picture visitors arriving at your site. Are they afraid of something they do not understand and seek products or information to help (medical and legal difficulties leap to mind)? Are they excited and anxious to find out anything they can (perhaps seeking marriage or college services or special information)? If they are seeking a product, is it a luxury or a necessary purchase and do they have their credit card in hand, or does much research and correspondence precede a sale?

The answers to these questions give you the initial direction for your site. Is there a particular expectation your visitors have of your site? A common theme you see on telecommunications sites is movement, usually from small, animated graphics. Why? Think about what you expect from a company involved in cutting-edge technology that moves data and voice around the world. You want a little excitement, don't you? Don't you want the site to grab you and shake you up just a little? This concept is how bells and whistles should be worked into any site — with a deliberate purpose and as part of building a specified mood.

Many retail product sites, such as Eddie Bauer (`www.eddiebauer.com`) and Crate and Barrel (`www.crateandbarrel.com`) create their site mood with product shots alone. That's what visitors are there for — to see the products these stores sell. In fact, if you visit the inside pages of these sites, you will notice that the site structure and appearance is quite similar. The site structure fades into the background in favor of the products.

On the opposite side of this issue, for movie sites, the mood is the product. Compare the Web sites for the movie, *Crouching Tiger, Hidden Dragon* (`www.crouchingtiger.com`) and *Tomb Raider* (`www.tombraider.com`). Warning: With slow connections, these sites require long download time. You don't have to see either of these movies to recognize the differences in style, even though both are adventure films with female lead characters.

The movie world sells mood — that is their product. They know how their visitors want to feel when they arrive at the site. The model comes from the movie, which has already inspired an interest for the visitor. Movie sites can be a fertile training ground for designers to learn about setting a mood. Major movie sites are generally very well done. Pay attention to how a theme is carried throughout the entire site. Study the extra features that are included on the site, such as behind the scenes glimpses for impressive effects.

Find the sites for several movies that you have seen and compare what the site designers have done to capture the mood of the movie. I am not implying that movie sites are good examples to bring into a corporate setting. Quite the opposite. But by studying such obvious mood creating sites, you can bring what you have learned about setting a mood to building the appropriate mood for your site.

I believe in writing down the details of a design. Artistic inspiration is wonderful and an extremely valuable talent. However, getting lost is too easy when creating any type of art, and in Web development losing the goal can be fatal to your site.

Exercise: Setting Your Site's Personality

Take the time to complete the following exercise, and you will probably refer to it many times as you design the layout and graphics for your site. At times, you may know instinctively what your site personality should be. More often however, the distinction between a perfect site to reach your goals and serve your visitors is a matter of subtle degree. Writing down where you are going is essential to keeping a strong identity and direction throughout your site.

On the CD-ROM   The exercise that follows also appears in an expanded version in the Chapter 6 folder on the CD-ROM included with this book.

1. Choose two Web sites that have a product unrelated to your site and list the mood that you "feel" for each one. List how you think the mood is created for each listed item.

2. Why will your customers be visiting your site?

3. List what your visitors expect to find. You should be able to list at least three expectations, unless you have a very simple, one-product site. However, do not let this list exceed six items.

4. Choose two Web sites of competitors or sites with a product that serves a similar customer group to your site. List the mood that you "feel" with each site and describe why you think that mood exists.

5. How do you describe the mood on your competitors' sites?

6. How will your site mood be similar to any/all competitors?

7. How will your site mood differ from any/all competitors?

8. What colors do you expect will deliver the mood you require? List at least three color combinations that would project the correct mood.

9. What site features can advance the mood you require? State a reason why the feature helps achieve your goals.

10. Considering your customer needs, the product you offer, and the mood requirements you have identified in this exercise, has a menu style started to come to your mind. If so, even if only fleeting pieces are there now, describe as much as you can. If not, try to jot down a few ideas.

Bossing Your Visitors Around

Okay, the time to be nice and accommodating is over. You have gathered and collected and surveyed and taken every visitor need under strong advisement. Now is the time to assert yourself. Well, maybe assert yourself a little — or better yet, assert yourself to help your visitors get what they need from your site. That should lessen the shock of my change in tone a little.

Visitors do not always know what they want when they arrive at a site. You have worked hard to make sure that you know what they want, so that you can place what they need where they cannot avoid it. On a twist of "build it and they will come" we must "place it where they cannot miss it." That is *your* job and one that site developers often mistake as their visitors' responsibility.

Caution Do not confuse what I am describing here with trying to force your visitors to seek information they are not already seeking. This section is about providing a visitor with non-thinking access to the place they want to be.

When you are considering your page design, use your site map, keep your mood in mind, and always remember why the visitor is there. However, you must also decide not only what content or menu items will be available, but also how visitors are likely to move through your site. You want to place the information they need right in front of them. Some of this direction naturally occurs with well-planned menus, plus teaser menu items to draw attention to specific content, but your mood must also come into play hand-in-hand with the site structure.

What are the tools you have to work with for attracting attention? You can change color, isolate a graphic element, make text larger, bolder, or animated. You can place links next to images, which always attract attention. You can use white space to make information stand out more. But which is the right technique? It depends completely on the mood of your site. A quite understated look does not need a dramatic enhancement of any element to draw attention—shifting a few degrees of color can do the job. However, a slight color change on a vibrant, fun, busy site has little attraction value.

You can see an example of how a subtle change can effect where attention will go in Figure 6-3. The gentle white and gray background enables the text to stand out well. A visitor's eye is drawn immediately to the text. But with higher contrast color for identical graphic elements, attention does not go to the text. Rather than the text taking center stage, the entire rectangular area grabs the eye and forces the visitor into a decision to seek the text. Sure you have their attention, but it is in the wrong place.

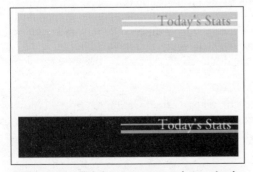

Figure 6-3: With low contrast color, as in the top sample, the eye is drawn straight to the text. In the lower sample with higher contrast colors, the eye is drawn to the black rectangle and the eye must "find" the text.

On a busy, high-contrast page, you may need animation to attract visitor attention. You can also reserve one color as the flag for visitors, such as red on a page that contains mostly dark colors. Even with high contrast colors and busy graphics, red and yellow stand out very well.

Each site has different requirements, but you must keep the mood that you are working with when you plan the method for attracting attention. Keep the same method throughout the site, and your attention getting method also adds to consistency, another critical element for creating a comfortable experience for your visitor.

Your Page is Heavy on the Left, Huh?

I cover many of the initial design planning considerations in this section—or at least those you need to know to create a great menu for your site. The final one that I want to discuss is balance. Although this is a little premature in the process to be fine tuning the ultimate balance on your pages, your menus are such a vitally important and visually heavy part of your page that a little pre-planning is not misplaced.

Pages that are not well balanced are uncomfortable for visitors. Think of sitting in a beautiful chair that is lower on one side of the seat than the other. No matter how you try to get comfortable, it is impossible. Visitors probably won't know why they do not read your page well or have trouble finding information, but may still leave for a more comfortable place. Balance is critical.

Visual weight

What has more "weight" on a page? A one-inch black circle or a two-inch light gray circle? Take a look at Figure 6-4 for a result that may surprise you. Although the black circle is only half the size of the gray circle, the black circle commands the space they share. Stand back from the image, maybe even across the room, to get the full impact of how strong that little black circle really is.

Color works in the same way. You can have a large graphic element in a light color and low contrast, and the element carries little weight. One word in heavy, black text can overpower that large image, or if placed at a distance, balance the visual weight on the page.

Texture can affect a graphic image weight, as can effects, such as drop shadows. This chapter must be the no-rules chapter—I again have to tell you that there are no hard and fast rules for visual weight. Even after years in many types of design, I cannot always predict exactly which elements in which color and in what scale will produce perfect balance.

Figure 6-4: The small black circle "weighs" more on the page than the gray circle at twice the size.

How much are your menu areas going to weigh? Keep this question in mind as you move to the design process. Because menus are such important elements of any page, they should have a starring role, but menus must balance with the rest of the page. Creating a balanced menu that stands out enough to be found, yet can allow the content to come forward when not in use is not easy. Keeping the fundamental idea of balance helps, however. A balanced page usually has met the ideal for a menu automatically. Continue on to learn how to test your balance and put it to use as you create your menus.

Testing for visual weight

While you have no tidy rules to apply to visual weight, you can use easy tricks to test your pages. Artists have been using these tricks for centuries, but Web designers often do not know of them, or do not think to apply the tricks to an image on a monitor. I do admit, some of these tricks are not easy to do. For example, a classic test of visual balance is to turn your page upside down. I strongly advise against turning a monitor upside down to test your page. I also recommend that you abstain from the most obvious variation of standing on your head in your office chair to turn *you* upside down. However, all is not lost, as there are few tricks we can use.

The easiest way to test your page for visual balance is to squint your eyes until the page is just a blur. After the shapes of your page elements are not distinct, all that is left is the pattern of color on the screen. Problems in balance show up clearly. My favorite testing method is to stand very far back from my monitor — out of my office to be precise. I can easily get more than 20 feet from my monitor with a clear view. As you step away, again the elements of the page become less distinct and the balance pattern becomes obvious.

I take this distance testing to another level when I think I have client-quality proofs. I sneak up on my pages. I work from home, so I will leave the page on the monitor and walk away for several minutes, perhaps making coffee or tidying up a little in the house. As I go by the office, I will just glance at the page. Although I am certain I look a little — let's say *unusual* — stalking a monitor, those fast glances can identify problems. If I can sneak up on my pages from several different directions and my eyes are drawn to the entire page, as opposed to one "problem" area, I can send the proof away with confidence. Consider the consequences before you try this in a crowded office!

In my past when fiber was my medium, a mirror was a valuable testing tool. Simply viewing your work as a mirror image can immediately show up balance problems. I have used this occasionally with intricate designs for the Web. Seeing a mirror image does help to identify balance problems, especially with vertical elements. Our surfing eyes are so comfortable with menus on the left side of the page that we can miss when they are too heavy for the other elements of the page.

Perhaps the easiest method, though it does involve a little time to train yourself, is to watch how you feel when you are working on your page. An unbalanced page can create a physical reaction. If you feel your head tipping in one direction when you are working on a page, it may be helping your eyes find a balance with the page. This method is the best way to auto-correct as you create your pages and is a valuable skill to develop, although not everyone can manage to master it. If your instinct for balance is not exceptional, test often, using one of the methods mentioned previously.

Controlling the Artist Within

Warning: Author on a soapbox!

Art is fun. Making pretty pictures can be a blast. Every person in the world should find a way to express his or herself through some form of art. Perhaps the world would be better. But everything has its place and time.

Unless you are creating a personal site for the express purpose of creating art and sharing it with the world, the bitter truth is that Web design done well is commercial art. Commercial art is — crass as it may sound — commercial. It is designed to sell. You may be providing information about a life-threatening disease, for no compensation, but you are still "selling" a product. You still have a duty to your visitors to provide a site that loads quickly, is intuitive to navigate, and speaks to the visitor's need for the product not your need to create beautiful pages.

If you are or want to be a professional designer, the previous paragraph is the best mantra you can adopt. The Web became popular with such a frantic flurry of new developments that newer, better, flashier became the norm. The Web is maturing now, and you can see that in many corporate sites. Many of the sites I loved because they were truly beautiful have now been replaced by attractive, functional sites that fly onto the screen. The corporate Web has started to realize that the Web is still first and foremost an information medium. The information may be how to buy a product through e-commerce, but it is information we demand.

Don't think that it is easy to design an attractive, simple site. In fact, I find it quite easy to make a show-stopping page if I don't have to worry whether anyone can use it. If I can work in a graphic program and just slice and create tables for a Photoshop creation... that is easy. Creating a site that is graphically attractive, simple enough to let the information shine through, and easy for a visitor to navigate through is skilled, hard work. That I can do it is how I make my living through design.

I repeat a plea from an earlier chapter — create a site where you can play and try all the techniques that interest you. When you are creating a site for the public, whether your goal is to sell high-ticket items or to share your club's latest news, place your visitor's needs first — always.

Exercise: Setting Your Graphic Direction

You can set the direction of your site's overall design by answering the following questions or by opening your favorite graphics program and working through the questions in graphic form. You may find that answering the questions in writing and then moving to your graphics program is an efficient way to start your site. You notice a repetitive question at the end of each point. Remember, that is why you have worked so hard to get to this point.

1. What are three potential color schemes for your site? Unless you are creating a specialized look, most sites will use at least three colors or shades of colors. Why is this choice appropriate for your site goals?

2. What is the logo for the page name? Are there design elements that can be borrowed from the logo (shapes, lines, circles)? Why is this choice appropriate for your site goals?

3. Where will the menu areas be? Why is this choice appropriate for your site goals?

4. Is content presented in column form? If yes, how many columns? Why is this choice appropriate for your site goals?

5. What font(s) will you use for graphic areas? Please hold the number of fonts to two families unless there is a very good reason for more. What font will you use for HTML text? What font size? Why is this choice appropriate for your site goals?

6. What will be used as your attention-getting element? Why is this choice appropriate for your site goals?

7. What balances what? For example, if you have a black menu with white fonts at the left, that is a lot of weight. What will balance that to the right? Hint: Plain text is unlikely to accomplish the balance, though two columns of text with icons to divide sections, or text broken into many headlines in a heavy font may work. Why is this choice appropriate for your site goals?

8. Do you anticipate any balance problems, such as many large images, heavy illustrations for a product? If so, how will you create balance? Why is this choice appropriate for your site goals?

9. What methods will you use to test your balance?

This exercise also appears in an expanded version in the Chapter 6 folder on the CD-ROM included with this book.

✦　　✦　　✦

Creating a Rough Comp

"**W**hen will you have the comps ready to view?" Uh, oh! You have a rough idea what they mean from the conversation, but what exactly is a comp?

As part of a well-planned project, you must create your graphics or project "look." This is when you experiment with color, layout, and artistic elements, as well as make critical decisions about your menus. Most designers, especially if working for clients, prepare an initial set of proofs for the project, usually in a vector or raster graphic program. These proofs are often referred to as *comps*, which is the term I use throughout this book.

Comps, which is short for *comprehensive layouts*, is an advertising agency term originally developed to describe a rough layout of an ad or a page for presentation to the design team and/or the client. The layout is not necessarily final, but is usually very close to what the final appearance will be. Often several comps are prepared for the same project to provide the client with choices.

Many professional Web designers have adopted *comp* as the term to describe the proofing process for a Web or intranet site. They prepare comps for client approval before creating graphics and rollovers for HTML pages; changes to graphic elements or page layouts are quick and easy in a vector or raster program. After the final look and layout is approved, designers can confidently move to the more exacting and time-consuming task of preparing graphics for HTML pages.

Comp layouts are usually prepared in raster or vector programs and exported as full-page JPG or GIF images. These images are most often placed in a very simple HTML page and uploaded to a folder on the designer's working site for online viewing. In the rare case that a client or member of the development team does not have Internet access, comps can be printed or copied to a CD-ROM for viewing.

Note   I make it very clear to my clients that graphic changes past the comp stage will add to the cost of the project. One small change can affect many images on the page and be doubled or tripled by requiring changes to rollover graphics. For my workflow, the comp stage is, by far, the most important stage.

I show you how to build efficient comps in several common graphics programs later in this chapter.

Establishing Menu Areas

Although every designer develops a personal method to create comps, some general guidelines can help you to save time and create a proof that can be easily converted to HTML. To reach the comp stage of a project, you must have some organization already in place. This organization can include a formal site map (see Chapter 5) but at the very least, the project should include the menu items that you determined in the early planning stages. In addition, you should have determined the overall look, based on the site's purpose and your visitor's needs (see Chapter 2 and Chapter 3).

Cross-Reference   If any of the terms in the following discussion are confusing, refer to the Menu Terminology section in Chapter 1 for clarification.

Main menu

Armed with the basic structure for your site, you can move ahead to planning menu areas. All sites will have a main menu, consisting of links to major areas. For small sites, this may be the only menu. I tend to focus on this menu before adding any subsidiary menus — through the main menu a visitor can reach every area of the site, making it the most important navigational tool.

Before you let your ideas run to the final appearance of your main menu, rein in and think of it first as an area. Trust me for a few minutes and I will explain why you should hold back now to save a lot of time later. Just decide where the menu will be: Top left? Top center? Top right? Left? Right? Somewhere else? (Not advised.)

In addition, take a guess at the amount of space you can allot to your main menu. Do you have a logo that will appear beside the menu at the top? If so, how much space does the logo require? Can the menu fit within the logo's height? How many menu items do you have? Keep that in mind as you decide how much space you need for your main menu. These details will become very important as you begin to create your comp.

Housekeeping menus

Containing items, such as contact and help functions, housekeeping menus are extremely important to your site success and visitor convenience (even though they are usually the demure areas on a page). I tend to keep my main and house-keeping menus close together, creating a one-stop area for critical information. However, do not take that idea as a rule. I have occasionally tucked the housekeeping menu under secondary menu items. If you have done your planning homework, you should have a good idea how often and at what stage your visitors will seek the housekeeping information.

See Chapter 8 for information on establishing how your visitors may use the site.

Secondary menus

Secondary menus usually provide additional choices for main menu areas. Although the menu items will usually be different for each of the main menu sections, to reduce confusion, secondary menus should appear in the same location with the same general appearance on each page. Before you create your comp, you should have a rough idea where you will place secondary menu items, and how much space they require.

When I started with Web design, the standard was to design for 640 x 480 pixel resolution as a minimum. I tended to place both the main and secondary menus at the top of the page, allotting most of the main page area for content and other important features, such as teaser menus.

However, many professional Web developers now design for a minimum resolution of 800 x 600 pixels. The extra 260 pixels (and many more at higher resolutions) provide too much width for content. Secondary menus are often placed at the left or right of the page to help keep content line length reasonable.

Teaser menus

Finally, you should establish where you will place teaser menus if your site plan calls for these powerful additions. Teaser menus are little pieces that can be placed anywhere on a page, even within the main content and call visitor attention to areas of the site they should not miss. Many sites, especially portal or information rich sites, allot an entire column to teaser menus. You may decide to place a few teasers under a secondary menu, in a right column, or sprinkled throughout your content like miniature advertisements.

Deciding where the teaser menu items will go before you begin creating a comp is not always necessary, but you must know if you *will* be using teaser menus, and how large they will be if you do. Teaser menus can be one line or several sentences — make sure you know how much space you require for your teaser menus.

Preventing battles between your left and right brain

Think of the menu areas as puzzle pieces that you will fit into place when you create a comp. I have created comps after my menu areas are well established, as I described earlier in this chapter. I have also created menu areas as I build the comp with very little advance planning for the menus. Planning ahead is much more efficient (concentrate on the design elements after you reach the comp stage.

You can always make changes, but every detail that is established firmly before you move to design seems to slide effortlessly into place. When I think back on the comps that were tough for me, there is one repeating theme: a lack of menu structure when I started to design. That just begs for a war between your right- and left-brain functions.

Please take a moment to separate menu structure from design structure. I have heard many designers take great pride in the fact that they allow the muse to rule, and that their sites "just happen." I have noticed something, though. These "just happen" advocates are never the highly successful designers I know. The designers who have reached great success pay attention to the site structure and navigation as a first priority. Ironically, it is that exact action that allows them the freedom to create great design.

I can't tell you how to create any one design. The bars and dots, images, and color backgrounds usually do "just happen," but they "happen" much more easily if you are not trying to ensure that you have a solid site structure at the same time. Computer-based designers are usually quite comfortable when working with either the right (creative) or left (logical) brain functions. However, focusing on one or the other at one time is more efficient. Creating a menu structure is a left-brain activity. Creating a design is very much a right-brain activity. Working on both at one time does not allow either the right- or left-brain function to rule — design by committee, which by definition, is design with compromise.

Can you do it all at once and still create a great site? Yes. Is it the most efficient way to design? Probably not.

Exercise: Getting Your Site Structure on Paper

The following short questionnaire will help you solidify your menu areas before you move your project to the comp stage. Although the questions seem almost ridiculously simple, you may be surprised at how things change as you attempt to write them down.

When I work through this process for a client, it never fails that I have to contact them for one more piece of information. Uncovering little omissions can save you hours in the design process, or in redoing graphics. (And because it is my job to uncover this information before I start the work, I cannot charge for correcting the resulting errors. And I hate working for free.)

You may want to print out a copy of this form from the file that is on the CD-ROM that accompanies this book or fill it in on the computer instead of writing in this book, especially as this exercise is a valuable one for every project.

On the CD-ROM   You can find a copy of this questionnaire in the Session 7 folder on the CD-ROM in the back of this book. You can choose to view the form in Word format (`menuarea.doc`) or in plain text (`menuarea.txt`).

Fill in every section, even if it is with a N/A (not applicable) or TBD (to be determined). If you work through this exercise and it does not help you, you have wasted a bit of time. But if you find that this little pause saves you time and uncertainty in the design phase on every project from now until... See my point? Give it a try.

1. What are the main menu items for your site? (List the names of the menu items.)

2. What is the best location for the main menu to meet site goals and visitor need?

3. Should the main menu be the focal point of the page (the first thing that a visitor sees)? If not, what page element will lead visitors easily to the main menu?

4. Does the main menu have the same appearance on the entry page as it does on interior pages? The same size? (Entry pages often feature the main menu in a more prominent position than on interior pages.)

5. Approximately how many pixels or what percentage of the page (width, height, or both as appropriate) do you estimate the main menu will require? (This is just a starting point.)

6. What are the housekeeping menu items for your site?

7. Does the housekeeping menu require high, medium, or low visibility? Why?

8. Considering the previous question, where do you think the housekeeping menu should be located, and at what size (pixels, percentage of the page, or in relation to another menu)?

9. What secondary menus do you require on the site? If the secondary menu items change with each main menu section, list each section separately.

10. Where will the secondary menus be located?

11. What percentage of the page or number of pixels do you estimate will be required for the secondary menu?

12. If the secondary menu items change for each main menu section, how will you maintain consistency (font, color, location, and so on)?

13. If you are planning teaser menus, where will they be located?

14. Do the teaser menu items require high, medium, or low visibility? Why?

15. If the teaser menus have a separate location, approximately what size should they be (pixels, percentage of page, or column)?

16. List any other information, such as required graphics, colors, or other elements that must be included with any of your menus.

If you have answered each of the relevant questions above, you are ready to move into creating a comp for your site.

Creating Comps with Graphic Software

It's design time! For me and for most designers I know, creating a new comp is probably the most exciting part of creating a site. You have worked through many tedious details and have a really good understanding of what you must do to accomplish site goals and meet visitor needs. Armed with your menu area breakdown, and often a site map, it is time to have some fun.

Yes, design is hard work. Yes, design can be exhausting. But it is fun to pull and drag color around a page, creating something from nothing. Or, it should be. When you are having fun, you are creating better design. Graphic design may not be your forte — many enter the Web development world from the programming side, not from an artistic background.

For naturally artistic people planning adds critical structure to the beauty they create. If you are not naturally artistic, or have yet to discover that you are, you will also find that solid site structure plans will help you. Because the details you tend to focus on are in place, you can turn your mind over to the design. (If the design phase of a project makes you nervous or uncertain, you may want to look at Chapter 9.)

The method used to create comps varies depending on which program you use; in reality, it also varies for every designer. As an example, I have chosen one method for each of several software programs that you can use as a guide. How you achieve a comp is not important, as long as you produce a representative image that reflects your idea for the final site.

Caution   When exporting comps from any program, make sure you turn on antialiasing as you export, and do not over-optimize. Comps are understood to be large files. It is better to have every color represented correctly for GIF files, and JPG images should have few or no artifacts for accurate proofs.

Creating a comp with CorelDraw or Illustrator

I do the majority of my early comps in an illustration program, such as CorelDraw from Corel Corporation or Adobe Illustrator. Vector programs work with an object based format, which provides one-click editing access to any object on the page.

For a small percentage of my work, I complete the proofing process in my vector program, and export the graphic elements directly from the program to the final GIF or JPG format. More often, I complete a rough comp in a vector program, providing client proofs directly from the vector program, and finishing the site in a raster program. Using this method, I keep the comp in vector format as long as there are likely to be changes.

Note   Although I love working in vector format, a vector cannot compete with the stronger tools for slicing graphics and creating rollover graphics that raster programs feature. I import the approved comp into a raster program to build the final site graphics. Although technically this is doing the same job twice, the time I save with vector flexibility in the initial design phase more than compensates for the short time it takes me to create the design again in a raster program.

Notes to create a comp in CorelDraw

1. Set your page to one of the preset Web page sizes in the drop-down menu or through the custom option. This page setup will create the canvas size you require and changes your rulers to pixel units.

2. Select the Websafe color palette to use only browser safe color. (CorelDraw: Select the Internet Explorer or Netscape palette.) If using safe colors is not important to you, creating your own palette is best by using the RGB selector.

3. Ensure that you keep all objects within the page frame. Objects outside the frame will not export correctly.

4. Create additional pages for multiple comps. Select all objects on the original page, copy and paste to a new page, making any changes you desire for the second proof. You can always delete any unnecessary pages later.

5. Export comp to GIF or JPG format for inclusion in an HTML proof page. To export one object, perhaps to test a rollover effect, use the Save Selected Only feature as you export to JPG or GIF format.

Notes to create a comp in Illustrator

1. Change the page units to pixels. Choose Edit ⇨ Preferences ⇨ Units and Undo. Change the text units to reflect the units you will use in your final page (pixels or points). Choose File ⇨ Document Setup to specify page size.

2. If you want to export only a few elements, build your page in layers. In order to export partial documents, turn off the visibility of the layers you do not want to export before exporting the comp or individual graphics.

3. Select the Websafe RGB color palette.

4. Use the Save for Web export to create JPG or GIF comps (export using JPG or GIF format for earlier versions).

Creating a comp in Photoshop, Paint Shop Pro, and Fireworks

More designers create comps in a raster program, such as Adobe Photoshop, JASC Software's Paint Shop Pro, or Macromedia's Fireworks, than by any other method. Web graphics are raster format, so comps usually become final working documents for site graphics. Raster programs are the powerhouses when it comes to automatically generating perfect rollover graphics, and easily slicing through large images. Moving, scaling, and changing color and stroke for objects is not quite as easy in a raster program as it is with vector format. However, effective use of layers, and the simple vector capability that has been added to modern raster programs makes editing much easier. Of course, nothing compares to a raster program for creating effects, such as shadows, texture, and dimension.

 Note   I included Fireworks in the raster section for this discussion, although it is technically closer to a vector program for drawing. When it comes to creating comps and graphic elements, however, Fireworks has all of the power to create sliced graphics and generate automatic rollover graphics.

Notes to create a comp in Photoshop, Paint Shop Pro, and Fireworks

1. Set the rulers to pixels. Set the Type units to pixels.

2. Set canvas size to desired final comp size.

3. Work in layers, erring to more layers rather than fewer (you can always merge layers. Photoshop: Use layer sets to organize your work. I use a layer set for each menu area.

4. Photoshop: Link layers for related menu areas before moving or transforming to apply the same edit to all layers.

5. Do not render text layers unless you cannot avoid it. If you must render a text layer, create a duplicate of the layer before rendering, and maintain the original layer. Turn off the layer visibility for the original.

6. Use guides to help align elements as you add them. Perfectly aligned layers are important when you progress to creating rollovers and your final page. (Photoshop: Linked layers can be aligned by choosing Layer ⇨ Align Linked and selecting the desired aligning parameter.)

7. Use the Save for the Web option to export JPG or GIF comps.

✦   ✦   ✦

Slim, Sexy Menus: Making Words Count

Understanding Text Menu Methods

Text menus get very little respect. Developers often toss them at the bottom of the page if, and only if, they are aware of accessibility issues and realize that some people still surf without graphics turned on. But text menus have a lot to offer and, in my opinion, we will see much more of this most sensible way to move visitors through a site. In this chapter, I try to convince you to give text a chance.

The Text Advantage

Text menus have two major claims to fame. First, if you compare the text that creates a Web page (HTML) to calories in food, text is the leafy vegetables: Use freely, and you still won't affect the overall size of the page. Graphics are the fats. Graphics still have a place on the page, but must be used with extreme caution, or the weight of the page balloons. Text menus are the true lightweights of the menu world.

Second, changing a text menu item is much easier than creating a new image. Menus are generally set up to be static, but how much of that norm results from the static nature of graphics? After you add text menus to your toolbox, you may find that there are places where menus can be more effective if changed with each season or phase of your business year.

We take a close look at text in this chapter. After you know how and why to use text, keep it in mind as you create your next site.

Not all text menus are ugly

Text creates tiny files. Even the smallest graphic is equal to dozens of tags and paragraphs of text. I don't think this is new information to any Web designer. However, as wireless technology becomes more and more common and Web surfers become bored with shuffling through a lot of art to get to the information, I believe that text as a design tool is going to become much more respected.

When you use Cascading Style Sheets (CSS) to control text, you can produce some very attractive menus. A graphic menu with rollovers and a nearly identical menu using text and CSS are shown in Figure 8-1. I include the final weight for all code and images to the right of each image.

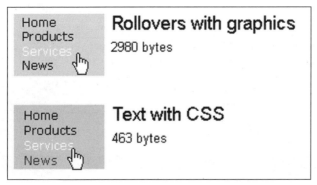

Figure 8-1: Two nearly identical menus. The top image features graphics and rollovers; the lower sample features text and CSS. The total weight for each menu, including JavaScript and CSS code, is listed.

At one time, my knowledge of CSS was light and coming from the print world, anything graphic seemed easy. However, if you are going to be a serious Web designer, whether professional or amateur, you must learn CSS. After you have CSS mastered, you will find that text menus are easier and faster than graphic menus — a bonus beyond the file size savings.

The trend is to text

Take a look at popular Web sites today and you probably see a trend toward more text menus. Successful retail sites, such as Amazon.com (`www.amazon.com`) are streamlining more and more of their site features into text. Webreference.com (`http://webreference.com`) has gone to a main page layout that is fully text, as shown in Figure 8-2. Andy King, formerly managing editor and always optimization guru, was the force behind stripping all excess weight from the page. He recognized that people were not visiting WebReference.com to see art, but to gather information, and he set out to get that information to them as fast as possible.

The WebReference.com logo is a graphic with two animated ads on the entry page, but the total weight of the page, including all code and images is well under 50K, even though a lot of information is on the page.

Figure 8-2: WebReference.com packs many screens of information onto its main page, but weighs less than 50K, even with the two animated ads.

WebReference.com is an information site. I am not implying that high fashion can be presented well in the same way, but many lessons can be learned from lightweight sites. Saving a few bytes on each page of a 500 page site adds up to major savings in bandwidth on a popular site. Bandwidth can be a very real and ongoing cost for a high-trafficked site. Using more text to save bandwidth is no different than choosing a car with good gas mileage to save money over the long term. So what's the big deal if you save 10K on a page? Suppose you save enough bandwidth to reduce your monthly bandwidth total by $50. Okay, maybe this isn't life changing, but project that over a year and that $50 turns into $600. I don't know if you are richer than I am, but $600 gets my attention.

Don't think that I am only referring to the top four sites in the world that can see this type of savings. If your site does as well as you are no doubt hoping it will, this is you I am talking about. Do the math. Calculate the total weight for an average page on your site. Calculate the bandwidth if that page is viewed 100 times, and then 1,000 times, and then 100,000 times. Multiply that by the number of actual or projected pages your visitors view before leaving the site. Take a deep breath and check your bandwidth limit with your host. I'm guessing that maybe I can talk you into paying attention to how you can save 10K, 20K, or even more on every page.

Cross-Reference   While I have your attention, make sure that you also pay close attention to Chapter 9, which focuses on CSS, a great code saver. Chapter 18 features the other big way to save bytes as it offers graphic optimization techniques and tips.

Keep text in mind. If you find yourself creating simple text menus in a graphics program, ask yourself whether you can do the same thing with text and CSS. The first time will take you much longer, unless you are a cross-platform CSS guru, but it is worth it. Even if you do not care much about bandwidth, the time you will save, and the flexibility you gain, is well worth the learning time.

Understanding Font Restrictions

I'm sure a few of you are muttering that there is no way you will use text for all of your menus. The selection of fonts you can use is too narrow. If you are one of the mutterers, you have a point. But remember two details: Not every menu must be text and most of the good fonts look really lousy on the Web anyway. What I am asking you to do is stretch your mind to the idea of text menus. Learn everything you can about what text can and cannot do, what CSS can and cannot do, and then make your choices.

Using text and text menus wisely

Text is not appropriate for every menu on every site. If we go to that extreme, people might stop paying to have pretty menus created, and I like my job! However, there are many other reasons past my job security that will keep graphics as an important element of Web development. Not all communication is about words. Photos and graphic images will continue to play an important role in creating mood and providing identity.

Beyond the practical marketing reasons for graphics to continue, Web surfers are human, and humans like to look at visually pleasing sights. Graphic menus will always have a place. The wireless researchers and developers are in a great race to offer higher bandwidth, working toward the capability to offer color pictures on wireless devices. The secret is finding where to use graphic menus to establish your mood and where text menus will do the job just as well.

However, increasing your font choice may be a poor reason to choose graphic menus over text. You really don't have as many fonts to work with as you think you do, even with graphics. In fact, many of the menus I see on the Web would be far better if the designer used a little more restraint in choosing a font. Again, a Web page is about communicating information. If you use a font that looks great but takes visitors several seconds to figure out the pattern of the letters so that they can read the word, well, that is just not good design. Artistic expression that interferes with communication has no place on a Web page.

Why graphic fonts fall apart on the Web

Very few fonts can hold their characteristics and legibility when they are displayed on a monitor. I included a large sample of the classic font Goudy in Figure 8-3. You can see the elegance and subtle variations that make this font a favorite for print designers. The second sample looks good. But the third Goudy sample is starting to fall apart for the same reason it looked great at a larger size (the variation in character thickness and the graceful serifs simply make the outline harder to see. The final sample features Helvetica, not as elegant and sexy as Goudy, but strong and clear at this size.

Goudy!

Goudy is a great font!

Goudy is a great font!
Helvetica is a great font!

Figure 8-3: Details that are clear at a large size become problems when the size is dramatically reduced. The effect shown here is similar to the effect low-resolution display has on text.

This effect is similar to the quality loss you can expect using text on the Web. You are looking at a sample that was printed at more than double the resolution of a monitor. More pixels, more detail. The reason most text looks bad on a monitor is not a mystery — the resolution is just too coarse to display the subtle variations in most fonts. Fonts, such as Verdana and Georgia were designed specifically to display clearly on the Web.

Cross-Reference You can read more about fonts, typography, and the best fonts for Web use in Chapters 11 and 12.

If you think I feel the way I do because I have not faced a struggle with this issue, you are wrong. I came from the print world. When designing for print projects, your skill with text is what defines you as a designer. Every bit of text control I have given up and every font I have abandoned because it will not hold up well for monitor display has gone painfully. It took a year, and I was bloodied and bruised before I gave up the fight to maintain some of my control over text. I have been a better designer since I threw in the towel and admitted that I had very little choice for text if I cared about communicating on the Web. Throwing in that towel also led to thinking more of text as a real tool for creating menus.

I am going to flip back to talking about real text now, not text that is filtered into a graphic before it lands on your page. Hopefully, I have convinced you that many of the fonts you would like to use are not appropriate for the Web.

Why is the selection of fonts for non-graphic text so bad?

Your choice of fonts to use as text on a Web page is pretty slim, and the reason has nothing to do with any one computer. The reason has to do with millions of computers and the lack of any way to predict what computer will be used to view your page. Fonts are not part of your page. When a visitor arrives at your site and loads a page, his or her computer searches through its fonts in order to display the text on the page. If you specified an obscure font that nobody has installed, your text will display in the default font, often a variation of Times Roman. In order for your page to be seen as you design it, the visitor's computer must have the font you specify installed.

The list of installed fonts that covers most computers in existence is not very long, especially because you must consider both Macintosh and PC platforms. Verdana and Georgia are top choices, as they were designed for the Web. Arial and Helvetica provide a sans-serif choice, and Times or Times New Roman are safe. Finally, you can specify Courier or Courier New and be assured that the receiving computer can display your page as intended. That's it!

The good news is that these choices offer the best of monitor display fonts. General wisdom is that sans-serif fonts are easier to read on the Web, which is opposite to common knowledge about print fonts, and most sites on the Web do feature sans-serif fonts.

Note Serif fonts are fonts that have little "feet" on the characters, such as Times New Roman. Sans-serif fonts do not have the feet. This sentence is set in Arial, a sans-serif font.

Tip I agree that sans-serif fonts are easier to read on the Web with one exception. Line spacing on a default sans-serif font is not good for legibility. If I must use a default font size for accessibility or to comply with company policy and cannot use CSS to specify line-height, I find that Times New Roman provides the best automatic balance between font size and line spacing. (See Chapter 12 for more about line spacing and font size.)

When you specify a font, specify several choices. The visitor's browser will proceed through the list of fonts you specify, stopping after it identifies a font that is installed on the visitor's computer. In case the computer does not have any of the fonts installed, you should also specify a generic font, such as sans-serif or serif, depending on the fonts you require. The CSS font specification for the menu shown earlier in Figure 8-1 is as follows:

```
font-family:Verdana,Arial,Helvetica,sans-serif;
```

This code tells the browser to display Verdana, if available, and then Arial, and then Helvetica if Arial can't be found. Finally, if all else fails, the system's default sans-serif font will display.

The list of fonts is restrictive, but on the bright side, choosing text for a Web site is a lot easier than it was for a print project. Accept it and don't try to spend your time searching for the perfect method to embed a font in your document. To date, you have no reliable method to accomplish this task and even if a great new method worked, it would blow the benefit of small file size through text to pieces. Henry Ford is reputed to have offered his customers a choice: "You can have this car in any color . . . as long as it is black." Henry did just fine.

Organizing Text for Legibility

Some terrible examples of text use are on the Web. Just because text appears as text does not mean that it is good. A vitally important principle of text you should always follow is to make sure that you are delivering a legible menu. Following this rule can help you to make decisions and can increase the professional appearance of your pages.

"Jaggie" text

HTML text is not *anti-aliased*. This term means that text appearing at more than approximately 12 points has some jagged edges, and very large fonts can be very rough, as shown in Figure 8-4. Although I am a perfectionist, I accept some slight rough edges for the file size savings or when frequent changes are required. Keeping font sizes down helps to minimize this problem. The effect is reduced with some background/text combinations, but be careful to keep enough contrast that the text is legible if you are using background color to reduce the aliasing effect.

Centered text

Centering text is one of the fastest ways to create a page that looks as if an amateur created it, yet centering text is a common sight. Centering text is almost never the right thing to do with content text and usually not the right choice if you are creating a vertically laid out menu. As boring as it sounds, left alignment is usually best for all text, although right alignment can be perfect for a list of menu items, especially if the menu is located at the left side of the page. Figure 8-5 shows a menu with left, center, and right alignment.

Headline
Headline
Headline

Text

Bold Text and *Italic Text*

Figure 8-4: HTML text is not anti-aliased. As the text size increases, the rough appearance of the edges also increases.

Figure 8-5: Identical menus with left, center, and right alignment. Note how left and right alignments provide a solid line at one edge, which helps your eyes follow the list.

As a test, cover the menus in sequence, looking at only one at a time. Note how your eye follows easily down the left-aligned text. This alignment is what your eyes expect — you reach the end of a line, and your eyes look for the next place to rest. Left-aligned text provides a predictable start for the next line. Right-aligned text with short lines, as in a menu, can do the same (right-aligned text for content is hard to read). At least you have a predictable end to the line. Centered text is hard for your eyes to resolve. Your eyes do not know where the line is ending or where to look to start the next line. Occasionally, a centered text menu does look good from a pure design standpoint, but it is never easy to read. I recommend you avoid center-aligned text for vertical menus whenever possible.

Underlines

The debate rages on — to underline or not. I come down solidly in the middle of this issue. First, and hear me roar on this point: It is *not* okay to underline anything on a Web page for any reason if you are not creating a link. Truth is, it is not okay in print, either, but it is deadly on the Web. When visitors see an underline, their instinct is to click the underlined item to get a reward. When nothing happens, the reaction is confusion — the last response you want to provoke.

Not quite so clear is whether links should be underlined. I believe that all links in content text should not only be underlined, but also be colored blue. You are reading this book to learn how to move your visitors efficiently through your site. Failing to use the one truly universal clue — blue, underlined text is a link — makes no sense to me.

However, I soften my stance when we are talking about text menus. If the underlined text works well visually and does not interfere with the legibility of the menu items, I think keeping the underline is good. However, a menu list, especially with mouseover changes, does indicate links. A list of text items placed at the left edge of a site is almost as strong a clue that the visitor is seeing a list of links, as is blue, underlined text.

Line height

Font size and line spacing is often misunderstood. Increasing font size is natural for beginners when they need to increase text legibility. But if that is done at the expense of line spacing, legibility drops. Eyes use the white space between lines to follow the words. Take that visual clue away, and separating the content of one line from another is very difficult. The samples shown in Figure 8-6 show what happens when line spacing disappears. The left sample is quite legible with large text. However, keep the same text size and reduce line spacing to save space, and the result is hard to read. Note how dropping the text size, shown in the right sample, actually creates a menu that is much easier to absorb with a quick glance — what a menu must deliver.

Figure 8-6: Increasing line spacing improves legibility. The smaller text on the right is easier to read than the large text in the center.

Although a text menu can look bad, just a few little tricks can create a text menu that is easy to use for your visitors and exceptionally easy to create and maintain for the designer. If you are interested in creating professional quality text menus, however, you must use CSS. Make sure you are up to speed with Chapter 9 in this book.

Tricks and Workarounds for Text in HTML

Now you know a few of the things *not* to do with a text menu. However, the ideas discussed in the previous discussion do not fully overcome the limitations of HTML text. You cannot use tabs in HTML text or easily add extra spaces between words (you can insert an extra non-breaking space), and your choices for alignment are left, right, center, and (please don't even think of using) justified. Not an impressive list for a creative mind. But a creative mind can use other tools to help whip HTML text into shape.

Tables

Using tables creatively can overcome many of the formatting problems with HTML text and gives you the creative freedom you seek. If you are comfortable with complex tables, you can accomplish most formatting that you desire. Figure 8-7 is a sample I adapted from a portion of a table on a client site. This is not a menu, but text was required — the results at the right of the table are returned from a database. For other design reasons, I could not use margins on the table, so every placement of this text is created with columns. I have included a sample with borders turned on so that you can trace the table pattern.

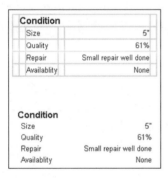

Figure 8-7: A table is used to create complex formatting. The top sample has the borders turned on so that you can see the table structure. The bottom sample is as the data appeared on the final page.

Coming out with a recommendation to use tables to force a page into a specific look makes me nervous. Please take my recommendation with the caution, which I show on other subjects. If you are going to use tables to create text menus, do it right. Make sure you understand tables well, from creating clean code to forcing table cells and rows to behave properly in all major browsers. Nothing is worse for a page than poorly created tables, and your text menu can become a liability on your page if the table does not display properly.

Caution   Don't go wild and create layer upon layer of nested tables (tables inside tables). Every extra layer adds problems for some browsers and makes troubleshooting a nightmare.

Custom bullets

Just because you are working with text does not mean that you are bound to have a boring menu. With CSS, you can place background colors, textures, and be very creative with borders for your text menus. You can also add bullets to unordered lists, which can be effective visual clues that your menu is an information spot. Figure 8-8 shows a custom bullet created with an image that displays in Internet Explorer and Opera and a square custom bullet that is substituted for the image in Netscape Navigator.

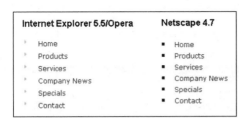

Figure 8-8: Custom bullets can make a text menu attractive.

All-caps

Creating some of your menu text in all-caps format is another way to create attractive menus. This is another suggestion that makes me nervous. All-caps is usually used poorly. Reading text that is all capitalized can be difficult when there is more than a word or two, but used judiciously, can help to organize a menu. Figure 8-9 shows one way that all caps can be used to separate headings from lower menu choices. Either of the samples shown here let visitors find the information quickly, but I think the all-caps version shown at the left highlights the sections with a little more power. I recommend that you type the caps rather than using CSS to create the effect. Typed caps are guaranteed to show on any browser. I like to use sure methods when one is available.

PRODUCTS
   Retail
   Commerce
   Food Service
   Industrial
SERVICES
   Accounting
   Project Management
   Human Resources

Products
   Retail
   Commerce
   Food Service
   Industrial
Services
   Accounting
   Project Management
   Human Resources

Figure 8-9: Two variations of the same menu. All-caps formatting draws attention well when used in small portions.

This section was just a small sample of techniques that you can use to make a text menu look great, although, I believe that they are key methods to keep in mind. When you start working with text menus, you will find a natural set of design tools for your style. Whatever you use to format menus, remember that text menus *are* menus. If your menu fails, your site fails. Commit to truly mastering any of the formatting techniques you use and test carefully across many browsers.

Exercise: Creating a Text Menu You'll Be Proud to Call Your Own

Are your fingers itching to hit the mouse? I created a short exercise to get you started developing text menus. For this lesson, you create a menu in your usual HTML editor using a pre-made CSS file to control your text. (You learn more about CSS in the next chapter.)

On the CD-ROM   You find the CSS files for this exercise on the CD-ROM included at the back of this book. Locate the files `textmenu8.css` and `bullet.gif` in the Chapter 8 folder. Copy the file to the folder on your computer where you are saving your work from this exercise. You also find a completed sample of the menu you will create, `textmenu8.html`, in the same folder.

To create a text menu, follow these steps (code examples follow written instructions in parenthesis where appropriate):

1. Open your HTML text editor and create a new document. Save the document as **textmenu8new.html**.

2. Make sure you copied the file `textmenu8.css` from the CD-ROM to the folder where the file you created in Step 1 is saved.

3. Create a table 170 pixels wide with 1 column and 6 rows. Set the alignment of the cells to top (`<td valign="top">`).

4. In the top cell, using the `<p>` tag, type **Products**. Make it bold. Set the table cell background to a tan color (`<td bgcolor="#CC9966">`). Repeat for the third and fifth cell, typing **Services** and **Contact**, respectively, and setting cell background to CCCC99 and FFCC33.

Note   Although I don't normally use the `<b>` tag in this setting, to reduce confusion with the CSS, I use bold for this exercise.

5. In the second cell, type **Retail**, **Commerce**, **Food Service,** and **Industrial**, each as a separate entry for an unordered list, as follows:

```
<ul>
  <li>Retail</li>
  <li>Commerce</li>
  <li>Food Service</li>
  <li>Industrial</li>
</ul>
```

6. In the fourth and sixth cells, repeat Step 5, typing **Accounting**, **Project Management**, **Human Resources,** and then **Customer Service**, **Press**, **Partners**, **Request a Quote**, respectively. Figure 8-10 shows how your document should look at this point in either Internet Explorer or Netscape Navigator.

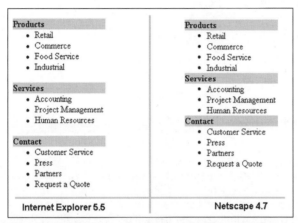

Figure 8-10: Before you add the CSS file to the document, your menu should look similar to one of these samples. Each browser displays unordered lists in a slightly different way, and default fonts can vary.

7. Add a link to each of the text entries. I used a # symbol as a null link, for example (`<a href="#">Products</a>`). You need each item to be a link in order for the CSS to be implemented properly.

8. In the `<head>` section of your document, add the following code:

```
<link rel="stylesheet" href="textmenu8.css" type="text/css">
```

This line of code activates the CSS file that you saved from the CD-ROM, and like magic, your menu should look like Figure 8-11.

Netscape 4.7 or earlier won't display the mouseovers or the image bullets. However, this is okay, because the links work, the hand icon indicates a link, and the menu displays properly. Internet Explorer and Opera support more CSS commands.

Note   If you are on your toes, you notice that this CSS style sheet controls all the links on the page. In Chapter 9, I discuss .class CSS styles, which we would normally use to define a menu. I wanted this sample to be very simple for those who are new to CSS.

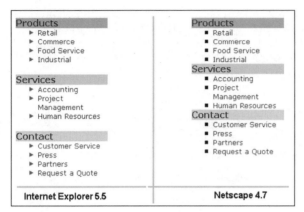

Figure 8-11: The final menu in Internet Explorer and Netscape Navigator

Experiment with different settings for the CSS commands to see how easy it is to change a menu or all menus on a site. That is the beauty of CSS. After your CSS file is perfect, you can change the style at any time, and adding or deleting menu items is as quick as typing in the new link and list item. The CSS handles all the formatting (a site maintainer's dream).

✦   ✦   ✦

Cascading Style Sheets: The Production Tool that Delivers on Promises

I can hardly remember a time that I did not use Cascading Style Sheets (CSS) when designing a Web site. In fact, my HTML font tag knowledge is becoming weak. In the beginning, I used CSS to control only a few attributes of my fonts, but as the Version 3 browsers started to drop away, I added more and more controls with CSS. I still do not use CSS for position-ing my pages for compatibility reasons, though I can hardly wait for the day that I can safely leave tables behind for good.

Tip   If you are working on an intranet site and know that your customers are all using browsers above version 4, espe-cially if they are all using the same browser, you have the freedom to stretch your CSS use fully into positioning.

Don't Make Another Page without CSS

The introductory paragraph hints at the direction I take in this chapter. CSS is a very big subject and for this book, I am only interested in promoting CSS to control text. But I want to make a strong statement about using CSS for text. If you are not, you are, quite bluntly, falling behind in the development world.

A few years ago, arguments could be made that CSS compromised cross-browser compatibility, but today, those arguments barely hang by a thread. New standards for HTML do not include <font> tags. Using HTML to specify all text formatting adds a lot of code to your page, invites inconsistency, and changes cannot be automated. CSS, on the other hand, adds very little code (especially if you are using a linked CSS file), guarantees consistency, and allows automated changes across an entire site by adjusting one file. What's not to love?

What is CSS?

CSS is so often discussed with HTML that I know some people do get confused as to what falls where between the two. So, before I tear off telling you exciting ways to control your text with CSS, perhaps I should start by giving an overview of exactly what CSS is.

I always try to find something in common use to compare a new concept to, and if you have experience with page layout programs or word processors, the following comparison will be fairly clear. CSS is used in the same way that styles are applied in other programs for page layout. For example, in Microsoft Word, you can define a style that specifies a font, the font color, line spacing, and many more attributes. After the style is defined, you simply tell Word that you want a paragraph to be in that style, and all attributes are applied at once.

You have two major benefits for working in this way. The first benefit is speed. You spend a little more time in the beginning creating the style, but from then on, you do not have to think about formatting or go through the required keystrokes to format a paragraph.

The second, and I think more important benefit, is consistency. This book is written in Microsoft Word with defined styles for every paragraph I write. The heading at the top of this section is my H2 style. I type the words for the subheading and click the H2 icon, as shown in Figure 9-1. Whenever I click this icon, the formatting is guaranteed to be exactly the same throughout the entire book. Better yet, the style template came from Hungry Minds' production department, so authors all over the world are creating documents with identical formatting. That's power!

CSS offers the same function. Although you can create CSS within a page, I always use a linked file. That linked file contains all of the information for the formatting of a site. Imagine that a year after you create a large site, you decide that you would like to increase the line spacing of the main content. One change to your CSS file and the entire site is updated.

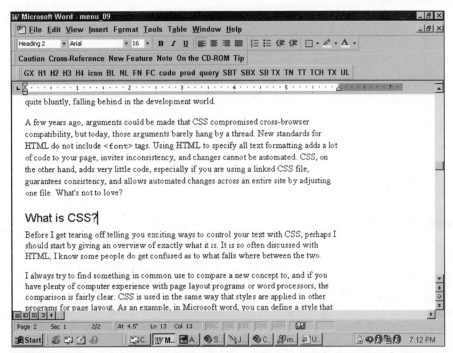

Figure 9-1: The page you are reading is shown here as it is being created. Note that the cursor is at the end of the heading paragraph and Heading 2 is shown in the Style field at the top of the page.

Exercise: Creating a CSS file

Through this chapter, I give you CSS commands rather than teaching you how to write CSS. That subject would, and has, filled entire books. By the time you finish this chapter, you will have the code for basic text and menu control with CSS. If you have not worked with CSS before and have not read Chapter 8, you may want to stop here and work through the exercise at the end of Chapter 8. You place a CSS file that is provided, which may help to fix the concept firmly in your mind.

CSS is actually very simple if you take the time to read through the code. Better yet, why don't you work through creating a CSS file that contains a simple <p> tag style.

To create a CSS file, follow these steps:

1. Working with a simple editor, such as Windows Notepad, create a new file and save it as ptagcss.css. In Notepad, you must select All Files from the Save As Type drop-down selector, or .txt will be added to the file name you specify.

2. Type the following code into your document:

```
p {font-family: Verdana,Arial,Helvetica,sans-serif; font-
size: 12pt}
```

3. Save the file.

4. To link the CSS file to an HTML document, place the following code in the head area of any document:

```
<link rel="stylesheet" href="ptagcss.css" type="text/css">
```

This link assumes that the `ptagcss.css` file is in the same directory as the HTML document. If it is not, simply add the correct path.

That's all there is to it. Now, any HTML document that you link to this file will display with Verdana 12 pt text (or Arial, and then Helvetica, and finally the system's generic sans-serif font).

Try adding this CSS file to an existing page. You have to remove any `<p>` tag formatting in the document, because font formatting overrides the CSS in a linked file. After you have all `<p>` tags under the CSS control, adjust the size from 12 pt to 10 pt and save the CSS file. Preview your page in a browser, and you will see the font size change. Repeat, but set the font size to 14 pt. It won't take many changes before you start to see how designers become raging CSS fans.

The ABCs of CSS for Text

Again, I want to remind you that in this chapter I focus only on using CSS for text. I do not discuss layers, or layers positioning, until Chapter 24, in relation to Dynamic HTML (DHTML). In fact, you will be looking at CSS to only control text throughout most of this book. I hate to leave the impression that what you cover in this chapter comes close to covering the full scope of CSS. On the other hand, one of the things that slowed my progress when learning CSS was sorting the text from the positioning information. The text portion is not at all complicated and is not dependent on positioning to work.

Tip

Now is an excellent time to become fully comfortable with CSS, including positioning. Stephanos Piperoglou, of WebReference.com, has an excellent column on HTML and CSS at `www.webreference.com/html/tutorials`. Another excellent source of CSS information is the HTML Writer's Guild site. It won't be too long before all CSS, including positioning, comes into true cross-browser compatibility. When it does, Web page design will take a huge leap. Be ready!

Using CSS for basic formatting

In HTML there are a few standard text styles, such as <p>, <H1>, and <ul>. The easiest CSS control simply assigns a style to control attributes for the styles that HTML recognizes.

I can't imagine a style sheet that does not include at least a <p> tag specification. The <p> tag is used to set the style for the main content text. You can use the <body> tag, but it is not always reliable in all browsers. When you look at each style separately, the mysteries become common sense.

```
p {
font-family: Verdana,Arial,Helvetica,sans-serif; font-size:
11pt
}
```

The p in the code represents the name of the style. The { (opening curly bracket) indicates the beginning of the style attributes. Font-family is the attribute that is affected and is followed by a : (colon). The font-family values are listed with commas between each listing. The ; (semi-colon) indicates the end of the values for that attribute. The routine is repeated for font-size, but a ; (semi-colon) is not required for the final listing. The style is completed with a } (closing curly bracket).

Whether the style is created in the format shown here, or as in the previous exercise does not matter — some people find it easier to use this format, as skimming through the many styles in a document is easy.

I include two more samples of CCS styles here. See if you can figure out what will happen after these styles are applied to a document.

CSS style sample 1:

```
ul {
font-family: Verdana,Arial,Helvetica,sans-serif; font-size:
10pt; color: #FF0000; list-style-type: square
}
```

CSS style sample 2:

```
h2 {
font-family: Arial,Helvetica,sans-serif; font-size: 16pt; font-
weight: bold; color: #000099
}
```

In the first sample, an unordered list is affected. The list selects Verdana first, then runs through Arial, Helvetica, and if none of the fonts are found, the browser displays the default sans-serif font. The font will be 10 pt, color FF0000 (red), and will have square bullets. The second sample sets the attributes for the H2 style, and I won't bore you with details — by now it is easier for you to read the style than my explanation.

That is really all there is to CSS style sheets when it comes to basic text formatting. I recommend keeping your first projects very simple, just controlling your text and getting used to updating text attributes at a later date. I recently updated a site that I created a year ago. All content and some menus were controlled fully by CSS with the original design. The reality of CSS power really hit home when I was able to update the site — in 30 minutes. The only change outside of the CSS style sheet was to strip out one font tag I had used to overcome an early browser weakness. The rest of the changes were accomplished in the CSS linked file. The next update will be even faster. Every change will be in the CSS.

Tip

What I needed in my early CSS days was a list of all the CSS font attributes. I think my learning curve flattened nearly instantly the day I found the plain, simple listing of CSS attributes at `http://htmlhelp.org/reference/css/properties.html`. Plus, `http://htmlhelp.org/reference/css` is an index for many CSS topics, with all information presented clearly and is an excellent resource that demands a bookmark.

WebReview.com has an impressive site as well. `www.webreview.com/style/css1/charts/mastergrid.shtml`, lists CSS attributes and saves hundreds of hours of trial and error or research with a compatibility chart. Wondering which CSS attributes work in Netscape Navigator 4.6? Check the chart. Browsers include Navigator 4 and 6, Internet Explorer 3 to 5.5 for PC and Macintosh, and Opera 3 to 5 for PC — an impressive list.

Exercise: Creating a Cascading Style Sheet

You created and linked a tiny style sheet to a document earlier in this chapter, but you now have the chance to create a style sheet that can control a full site. I have added a few unusual formatting styles in this exercise, such as an accent line, margins, and padding on your H1 definition. The H2 and H3 are basic and straightforward, and you can skip the more involved pieces of the H1 styling if it seems too tough.

On the CD-ROM

On the CD-ROM included with this book, locate the Chapter 9 folder. Copy the file `firstcss.html` from the CD-ROM to the folder where you save files for this exercise. I also include a completed copy of the CSS style sheet file that you will be creating in this exercise (`firstcss.css`).

To create a full style sheet, follow these steps:

1. Create a new document in a simple text editor and name it **firstcss.css**.

2. Add the `<p>` tag style as follows:

```
p {
font-family: Verdana,Arial,Helvetica,sans-serif; font-size:
10pt; color: #000000
}
```

3. You define the <H1> tag in the next step. Add the <H2> and <H3> styles as follows:

```
h2 {
font-size: 16px; color: #000099; font-family:
Arial,Helvetica,sans-serif; font-weight: normal;
}

h3 {
font-family: Arial,Helvetica,sans-serif;font-size: 12px;
font-weight: bold; color: #CC0000
}
```

4. The <H1> tag definition is similar to the <H2> and <H3> definitions shown previously, but I have reduced the line spacing for <H1> by using a negative margin style. I also added a horizontal line and moved that line further from the text with a padding value. Type in the code as follows:

```
h1 {
font-family: Arial,Helvetica,sans-serif; font-size: 18pt;
font-weight: normal; color: #000099; margin-bottom: -10px;
border-bottom: 1px solid #CC0000; padding-bottom: 5px
}
```

5. Finally, add the link and rollover styles as follows:

```
a:link { color: #0000CC }
a:hover { color: #CC0000}
a:visited { color: #990066}
```

6. Your style sheet is complete. Save the file.

7. Open the file, firstcss.html that you copied from the CD-ROM. In the head area of the document, add the following to link your style sheet to the document and then save the file:

```
<link rel="stylesheet" href="firstcss.css" type="text/css">
```

8. Preview your document in Internet Explorer, and your results should be very similar to those shown in Figure 9-2. The line, padding, and margin effects show in all current browsers, but sporadically through earlier versions.

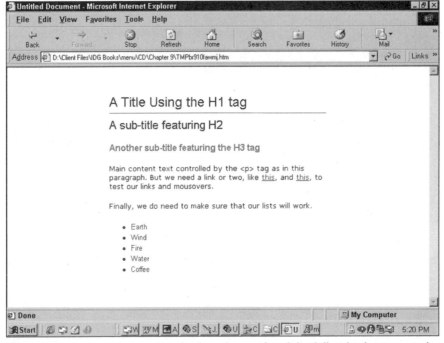

Figure 9-2: Internet Explorer 5.5 displays the results of the full style sheet created in this exercise.

Updating and Sharing CSS Files

I hope you are feeling a little smug right now. I told you it was not so hard, and by now, you might just be starting to believe me. Oh, I admit there are a lot of different attributes to remember, but I gave you the tools earlier to deal with that. Print one of the list pages and keep it beside the computer when you are working. As soon as you understand the syntax, working with CSS for text formatting is really just a fill-in-the-blanks job.

Watching your first CSS page leap into order, as you would have seen with the last exercise, is a treat and gives you an idea of how powerful a tool you have just discovered. That reality hits again the first time you make a change to a CSS file.

Exercise: Changing a CSS file

To get the true impact from the next steps, why not create a few sample pages, all linked to the CSS file `firstcss.css` that we used for the last exercise. That way, when we make the changes, you get the full impact of the linked CSS file.

To update a CSS file, follow these steps:

1. Open the CSS file `firstcss.css` in a text editor.

2. Change the font-size value in the `<p>` tag to `12pt` as shown here:

```
p {
font-family: Verdana,Arial,Helvetica,sans-serif; font-size:
12pt; color: #000000
}
```

3. Change the `<H1>` tag font-weight value to bold, and the border-bottom value to `2px` as follows:

```
h1 {
font-family: Arial,Helvetica,sans-serif; font-size: 18pt;
font-weight: bold; color: #000099; margin-bottom: -10px;
border-bottom: 2px solid #CC0000; padding-bottom: 5px
}
```

4. Save the CSS file and open the linked HTML documents if they are not already open. Preview the results to confirm that the changes have taken place. Check each document that is linked to the CSS file, and the same changes appear in each one, even though, technically, you have not even touched them.

Sharing a CSS file

It may or may not have occurred to you yet, but the CSS file you created earlier in this chapter is an independent file. Although you created it for a specific document, and the document is dependent on the CSS file for formatting, the CSS file is in no way dependent on the document.

I often start a new site with a style sheet from an old site. We all have our own styles, and most often, do not vary much in the attributes we control with CSS. Quite honestly, I do not change all that much that is CSS responsibility from one site to the next.

To share a file with another site, simply open the CSS file and immediately save it as a new name in the folder for the new site. I then make any adjustments for the new site in the new file and link the new name to the documents in the new site.

Caution   Make sure you save the CSS file with a new name the *instant* you open it. While CSS saves much time because it is only linked to your document, overwrite the old CSS and you may lose a lot of work. Forgetting to save to a new name is very easy after you have been working for a while.

Class Styles in CSS: Complete Freedom!

As you may have discovered, there is a drawback in using CSS styles to control HTML styles. When you are working with tags, such as `<p>` or `<H>`, you are working with a paragraph at a time. What if you only want to change the style for a few words at the beginning of a paragraph? Or, what if you want the `<p>` tag to be different for one of your columns? Enter Class styles.

Class styles can be thought of as floating styles that you apply when and where you want them. I find that with each site I create, I define more Class styles. Class styles are perfect for teaser menus. You can create a style used throughout the site to identify that the teaser menu item is special, not part of the regular content. You have no problem remembering whether you used Arial or Verdana, 16 or 18 pt line spacing on the first teaser menu you create. Assign the style and you can be sure that page 50 has the exact same teaser menu style as the teaser menu on page 1.

Remember the other bonus, as well. If you reach page 52 and decide that you really hate the color, font, line-spacing, line, border, or anything else about your Class style, open your CSS file, make the changes, and voila! All pages reflect the changes. I suspect you may be getting the idea that I really like CSS.

What's with the "." in .class?

The period in ".whatever" makes the style available to all HTML styles. For example, if you create a Class style and name it .italic, specifying nothing but that the style adds italics, you can apply that style to a `<p>` tag or one of the `<h>` tags without affecting any other attribute of that style. Following is the code I'm describing:

```
.italic {
    font-style: italic;
}
```

This is the entry in the CSS style sheet. To apply the style to the text in the HTML document, you can place the .class style in the tag controlling the text, such as this: `<p class="italic">`, and the entire paragraph appears with the `<p>` tag attributes, plus the attributes of the .italic Class style.

If you do not want the entire paragraph in italics, you can add the .class attributes by using a `<span>` and `</span>` tag as follows:

```
<span class="italic">point</span>
```

In this case, the word *point* adds the attributes of the .italic Class file to the attributes that are already present. I have included all the text code that creates the look in Figure 9-3 for your perusal. Study how the .italic style appears in the HTML code, and observe the effect in the resulting page.

Note
I highlight all code related to the .class style additions in bold type. This highlight is to help you identify the exact code, not as the code appears in the document.

```
<h1>Headline in H1 style, but wanting to make a <span
class="italic">point</span>!
    </h1>
    <p>Text controlled by a &lt;p&gt; tag, but also wanting
to make a <span class="italic">point</span>.
    Of, course, it must make the <span
class="italic">point</span> twice, since it is smaller
text.</p>
    <p class="italic">And if things get really heated, why
not just take an entire paragraph of text and make a point with
it.</p>
```

> **Headline in H1 style, but wanting to make a *point*!**
>
> Text controlled by a <p> tag, but also wanting to make a *point*.
> Of, course, it must make the *point* twice, since it is smaller text.
>
> *And if things get really heated, why not just take an entire paragraph of text and make a point with it.*

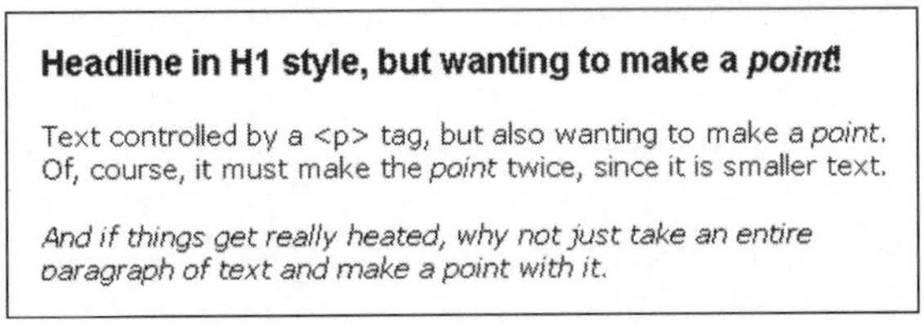

Figure 9-3: Results of adding the .italic Class style to several words and to an entire paragraph

Exercise: Creating a .class style

Creating a .class style is almost the same as you have already done with creating styles for the HTML style tags. This time, you get to choose your own name, however, and you do not have to be thinking about the appearance on the entire page of the values you use. Remember, .class files are applied wherever they are needed and do not affect anything other than where you specify they should be.

On the CD-ROM
On the CD-ROM included with this book, locate the file `class.html` in the Chapter 9 folder. Copy this file to your working folder. A file with the completed exercise, `classfinal.html` is also found in the Chapter 9 folder.

Note
You start this exercise creating a new CSS file from an existing one. If you did not do the previous exercise, simply open the file `firstcss.css`, which is also located in the Chapter 9 folder on the CD-ROM.

To create a .class style, follow these steps:

1. Open the file `firstcss.css` in your text editor. Save the file as **classtest.css**.

2. Scroll to the bottom of the document and add the following code:

```
.testclass {
    background-color : #000099;
    line-height : 16pt;
    border : thin solid #CC0000;
    color : #FFFFFF;
    padding : 5
}
```

This code adds a blue box with a red border to the text, as well as increases the line spacing, and changes the text to white whenever the .testclass style is applied.

3. Save the CSS file.

4. Open the file `class.html`. In the head of the document, insert the following code:

```
<link rel="stylesheet" href="classtest.css" type="text/css">
```

5. Apply the .testclass style to the word "true" in the left column of the table as follows (I include the code for the entire paragraph):

```
<p>So <span class="testclass">true</span>!</p>
```

6. Apply the .textclass style to the paragraph in the right column. This time you want the style to apply to the entire paragraph, so that you add the .testclass style to the `<p>` tag as follows:

```
<p class="testclass">And if things get really heated, why not
just take an entire paragraph of text and make a point with
it.</p>
```

7. Save the document and preview it in Internet Explorer. Your results should be similar to those shown in Figure 9-4. Results vary in other browsers.

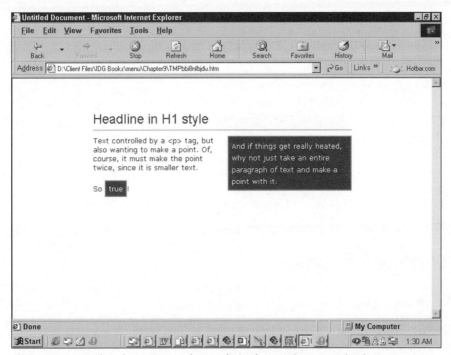

Figure 9-4: Results of creating a .class style in the previous exercise in Internet Explorer 5.5

Creating Mini Page Environments with DIV Styles

Assigning styles to HTML tags and creating flexible CSS control by using .class styles gives you all you need for most tasks. However, suppose you want to use CSS to define a menu area, but you want the link colors to differ from the main page link specifications? That power is possible by assigning CSS styles to the <div> tag. The specific style you create is included for any content that falls between the <div> and the </div> tag.

Using CSS with ID styles and <div> tags

If you have followed this chapter so far, you will have little trouble learning to work with the CSS and the <div> tag. All of the rules for specifying colors, font sizes, backgrounds, margins, or any other CSS style are exactly the same. You can place the style sheet in a linked file as you did in the previous exercise.

The difference appears when you apply the style to your document. Instead of specifying an HTML style, such as `<p>` or H1, or a `<span>` identifier, you order the browser to read the style sheet by placing a call for formatting in the `<div>` tag, using the code:

```
id="yourstylename"
```

The reference to `"yourstylename"` refers to a name that you create for your style.

To place the style in the document, your code is as follows:

```
<div id="topmenu"></div>
```

The name `"topmenu"` is one I made up, and the content for this section goes between the `<div>` and `</div>` tags.

Creating the style

Here is where we see the power in this method for using CSS. To create a special set of formatting for a menu area, you only need to learn one more way to define a CSS style. Creating an ID style is almost the same as creating a .class style (see previous section in this chapter), but instead of using a .yourname convention, you use #yourname. The name you specify, without the # character is the name you use to call the style in the `<div>` tag.

You can add the #yourname title to any existing style, including the most common use for this method to change the link formatting. Earlier in this chapter, you defined `a:` link and `a:hover` formatting, to affect the appearance of a link when inactive and when the mouse passes over it. With an ID style, you can create the same formatting that only applies when the ID is used in a `<div>` tag. The syntax for an ID style named "topmenu" is as follows:

```
#topmenu A{
text-decoration: none; font-size: 13px; font-family:
Arial,Helvetica,sans-serif; color: #FFCC99; text-decoration:
none
}

#topmenu A:hover { color : #FF6600}
#topmenuA:visited {  color: #FFCC33 }
#topmenuA:active { text-decoration : underline; ; color:
#FFFFCC }
```

Read through the code to see what each entry does. #topmenu A defines the link formatting, which stays in place for all states of the link unless changed for another state. #topmenu A:hover changes the color when the mouse is passed over the link. #topmenu A: visited changes the color of the link to show the visitor has been to that page. #topmenu A:active changes the color of the link on the active page.

Apply the style to a <div> tag

After you have your CSS defined and included either in a separate CSS file or with your main CSS file for the page, you simply specify where the #topmenu formatting is to be used. In the following example, menu items are listed vertically and enclosed in a <div> tag with the topmenu style applied.

```
<div id="topmenu">
<p>Home<br>
   Products<br>
   Services<br>
   Company<br>
   Contact<br>
   Links</p></div>
```

By adding that one piece to the <div> tag, the topmenu formatting overrules any other CSS formatting.

Adding style is that easy. Define your ID style and apply the style to a <div> tag. You have no limit to the number of ID styles you can use in a page, although keeping pages as simple as possible is always a good idea. I usually have no more than two ID styles defined in a site. Usually one controls a main menu, and the other controls a side menu. One works if the background for the menu is the same. I find that I usually have one menu on a colored background and one on a white or a light color, which demands different formatting.

Working with a CSS Editor

As a final word on this subject for a while, I would like to make you aware that good editors for CSS are available. Most major HTML editors have some CSS editing capability included with the programs. Some of the features I have used are wonderful, and they do save time.

You can also test, and, if satisfied, purchase a stand-alone CSS editor. TopStyle, by Bradbury Software (www.bradsoft.com/topstyle), deserves its status as a popular choice for many designers. The program assists with writing the CSS styles, although you do need to fully understand the concept of CSS. In addition, a preview of the styles in the document is shown as you work, and most choices you make are click and select. See Figure 9-5 for a screen shot of TopStyle in action.

Caution   As I think is true with any type of code editor, the more knowledge you have of the code that will be added, the more success you have with editors. CSS is no exception. At the very least, you must make sure that you understand CSS well enough to understand *every* line, even if you use an editor to create those lines. I cannot think of one document I have created, HTML or CSS, that has not required hand editing to achieve the best results.

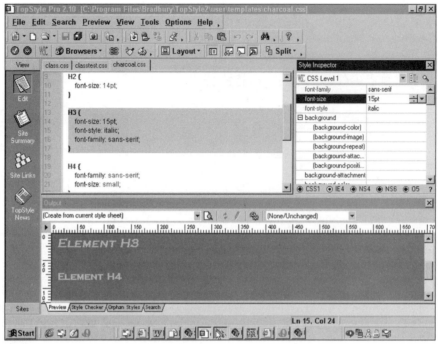

Figure 9-5: The CSS editor TopStyle Pro 2

✦   ✦   ✦

Lightweight Champs: Text Menus That Fly onto the Page

As a Web designer, you've no doubt heard of server side includes (SSI), a popular technique to include information contained in one document into many with a simple code reference. SSI is used often to create menus, especially text menus. I can remember hearing about SSI, thinking it sounded exotic, but assuming the method was difficult. Everyone who talked about it, spoke with reverence, and swore they would never do another site without SSI. It had to be difficult, because nobody ever seemed to provide much detail. Truth is, they were not giving detail because SSI is so simple there are few details to give.

The only difficulty with SSI is its concept. After you have that fixed in your mind, you have a few terms to learn and a tiny amount of code. I now understand why those who talk about SSI have such reverence in their voice. SSI is a one-size-fits-all solution for many automation tasks, especially because it is cross-browser safe (the server does the processing.

Working with Server Side Includes

The concept behind SSI is not really so tough. SSI is nothing more than a line of code in your HTML document that tells the browser to find a file and put it in a certain spot when it displays the page. Just like placing an image, but instead, you are placing a piece of HTML into a certain location on your main page.

The *server side* part of SSI indicates that the information called for by the SSI code is processed by code on the server (more about this in the next section). The "includes" is just as it sounds. The line of code in the page that is being displayed says, "Browser, go get (include) the stuff from file x and put it in this spot." Figure 10-1 shows how the process works.

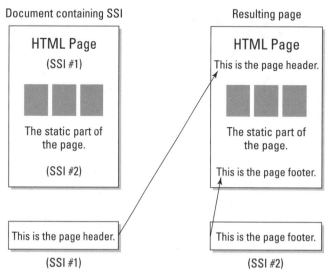

Figure 10-1: Server Side Includes in action. Content from separate files is placed into the HTML document as called for by the SSI codes.

Understanding and placing the codes

In order for SSI to work, your server must be SSI enabled. For those of you who aren't running your own server, a call or note to the technical people at your hosting company will give you the answer to whether you can use SSI. The majority of commercial hosts offer SSI processing. If your host does not offer SSI, you will have to change hosts in order to use it, which I urge you to consider.

Placing code in your main page

Check out the code placed in the main document (the document that is displayed by the browser) separately from the pages that contain the information that is to be placed.

SSI is called into action with an HTML comment tag and a # symbol, such as this:

```
<!--#comment -->
```

The comment tag prevents the line of code from being displayed by the browser, but the comment tag plus the # sign is read by an SSI enabled server as a command to do something. You can call many commands with this code, such as the date, where your visitor was before coming to your page, even to run a script, but for the topic of this book, I am most interested in calling a file.

Now that you have the SSI server's attention with the comment tag and # symbol, you must tell it what to do. You may shake your head at how easy this is, but you, well, just put in the desired file name after an equal sign as follows:

```
<!--#include file="filename.html" --> or <!--#include
file="textfile.txt" -->
```

Suppose you have a piece of text on hundreds of pages that you need to update a few times a week. Instead of a tedious and time-consuming task each time, you can simply call the information from a file with an SSI command. If the file name is `latenews.txt`, you would insert the following code on each page where you want the text to display:

```
<!--#include file="latenews.txt" -->
```

Tip   Some servers require that you place a command in the file name as an alert to look for SSI commands. Changing the .html extension to .shtml will always work if your server is not processing the SSI with an .html extension to the file name.

Creating a file to use with SSI

Your text file must contain exactly what you want to have displayed where the code is placed. Figure 10-2 shows a Notepad file containing the text and <p> tags that will be inserted in the main document.

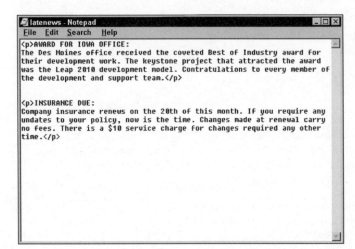

Figure 10-2: The text file called to create the page shown later in Figure 10-3

Putting it all together

Your work is complete at this point. Putting it together is done through the SSI processing on the server. If you have created your files correctly, your page will display the text in the external file in place.

Note Unless you use an HTML editor that will simulate SSI results, such as Macromedia Dreamweaver, you must upload the files to your server to test the results.

Just to review, I included the code that forms the table cell where the SSI resides. In Figure 10-3, I added gray shading to the area of the page represented by the following code:

```
<td bgcolor="#CCCCCC">
    <!--#include file="latenews.txt" -->
</td>
```

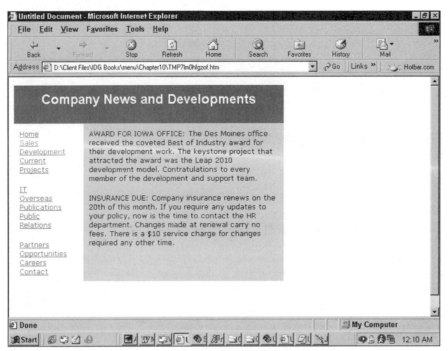

Figure 10-3: Final page shown with the shaded area representing the cell where the SSI command is placed by calling the text from the file shown in Figure 10-2

How's that for simple? In the previous example, changes to all 100 pages containing the SSI are instantly done, simply by editing the Notepad file.

Updating SSI files

Someone notices that the headlines are not standing out from the text. Adding a `.class` CSS command to the headlines, such as this

```
<p><span class="newstitle">AWARD FOR IOWA OFFICE:</span>
```

creates the new look on all pages containing the SSI include code. Figure 10-4 reflects the change in the text file.

Cross-Reference

Chapter 9 covers CSS styles and `.class` files in detail.

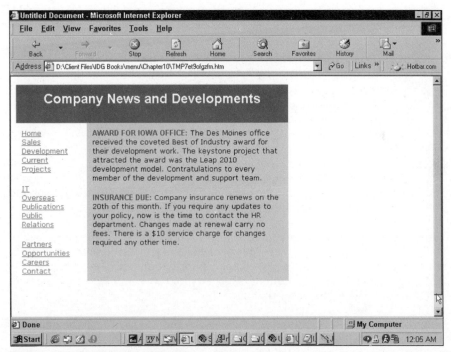

Figure 10-4: Adding new formatting to the text file that is inserted by SSI updates all pages that contain the include code

On the CD-ROM

The HTML page and text file shown in Figures 10-2, 10-3, and 10-4 are included in the Chapter 10 folder on the CD-ROM included with this book. The HTML page is `ssitestpage.shtml`, and the text file is `latenews.text`. You must place these files on an SSI-enabled server, or test in a program that simulates SSI processing. If the HTML file is simply opened in a desktop browser window, the text file will not be included in the display.

Exercise: Creating and Implementing an SSI Menu

Explaining a very simple procedure took a lot of words. Try the following exercise to create a text menu and you will realize that, with the background you now have, SSI truly is a very fast and simple tool that you will use over and over.

On the CD-ROM Before starting this exercise, copy the following files from the Chapter 10 folder on the CD-ROM included with this book to your working directory: `mainmenu.shtml`, `menussi.html`, `menucss.css`, and `space.gif`. All of the files must be placed in the same folder.

To start, open the two documents that will create the final pages. You should take a look at the content of these files before you move ahead with the rest of the exercise.

1. Open the file `menumain.shtml`. This document will be your main display page.

2. Open the document `menussi.html`. This file is the SSI file that will be called into the main display page. Because this file will contain only the include information, do not rename the file to an `.shtml` extension no matter what your server requirements.

I prepared documents for you to use for this exercise, leaving only the SSI code to add to the main document. There is nothing new to learn about SSI in the construction of the pieces used to form the documents to this point. However, I would like to point out why I created the document containing the SSI in this way.

When you insert an SSI command in your main document, calling on a file to be placed in that location, you are asking for everything in that document. Notice that `menussi.html` does not have page display information (such as background) or font information. When the content is placed into the main page, it will be under the influence of the style sheet for that page.

I could have placed the CSS `<div id="menu">` and `</div>` tag in the main document, enclosing the SSI command. The style details will be read from the main document's style sheet, but I like to keep the style tags with the SSI content when I can. Remember that anything in the document `menussi.html` can be edited and changes will automatically appear globally.

Keeping the SSI content files as clean and simple as possible is important. Thinking through the setup of the SSI content and receiving document is also essential. Test the results of the SSI finished page and edit the content on one or two documents before you apply the SSI command to hundreds of files.

After you are familiar with what each document contains, you can move on to adding the SSI command as follows:

3. In the main document, `menumain.shtml`, locate the code for the first cell in the second row of the table as shown here and insert the command `<!--#include file="menussi.html" -->` between the `<td>` and `</td>` tags. The code is as follows:

```
<td width="100">
    <!--#include file="menussi.html" -->
</td>
```

4. Save the file. Your results should look similar to Figure 10-5 in Internet Explorer. Remember that you must upload the file to the server if your editor will not display a simulated SSI result.

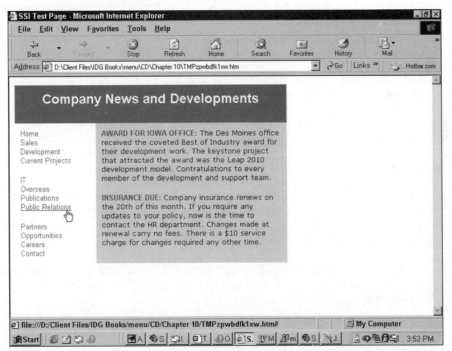

Figure 10-5: Final page displayed in Internet Explorer. Note the mouseover effect shown in the menu. This effect does not display in Netscape Navigator.

On the CD-ROM

I include a copy of the finished file, `mainmenu_done.shtml`, in the Chapter 10 folder on the CD-ROM included with this book.

And that's it folks. If you are interested in firming up your skills with SSI, why not create your own SSI content files to fit into the main document you used for this exercise. Create any HTML or text file and save it. Remember to leave out any commands that will be present in the main document. You cannot have two body tags on a page. If your SSI content page has a body tag, it will be added to the main document, wrecking the page.

Using HTML Editor Automation

Hot on the heels of SSI's gaining popular use, HTML editors, such as Macromedia Dreamweaver started to include a similar capability, but processed by the editor. The idea is the same. You create a file that contains the content you want to place into a spot on a page. You then tell the editor to include the contents of that file when the page is displayed. Functions, such as Dreamweaver's Library Items or Adobe GoLive Components are modeled after the concept of SSI and do not require any special server capability.

However, these automation tools are proprietary, meaning that you must use the original program to create the files. Editor-specific functions are fine when a site is built and maintained by one person or created and kept up by a team that uses the same editor. I do not often use automated tools like this for client work. Currently I do not offer ongoing maintenance for Web sites, and cannot box clients into working with only one editor. For sites that I build, run, and maintain for ongoing clients, I do not hesitate to take advantage of proprietary tools. They do work very well.

An SSI command works because the instructions or path to the content is included within the command. HTML editors include the actual content in the main document markup, but surround the automated content with specialized code that only that editor can understand. Updating content is accomplished through this proprietary code. The link for the automation can be broken, but of course, you lose the ability to update the content from one location.

Caution   The following automated features are specific to Dreamweaver and require that you are working within a defined site. See your manual for instructions on how to create a site.

Dreamweaver Library Items

To practice the concept and method for creating automated elements in Dreamweaver, you will work through the same example as we used earlier in this chapter in the SSI exercise. The structure and content of the sample page is the same, however, I added color changes to prevent confusion. You will create a Library Item for both the menu and text content, each using a different method. The end result for the content areas of the document will be the same as for the SSI sample.

On the CD-ROM Copy the file `dwlib.html` from the Chapter 10 folder on the CD-ROM included with this book to the working folder on your computer. If you have not already copied the following files onto your computer with the previous exercise, you will also require `menucss.css`, `menussi.html`, and `space.gif`, also found in the Chapter 10 folder on the CD-ROM.

Creating a Dreamweaver Library Item from existing content

To create Dreamweaver Library Items from existing content, follow these steps:

1. Open the document `dwlib.html` in Dreamweaver and choose Window ⇨ Assets to open the Assets panel.

Note You will create a Library Item using the text in the right column. The text content in the right column will be automated so that changes can be made across many pages. You will create a Library Item from the existing text in the right column. Future changes to this text will be made to the Library Item and changes will be reflected anywhere the Library Item has been placed.

2. Highlight the text in the right column. In the Assets panel, activate the Library Item tab by clicking the bottom symbol (open book) at the left of the panel. To create the Library Item, click the triangular symbol at the top right side of the panel to open the menu. Choose New Library Item or click the button with a + symbol at the bottom of the panel. An alert window opens (providing you have not disabled the alert at an earlier time) reminding you that CSS style sheet information is not copied with the selected content.

3. The Assets panel now shows a listing with the title selected. Type **news** to name your Library Item. Your screen should be similar to the screen shown in Figure 10-6.

4. Open a code view in Dreamweaver and see what has happened to the content code. `<!-- #BeginLibraryItem "/Library/news.lbi" -->` appears at the beginning of your content area, and `<!-- #EndLibraryItem -->` appears at the end of the content. Dreamweaver uses this code to update your Library Items automatically.

Caution When using the Clean Up HTML command, make sure you do not request that Dreamweaver comment tags be included. If you remove Dreamweaver comments, you lose both Library Item links and links to templates.

5. To check or edit the Library Item, double-click the library listing in the Assets panel. A Dreamweaver document opens with the Library Item content displayed. Note the window title, which includes `<<Library Item>>` as well as the Library Item name. Note also there are no page commands, such as background — only the specific content. Although the alert window advised that CSS styles would not be copied, that warning refers only to the page CSS or a linked file as you are using for this exercise. `<span>` commands, as are included with this text, are included (use a code view to confirm that the `<span>` tags are still there).

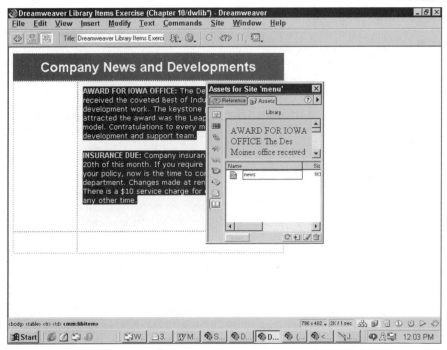

Figure 10-6: Dreamweaver Library Item created from existing content

6. Edit the content of the file by clicking at the end of the last paragraph to place your cursor and type **Call 555-1212 for more information.** Choose File ⇨ Save. An alert window appears asking if you would like to update the listed files. Click OK, and the change you made to the Library Item appears on your page. Close the Library Item window.

7. Finally, create a new document. With the Assets panel open and the Library Items tab active, click and drag the Library Item onto the screen. The contents of the Library Item appear on the screen with no formatting and stretching across the page. That is all you must do to place this item over and over again. Any edits are done as described in Step 6 and are reflected on every page that contains the Library Item.

8. Save the document as dwlib.html.

Creating a Dreamweaver Library Item from scratch

You have just completed a Library Item by selecting content. You can also create a Library Item from scratch in a very similar way to creating SSI content as discussed earlier in this chapter. When you create a Library Item from existing content, Dreamweaver does much of the thinking for you. However, you should understand how Library Items work in order to create one from scratch.

You must always remember that Library Item content is only a piece of a page. It is essential that you do not include page commands as you create a file, which means you must remove the page code that Dreamweaver places by default.

In the exercise that follows, you create a menu in HTML format, and then copy and paste the code into a new Library Item.

To create a Dreamweaver Library Item from scratch, follow these steps:

1. Open the file `menussi.html` and `dwlib.html` (if they are not already open).

Note

> You are using prepared content for this exercise for simplicity, but the next few steps could just as easily be hand entered and formatted by using any of Dreamweaver's commands. Make sure that you do not add page commands, however.

2. Open a code view in the `menussi.html` document and select all the content. Choose Edit ➪ Copy or Ctrl + C (Windows) or Command + C (Macintosh) to copy the content to the clipboard.

3. Activate the `dwlib.html` document and open the Assets panel. Click the Library Items tab in the toolbox at the left of the Assets panel, and click the New Library Item button at the bottom of the Assets panel to create a new Library Item. Type **menu** to replace Untitled in the new listing.

4. Double-click the menu Library Item. The Library Item editing window opens. Check a code view, and you can see no code is entered.

5. Choose Edit ➪ Paste or Ctrl + V (Windows) or Command + V (Macintosh) to paste the content from the clipboard into the document.

6. Save the Library Item document and close.

7. Return to `dwlib.html`. In the Assets panel, click and drag the "menu" Library Item to the left column to place the menu.

8. Save the file as `dwlib.html`.

You now have an updateable menu in place. You can repeat Step 7 to place your menu on any page. To make changes, you simply double-click the "menu" Library Item in the Assets panel and make changes to the content. When you save the changes, you will be given a list of documents containing that Library Item. Clicking update makes the changes to any placed Library Item.

Adobe GoLive Components

Adobe GoLive uses individual components to deliver automation just as SSI. As with Dreamweaver's Library Items, Components can be updated only within GoLive, so caution must be used to ensure that everyone has GoLive if you are working in a team setting, or, if another designer will maintain the site, the designer has access to GoLive. If not, SSI is a better choice.

However, Components do offer a lot of power if you are designing a site that you will maintain, or if the entire team will be using GoLive. You can create a small piece of HTML and use it over and over in documents. Updating the document will show in every document containing the Component.

On the CD-ROM

Copy the file `golivecom.html` from the Chapter 10 folder on the CD-ROM included with this book to the working folder on your computer. If you have not already copied the following files onto your computer with the previous exercise, you will also require `menucss.css`, `menussi.html`, and `space.gif`, also found in the Chapter 10 folder on the CD-ROM. These files must be in the folder you are using for this exercise.

Creating a GoLive Component

GoLive creates Components from blank documents, so whether you are creating a Component from existing content or creating one from scratch, the process is the same.

To create a GoLive Component, follow these steps:

1. Open the file `golivecom.html`. You create a Component for a menu that is placed in the left column. Also open `menussi.html`. You use this file to copy the code for the Component content.

2. With the Source view active for `menussi.html`, select the content contained between the `<div>` and `</div>` tags, but not including those tags. The `<div>` tags are already in the main document.

3. Choose Edit ⇨ Copy or Ctrl + C (Windows) or Command + C (Macintosh) to copy the content to the clipboard. Close the file.

4. Choose File ⇨ New to create a new document.

5. With Layout view active, click the Page icon located just below the Layout tab. If the Inspector window is not open, choose Window ⇨ Inspector to open. Click the HTML tab and then click the Component button at the bottom of the Inspector window (it may already be grayed out.) See Figure 10-7 for the correct settings.

6. With the Source view active, locate the following code:

```
<body bgcolor="#ffffff">
      <p></p>
   </body>
```

Delete the `<p>` and `</p>` tags and ensure that the cursor remains between the `<body>` and `</body>` tags.

Figure 10-7: The correct settings to create a Component document in Adobe GoLive

7. Choose Edit ➪ Paste or Ctrl + V (Windows) or Command + V (Macintosh) to paste the content from the clipboard into the document.

8. Choose File ➪ Save As and the Save As window opens. Click the icon in the bottom right corner of the window (Windows) or top (Macintosh) and select Components from the popup menu, as shown in Figure 10-8. Type **menu** as the file name. Click Save to save the component and then close the document.

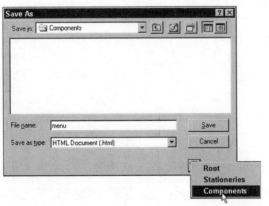

Figure 10-8: Saving a document as a Component in Adobe GoLive

9. If the Objects window is not open, choose Window ➪ Objects to open. Click the Site Extras tab or use the side menu popup to activate the Site Extras window. Select Components from the drop-down menu at the bottom right of the Site Extras window. An icon should appear on the screen, and holding your mouse over the icon should reveal the name menu.html at the lower edge of the Site Extras window. This is the component you just created, and it is available to insert into any document in your site.

Using GoLive Components

Now that your Component is completed, you can place it anywhere, in any document, within the site.

To place a Component in a document, follow these steps:

1. To include the Component in your document, click and drag the `menu.html` icon from the Site Extras window to the desired location, as described in Step 9 of the previous exercise. The menu should fall into place and can be changed from the Component document at any time.

2. Activate the Preview view to see your results, which should be similar to the results shown in Figure 10-9.

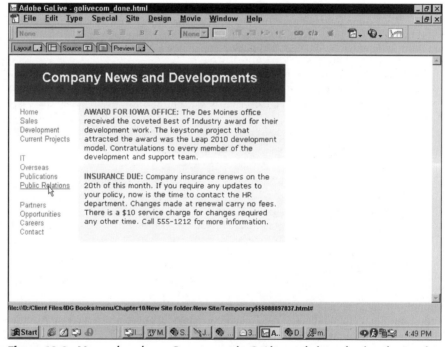

Figure 10-9: Menu placed as a Component in GoLive and viewed using the Preview view

✦   ✦   ✦

Creating Tiny Text You Can Actually Read

What is one sure way to provide a wide selection of navigation options for your visitors, yet still have room for the most important part of a Web site—the content? Use tiny text. Using small text to create menus lets you pack a lot into a small space. But it is not easy.

Working with small text is like walking through a minefield. Any designer can specify a small type size as he or she creates graphics, but it takes specific knowledge to make that text legible, fit with the design, and most importantly, stand out enough to attract attention.

In this chapter, I look at the pitfalls that surround using small text and provide some proven solutions. As with all graphic topics, however, if you are looking for 10 rules on how to use small text successfully every time, you will be disappointed. Color, texture, and other graphics vary too much from site to site to ever have hard, fast rules. With the guidelines in this chapter, however, you will have the tools to find the perfect solution for every Web site you create.

Why Does Tiny Type Look So Bad?

Antialiasing is the one word answer to most problems you see with tiny type and is one of the most important concepts to understand when we are talking about small text. Bear with me for a few paragraphs if you are already familiar with antialiasing. Antialiasing basics are so important when working with text that I want to make sure everyone understands exactly how antialiasing works. Without this understanding, it is hard to follow any workarounds.

Antialiasing prevents jaggy edges. Because raster images (GIF, JPG, and PNG are raster formats) are created with pixels, which are square, diagonal lines or curves look rough in raw pixel format. To overcome this rough, or jaggy effect, antialiasing mixes the object color with the color behind the object to create pixels of mixed color where they meet. This effect tricks the eye into seeing smooth curves or lines, rather than square pixels. See Figure 11-1 for a magnified view of antialiasing at work. The top sample has no antialiasing and the bottom sample has Adobe Photoshop's Crisp antialiasing command applied. Note how the edge pixels have been combined with a shade of white. Figure 11-2 shows the same characters at actual size.

Figure 11-1: The Sevenet 7 sample from Figure 11-2 magnified. The top sample does not have antialiasing applied. The lower sample features Photoshop's Crisp Antialiasing command.

Figure 11-2: The effect of antialiasing on two fonts. The top sample is Sevenet 7, a font designed to be used without antialiasing at a specific size. The lower sample is Arial shown at a small and large size. In both cases, the left sample has antialiasing turned off. The right sample has Photoshop's Crisp Antialiasing command applied.

Every font behaves differently with different levels of antialiasing. To make antialiasing even more challenging, the color of your text and background also affects the appearance of your antialiasing. Simply choose the settings that give you the best appearance. Make sure that you apply the same setting to text that is intended to match throughout the pages of your project. You may want to make a note of the settings you use for antialiasing on a large, multi-page project.

In Figure 11-3, I used different settings for antialiasing in each line, but the same settings for the black and gray type on each line. Note how the same settings deliver different results for each color combination. A few rules, other than using what looks best, can be applied to antialiasing. Common advice recommends that text under 10 pts should be used without antialiasing, but I have seen exceptions. I have also seen 14-pt type that looks best with no antialiasing.

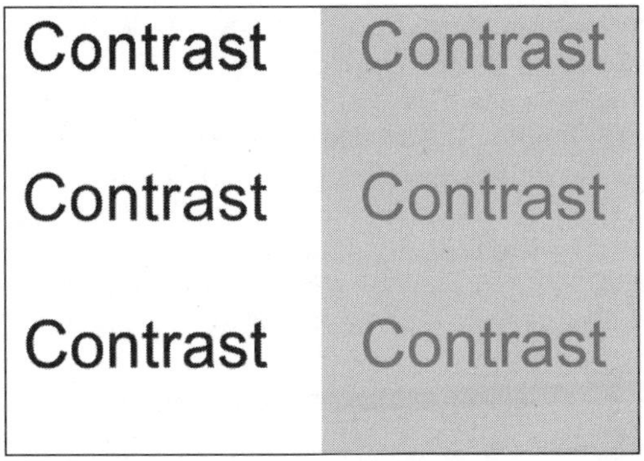

Figure 11-3: Antialiasing settings in Photoshop from top to bottom: None, Crisp, and Strong. Note how the low contrast type at the right has a different look from the high contrast type with each antialiasing setting.

Although I have no secrets for you to guarantee great results with a specific formula, just understanding that antialiasing plays a major role in small text quality will help you to achieve better results. Some fonts behave better at small sizes than others for monitor display, and any Web designer should always be watching for text that is terrific when tiny.

Building a Font Library for Tiny Type

As a Web designer, you are probably a fontaholic. Few designers of any medium are not captured by the allure of fonts and the millions of variations of fonts that exist. Add the almost unlimited number of free and very low-cost fonts available on the Web, usually with instant download, to the natural compulsion to present words in a "new" way, and designers have little defense against becoming fontaholics.

Using a screen font

However—and this is a big however—not many fonts can stand up at small sizes for a 72 dpi display. In addition, featuring more than two font families on one page is never a good idea (*never* more than three). On the Web we are restricted to a limited range of fonts to use for HTML text, so you already have one font that is non-negotiable on any page. The sad truth of the Web design world is that in a wonderland of font choice, little of that choice is practical. In order to be a successful designer, defined by the ease with which your visitors can find information, you must use serious restraint in choosing fonts.

The small font world is one where more is good, however. The explosive growth of the Web has instigated an entirely new class of font designed to be used at specific sizes. Known as *screen* or *pixel fonts*, this new class of font can instantly improve the legibility and professional appearance of small menu item fonts.

Caution   Throughout this section, the fonts I refer to are fonts that are used as graphics. Screen fonts fall under the same restriction as all other fonts for HTML text, in that they must be installed on the user's computer in order to display. Screen fonts are found on very few computers outside those used by designers.

Screen fonts are designed to be used at a specific size. Do not use antialiasing with screen fonts. They are designed to appear crisp and clean without antialiasing by using only the pixels available for a 72 dpi display. I include several sources for small fonts in the next section. Make sure you pay close attention to the specified size for each font you purchase or download. If you have a master Web design notebook of any kind, make sure you write down this information. These fonts will not work at any other size but the specified one.

Tip   Web Page Design for Designers (`http://wpdfd.com`) provides a wealth of other information for professional designers. It is also one of the best online resources for screen fonts and screen font information I have found. Specific screen font information is found at `http://wpdfd.com/wpdtypo3a.htm`.

Screen font resources

One of the most popular screen fonts is Mini 7, created by Joe Gillespie of Web Page Design for Designers, shown in Figure 11-4. I included a sampling of this amazing small font collection. I have not included the extras part of the font family, which includes many kerning and decorative tools. Joe also created a font family called Tenacity, designed to be used at 10 pixels. See Figure 11-5 for a sample of the variations included with this font. Joe continues to produce new screen fonts, and while they are not free, the entire collection is available for $25, or individually for $8 to $15. Visit `http://wpdfd.com/MiniFonts.htm` to view and order any of these fonts.

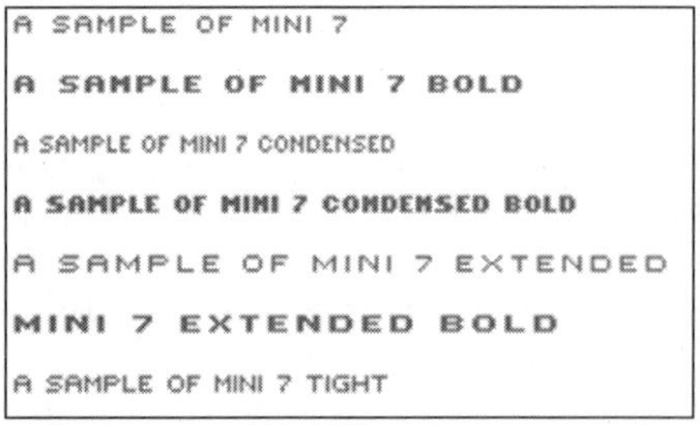

```
A SAMPLE OF MINI 7

A SAMPLE OF MINI 7 BOLD

A SAMPLE OF MINI 7 CONDENSED

A SAMPLE OF MINI 7 CONDENSED BOLD

A SAMPLE OF MINI 7 EXTENDED

MINI 7 EXTENDED BOLD

A SAMPLE OF MINI 7 TIGHT
```

Figure 11-4: Joe Gillespie's Mini 7 family.

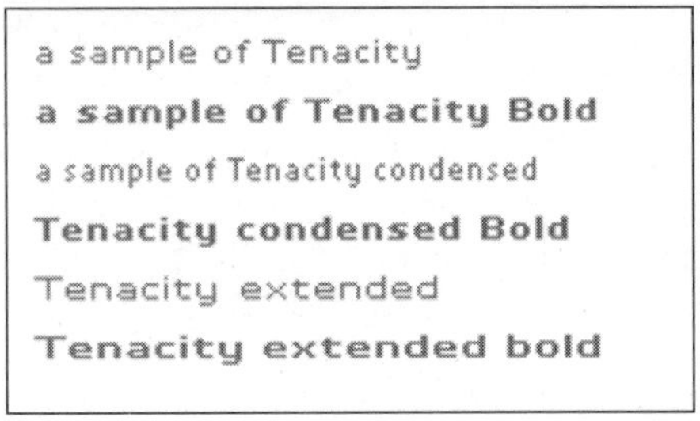

Figure 11-5: The Tenacity family of screen fonts, also by Joe Gillespie

The 04 Bitmap font family, shown in Figure 11-6, provides plenty of variety in style. The fonts are created by Yuji Oshimoto and can be downloaded at `www.dsg4.com/04/extra/bitmap/index.html`.

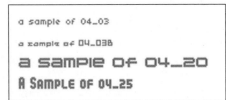

Figure 11-6: Several samples of the 04 Bitmap screen font selection, created by Yuji Oshimoto

Another wonderful font is Intermosaic, by ShyFonts (see Figure 11-7). Although the original Shyfonts site has been discontinued, the fonts can still be downloaded from `www.moorstation.org/typoasis/designers/shyfonts/shy01.htm`.

Figure 11-7: Intermosaic, by ShyFonts, a reliably legible screen font

Try this selection of fonts and if you still want more information or want to test even more pixel fonts, you can visit WebSite Tips (`www.websitetips.com/fonts/index2.html`) for a comprehensive listing.

The exercises that follow get you started with pixel fonts. Experiment and see how you can improve your menu creation or perhaps work with small fonts for the first time. Each of us is attracted to different fonts, so there can be no "good" or "bad" pixel fonts. Just remember the restrictions and methods for a quality product—a giant step toward professional and efficient menus.

The Other Side of Antialiasing

In this chapter I have been talking about small type, and the exercises that follow are about creating tiny text, but I do want to take a short side trip while I am on the topic of antialiasing. HTML text does not have any antialiasing. You must work without antialiasing for clear type in tiny text, but on the opposite end of the scale, must work around the lack of antialiasing in larger HTML text—opposite sides of the same problem.

Caution   I am about to discuss using graphic text to replace HTML text, but I want to enforce that this is a topic only for headlines or menu items. Graphic text has *no* place in content delivery on the Web. I am adamant enough on this point to say that graphic text use on the Web reflects negatively on the designer's understanding of the Web. If you are presenting content text as graphics, you are ignoring the vast numbers of surfers who have slower Web connections, like me, who have no choice of connection speed. You are allowing your need for graphic control to overwhelm true skill development for this medium. You are robbing yourself of the potential to be a professional designer.

I include an extreme example in Figure 11-8. The top sample of the word *product* was created in a graphics program and included in the HTML page as an image. The second sample is Times New Roman HTML text, created to resemble the graphics text as closely as possible. The text created with a graphics program and antialiasing added, is undisputedly superior.

Serif fonts, such as Times New Roman, perform poorly without antialiasing at headline size. If you must use HTML large text, and I always advise that you use text when possible (especially if the large text is part of a menu system), results are often better with sans serif fonts, such as Verdana or Arial. I find that Arial's taller, slightly square characters perform quite well at larger sizes for non-antialiased text, as you can see in the third sample in Figure 11-8.

Products

Products

Products

Figure 11-8: Times Roman is featured in the first and second sample, with and without antialiasing, respectively. The third sample is Arial. Note how the characters in Arial are less "jaggy" than the same characters in the non-antialiased Times Roman sample.

I have said before, and will again, that Web design is constant compromise. HTML text loads instantly, and is easily edited, but the lack of antialiasing creates quality problems at larger sizes. Graphics programs are often used to create text menus containing small fonts, but you must be able to remove antialiasing from the text as you create the graphics, or the result will be fuzzy. Tiny fonts are often illegible, unless a special font is used.

Background texture or color, when combined with text color, creates a unique combination every time you create a menu. Experiment, observe what works for your style, and each time you create a new menu, try several variations before you settle on your construction method. I strongly recommend finding at least one screen font that works well with your style, so that you can create crisp, legible menus with very small type. To get you started, the exercises that follow step you through creating a small sample menu with Tenacity Condensed, a screen font from Joe Gillespie.

Before starting this exercise, copy the font, Tenacity Condensed, with file name `Tencond.zip`, located in the Chapter 11 folder on the CD-ROM that accompanies this book, to your hard drive. Unzip the file and install the font in the usual way for your computer. (This step is unnecessary if you have Tenacity Condensed already installed on your computer.) Tenacity Condensed is part of the Tenacity family package available through Web Page Design for Designers (`http://wpdfd.com`). Thanks to Joe Gillespie for making this font available to complete this exercise.

Exercise: Creating Tiny Text in Photoshop

The following exercise creates a very small sample menu using Tenacity Condensed, a screen font designed to be used at a 10-pixel size. Just for interest, you may want to change the size of the font to 8 or 10 pixels to see the effect.

Create a tiny text menu in Photoshop as follows:

1. Create a new document at 200 pixels by 25 pixels, 72 dpi resolution, RGB color, and with a white background.

2. If your type units are not set to pixels, choose Edit ⇨ Preferences ⇨ Units and Rulers or double-click the ruler and choose Pixels for the Type units.

3. Activate the Type tool and set the font to Tenacity Condensed, 10 pixels. Set Antialias to None in the Toolbar and color to #000066.

4. Type **Home | Products | Contact** (| is typed as Shift + \). Center the text in the document. Your text should be crisp and clear and closely resemble Figure 11-9.

5. Save the document for future reference. It is easy to forget exactly how to work with screen fonts if you do not work with them often. The most common error is to set the size in points rather than pixels. Keeping a sample copy of a perfect screen font result will jog your memory.

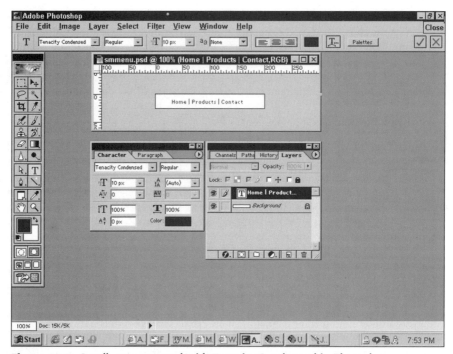

Figure 11-9: Small menu created with Tenacity Condensed in Photoshop

Exercise: Creating Tiny Text in Paint Shop Pro

I have good news and bad news for users of JASC Software's Paint Shop Pro. The bad news is that you cannot set your text to pixel sizing, and cannot even cheat by adjusting the point sizing to approximate the pixel sizing, because you cannot use decimal point sizes for type. The result is that screen fonts cannot be used as predictably as with other programs. The good news, however, is that the antialiasing setting is excellent, and you can achieve good results using regular fonts.

To create a small menu using regular fonts and antialiasing in Paint Shop Pro, follow these steps:

1. Create a new document 200 pixels by 25 pixels, with a white background, 24-bit color, and 72 dpi resolution.

2. Activate the Text tool and click in the document to open the Text Entry window.

3. Select a simple font, such as Arial, Helvetica, or Verdana, and set it to 9 pts. Make sure antialiasing is turned on and type **Home | Products | Contact** (| is Shift + \). Click OK to check the results. Try setting the Kerning value to 50 to

see if the text is easier to read. You must return to the document window to see any changes. See Figure 11-10 for the settings.

Although the results are not as smooth and crisp as when a screen font is used, Paint Shop Pro's gentle antialiasing produces an acceptable result for small text.

Figure 11-10: Settings for creating small text in Paint Shop Pro

Exercise: Creating Tiny Text in Fireworks

Macromedia Fireworks has excellent controls for using screen fonts. The text is specified in pixels, and you have a no antialiasing setting that delivers perfect results for any screen font.

To create a sample menu using Tenacity Condensed, a screen font designed to be used at 10 pixels, follow these steps:

1. Create a new document, 200 pixels by 25 pixels, with a white background and 72 dpi resolution.

2. Activate the Text tool and click in the document to open the Text Editor window. Set the text for Tenacity Condensed, size 10, and No Anti-Alias.

3. Type **Home | Products | Contact** (| is Shift + /). Figure 11-11 shows the Text Editor window with the menu entries completed.

4. Save the document for future reference when working with a screen font.

There is not a lot different in using small fonts from regular text entry, but becoming familiar with the process and understanding how and why screen fonts deliver such great results is a good idea.

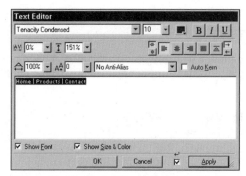

Figure 11-11: Text editor window with Tenacity font specified and the text entered

But screen fonts and tiny text is just the edge of the type world. Chapter 12 takes you further into the art of typography and can help you to achieve some of the professional results you may have seen but could not put your finger on why they looked so much better than the next site. Often the answer to that puzzle is typography.

✦   ✦   ✦

Typography Counts for Menus

For those of us who came to Web design from a print background, a great shock awaited. We worked so hard in our print work to perfect typography — the standard by which print design is measured. As we started into Web design, we discovered that we had almost no control over text, not even the text size or length of the lines. Years of dedicated learning down the tube . . . or is it?

In my tours of great Web sites, I started to notice that the sites that caught my attention and had balanced and attractive designs had perfect typography. Not in the body text, obviously (sorry if you thought I had the magic bullet), but in the headlines and menu items. We do have control over our graphic text. The other aspect I noticed was that many sites missed being great sites because the designer had just "typed" and not used "typography." There is a huge difference when text is carefully crafted.

This chapter covers the basics of typography and shows you the controls in graphics programs to reach a higher level of text presentation. If you are serious about producing professional sites, I strongly recommend that you carry on past this chapter and study typography as an art. Although all sources I have seen for typography to date are specific to the print industry, the principals of headline typography, the only type really open to Web designers, applies equally to the Web.

What's Typography Doing on the Web?

I can hear you muttering about me taking you on a roller coaster ride through the text discussions in this book. First, I tout HTML text menus as if they were the answer to everything Web. Then, I teach you how to do tiny type, which is a graphic form of text. Then I lament the lack of control you have with HTML text, and here I am saying typography on the Web is something you should know. Remember the Web being a steady stream of compromise? It's here again.

First, if you can accomplish site goals with HTML text, do it! I am not the least bit ambiguous about that point. However, if you are going to do graphic text and that is also a valuable part of both the artistic and practical side of the Web, then doing it right is important. Beautiful text attracts attention and can act like road signs, directing your visitor to the right place at the right time. It can help you set the mood for a page and separate many different headings with different type treatment.

Typography is also the solution for one of my pet peeves — fonts that look great but cannot be easily read. The excuse for using a font with questionable legibility is often "but it is setting a mood." Effective typography can also set the mood, but doing so by using characters that are familiar to a visitor's eyes.

So if you think typography is something you only need to know if you are going to go into the print side of design, think again. In just a few pages, I am hoping that I can show you why you must add typography to your skills if you want to improve your skills.

The World's Fastest Typography Course

To say that I can't do the field of typography justice in a few pages is a laughable understatement. However, as in most complicated subjects, a few critical techniques can improve the quality of your work very quickly. That is where we will focus our attention: to get you kick started with typography and perhaps interested enough to carry on.

Tip   The *Non-Designer's Type Book* by Robin Williams (Peachpit Press; 1998) is highly recommended reading for anyone interested in typography. The book is geared to print production, but with the tools you will have at the end of this chapter, you will be able to create any of the effects featured.

Understanding the power of spacing

The default settings for line and character spacing can usually be improved. There are few times that I create a menu or menu heading that some adjustment is not necessary. Your eye can quickly become trained to watch for places to improve your spacing simply by focussing on the topic.

Character spacing

Take a look at the samples in Figure 12-1. In the first sample, I loosened the character spacing just a little and tightened the normal spacing for the second sample. (Character spacing is called *kerning* and/or *tracking* in many design programs and the commercial print world.) Notice how the second example seems to hold together better as a word. Sometimes, for style reasons, you want more space in your words. That should be deliberate and to reach a certain goal. Most times, you want your characters to be close together without crowding.

Figure 12-1: Tighter spacing usually helps the characters of a word hold together as a unit.

Leading or line spacing

One of my pet peeves in text work of any kind is line spacing that is far too wide. Look at the first "Shop Smart" sample in Figure 12-2. The default line spacing, which is called *leading* (rhymes with *sledding*) in some programs, is usually far too large for large type sizes. Too much space makes it difficult for the eye to see the headline as a unit. In the second sample, I tightened the spacing. Cover one and then the other with your hand and pay attention to how you read each sample. You will find that when the line spacing is large, you tend to read each word individually, rather than seeing the phrase as a unit.

When we are talking only about character or line spacing, the best guide is your eye. Unfortunately, the effect of poor typography is very subtle. You may have to read the headline twice if the line spacing is too large, or the character spacing too tight, but you are unlikely to blame the type. As a designer, though, if you start to focus on your typography for your display text, you will soon discover that your page design improves. With this tiny "heads up" on spacing, you will already be better text designers, simply because you are now alert to watch for gaps.

Shop
Smart

Shop
Smart

Figure 12-2: Default line spacing, as in the top sample, is too wide for large type. After the spacing is tightened, reading the headline as a unit is easier.

Character combinations and spacing

In addition to character and line spacing, you must also watch for gaps or crowding in words caused by various letter combinations. With the proliferation of freeware and shareware fonts, the way that characters pair together is not always attractive. You do not have to forgo the font you want, just watch for ways to improve the appearance.

Take a look at Figure 12-3. The samples on the left of each row have loose spacing, and the right sample has tight character spacing. The upper case example with tight character spacing is too tight, and the different angle of the characters is not attractive. It is also cramped, making it hard for the eye to separate the two letters (although this character pairing often requires tighter spacing). The first sample is a little too loose and would be better with a slight tightening. In the lower case sample, the tighter version works much better.

Note   In print work, you tend to work only with professionally designed fonts, which give you the freedom to set large passages of text in your choice of font(s). Changing the spacing for several combinations of characters in 60 pages of text is not practical. In Web design, our font use is only to display text, so adjusting the letter pairs or entire passages when necessary is reasonable. Many former print designers will cringe at the idea of a freeware font, but for Web work, the reasons you always use professional, high-quality fonts in print just do not exist.

Figure 12-3: Tight and loose character spacing for upper and lower case letters in the same font

Understanding the design factor of typography

We have talked about leading (line spacing) and kerning (character spacing) but there are other controls you will need to perfect your typography skills. In addition to moving characters and lines in relation to other characters and lines, you will also want the ability to move letters in the same word or phase up or down. I cover a few examples of where you would move the characters (shifting the baseline) but you have many other appropriate reasons to use this shift.

Baseline shift

The *baseline* is the line where the bottom of the characters line up. Letters, such as *y* or *g* have descenders, which is a portion of the letter that falls below the baseline. In Figure 12-4, the top sample is created with a default baseline position and the fine gray line marks the baseline. The second sample is the same text, but the baseline has been shifted by 10 pixels.

The baseline shift is an important part of creating well-crafted typography. See the two samples in Figure 12-5. In each, the top version features default settings. In each lower sample, the entries have been carefully nudged into correct form with kerning and baseline shift. For the "Friday" sample, note how the parentheses are not in the middle of the word. A slight adjustment to the baseline for each of the parenthesis corrects the balance. Character spacing was tightened between the "F" and "R" and for both the "A" and "Y". You could certainly get away with the top sample, but look at how much better the lower sample looks.

The changes are even more dramatic in the price sample. Again, I raised the parenthesis baselines by a small amount. The entire entry is kerned heavily with the "7" and "4" receiving even more to take advantage of the nesting shapes. The "99" was reduced in size, with the baseline raised to match the top of the other characters. Arguing with the value of good typography is hard when you see the difference between the original and the one that uses typography methods.

Figure 12-4: Gray line represents the baseline for text. In the lower sample, the text has been raised 10 pixels above the baseline.

Figure 12-5: Kerning and baseline adjustments create the second version from the first for a professional appearance.

Typographer's quotation marks

Although quotation marks are not usually associated with menu items, I did not want to leave this issue out of any typography discussion. When creating a quote in graphics, you should be using typographer's quotes, and not the keyboard quote marks " and ' (see Figure 12-6). Typographer's quotes are stylized marks that are also known as *curly* quotes or *smart* quotes. See the sidebar for the keyboard commands to create these symbols.

Figure 12-6: Keyboard characters (top). Typographer's quotes (bottom). Italic keyboard characters to simulate correct inch and foot symbols (prime markers) (bottom).

I created a sample with straight typing and one with typography adjustments to illustrate the dramatic difference small adjustments can make. (See Figure 12-7.) The correct quotes are much more attractive than the typed quotes. Observe how much difference it makes to align all of the text and enable the quotes to stand outside the text. For the small amount of text we are working with as graphics, achieving this look is easy by simply inserting a space and adjusting the kerning of the space until the text lines up. I also reduced the line spacing to create a more unified appearance.

Typography is often seen as as a perfectionist obsession, but when you see the difference a little work can make to a page, you will never treat type casually again. The exercises that follow give you the techniques you need to create such typography effects.

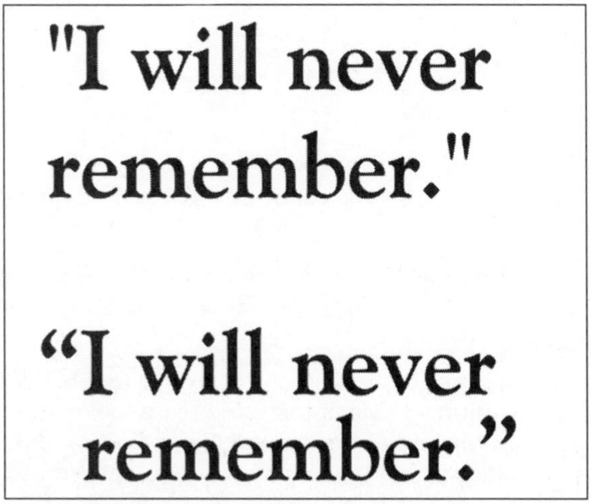

"I will never remember."

"I will never remember."

Figure 12-7: Top version uses default values. Bottom version has correct quote form, aligned text, and reduced line spacing.

Keyboard Shortcuts for Typographer's Quotes

The PC keyboard shortcut to create typographer's quotes in any program is ALT + 0147 for opening quotes and ALT + 0148 for the closing quotes. Single opening quotes are ALT + 0145 and closing ALT + 0146.

For the Macintosh, the keyboard shortcut is OPTION + [for opening quotes and OPTION + SHIFT + [for closing quotes. Single opening quotes are OPTION +] and closing OPTION + SHIFT +].

Exercise: Working with Typography Techniques in Photoshop

You work through creating a text quotation in order to cover every typography technique I have covered. Step through it one technique at a time, and you will have all the control you need to create fine typography using Adobe Photoshop. Refer to Figure 12-8 for the location of typography tools through the exercise.

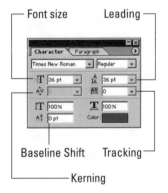

Font size   Leading

Baseline Shift   Tracking

Kerning

Figure 12-8: Typography tools in Photoshop

1. Create a new document in Photoshop, 300 pixels by 200 pixels, 72 dpi, and with a white background.

2. Activate the Type tool and set the type to Times New Roman (or Times), size 36, with Crisp Antialiasing, and color 663300. Type **Whenever**. Press Enter to insert a hard return and type **I call.**

3. Insert your cursor at the beginning of the text within the same text block and type Alt + 0147 (Windows) or Option + [(Macintosh) to create the opening quotes ("). Insert your cursor at the end of the second line, following the period and type Alt + 0148 (Windows) or Option + Shift + [(Macintosh) to create the closing quotes.

4. If the Character window is not open, choose Window ⇨ Show Character to open. Select all the text. In the Character window, set the leading to 36.

5. Set Tracking to 10 to loosen character spacing across the entire selection.

6. Check spacing between individual characters. If the spacing is not perfect, insert your cursor between the characters you want to adjust and set the Kerning value that gives the best result. Positive numbers increase spacing between characters. Negative numbers decrease spacing.

7. Drag a guide to line up with the left edge of the "W" in the first line of type. Use your spacebar to move the "I" to line up with the guide. You may need to insert your cursor in front of the "I" and increase or decrease kerning value to line the characters up perfectly. In Figure 12-9, I used two spaces and a Kerning value of -50 to line up the characters.

8. Select only the opening quote character, and specify 5 for the Baseline Shift value. Doing this raises the character by 5 pixels. Repeat for the closing quote character.

9. Check that your results are similar to those shown in Figure 12-9 (magnified view). Save the document in PSD format for future reference.

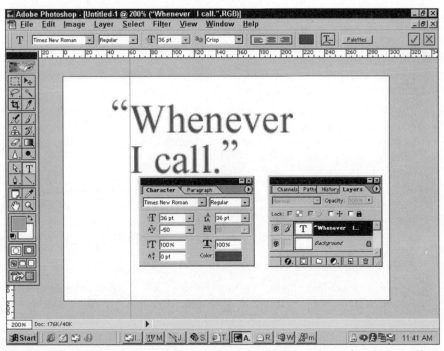

Figure 12-9: Adjusting the spacing and Kerning values to line up characters in Photoshop

Exercise: Working with Typography Techniques in Paint Shop Pro

Paint Shop Pro from JASC Software offers plenty of typography power. Move the Text Entry window to the side so that you can see your document as you work. Make sure that the preview button in the lower right corner of the window is on, and you can see changes as you make them.

Create a text quotation that requires all typography tools in Paint Shop Pro as follows:

1. Create a new document, 300 pixels by 200 pixels, 24-bit color, with a white background, and 72 dpi resolution.

2. Activate the Text tool and click the document to open the Text Entry window. Set the type to Times New Roman (or Times), size 36, with Antialiasing, and color 663300. Type **Whenever**. Press Enter to insert a hard return and type **I call.**

3. Insert your cursor at the beginning of the text within the same text block, and type Alt + 0147 to create the opening quotes ("). Insert your cursor at the end of the second line following the period and type Alt + 0148 to create the closing quotes (").

4. Select all the text and set the Leading to -10.

5. With all text still selected, set Kerning to 5 to loosen character spacing across the entire selection.

6. Check the spacing between individual characters. If the spacing is not perfect, insert your cursor between the characters you want to adjust, and set the Kerning value that gives the best result. Positive numbers increase spacing between characters. Negative numbers decrease spacing. Click OK to accept the changes you have made in the text.

7. Draw a vector line to act as a guide and place it at the left edge of the "W." Open the Text Entry window again and position the window so that you can still see your document. Use your spacebar to move the "I" to line up with the guide. You may need to insert your cursor in front of the "I" and increase or decrease the Kerning value to line the characters up perfectly. In Figure 12-10, I used two spaces and a Kerning value of -120 to line up the characters.

8. Delete the guideline, check that your results are similar to those shown in Figure 12-10 (magnified view), and save the document in PSP format for future reference.

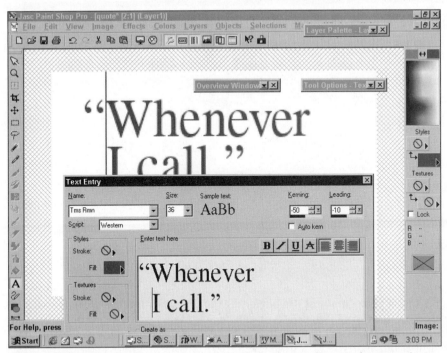

Figure 12-10: Adjusting the spacing and Kerning values to line up characters in Paint Shop Pro

Exercise: Working with Typography Techniques in Fireworks

Macromedia Fireworks has powerful typography tools, and you can view results as you make changes by keeping the Text Editor window off to the side so that you can always see the document. Refer to Figure 12-11 for the location of typography tools through the exercise.

To create a text quotation using all the typography tools in Fireworks, follow these steps:

1. Create a new document, 300 pixels by 200 pixels, with a white background, and 72 dpi resolution.

2. Activate the Text tool, and click the canvas to open the Text Editor window. Set the type to Times New Roman (or Times), size 36, with Crisp Anti-Aliasing, and color 663300. Type **Whenever**. Press Enter to insert a hard return and type **I call.**

Kerning   Leading

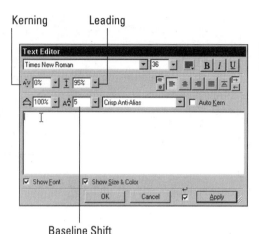

Figure 12-11: Typography tools in Fireworks

Baseline Shift

3. Insert your cursor at the beginning of the text within the same text block, and type Alt + 0147 (Windows) or Option + [(Macintosh) to create the opening quotes ("). Insert your cursor at the end of the second line following the period, and type Alt + 0148 (Windows) or Option Shift + [(Macintosh) to create the closing quotes (").

4. Select all of the text and set the Leading to 95%.

5. With all text still selected, set Kerning (called Range Kerning when multiple characters are selected) to 2% to loosen character spacing across the entire selection.

6. Check the spacing between individual characters. If the spacing is not perfect, insert your cursor between the characters you want to adjust and set the Kerning value that gives the best result. Positive numbers increase spacing between characters. Negative numbers decrease spacing. Click OK to accept the changes you have made so far, and return to the document.

7. Pull a guide to the left edge of the "W." Open the Text Entry window again and position the window so that you can still see your document. Use your space-bar to move the "I" to line up with the guide. You may need to insert your cursor in front of the "I", and increase or decrease the Kerning value to line the characters up perfectly. In Figure 12-12, I used one space and a Kerning value of 22% to line up the characters.

8. Select only the opening quote character and specify 5 for the Baseline Shift value. Doing this raises the character by 5 pixels. Repeat for the closing quote character.

9. Check that your results are similar to the results shown in Figure 12-12 (magnified view). Save the document in PNG format for future reference.

Figure 12-12: Adjusting the spacing and kerning values to line up characters in Fireworks

✦   ✦   ✦

Text and Design

Does it seem as if I am hung up on text? I probably am. If it were not for my love of direct communication, which is where text differs from any other art tool, I would probably be a painter or a sculptor. If you are a Web designer, you should also have a huge soft spot for text and for finding the ways that bring text to your visitors in an exciting and useable form.

The fun and skill in design work comes from identifying the elements that are required and presenting them in a useful and exciting way. Text makes up a considerable portion of any effective Web site. In this chapter, I offer many new ideas for presenting text as part of a menu system and will even side track a little into using text to attract attention to an area of the page. Remember, while menus are critical to the success of your site, they are just one part of the whole on any Web page.

Where Does Text Fit into Design?

Text delivers the message. You can evoke mood with graphics or provide graphic icons to help people get to a different spot on your site, but the responsibility for getting your message into the minds of your visitor falls to text. However, that is not the extent of what text does for a Web site. Text plays two additional roles: It can provide site consistency and design benefits.

Providing consistency

Text plays a vital, important role in providing consistency for your site. Text is the one element that will be on every single page of every single site on the Web. Within one site, you can have pages that are meant to build the mood and others that are meant to be down-and-dirty business pages. But each has text. What better place to apply one of the most important elements that can convert a "bunch of pages" into an effective site — consistency.

When you add unique characteristics to text, whether color, justification, or a graphic presentation, you can present that element on every page of your site. This consistency provides your visitors with instant, visual clues that they are on the same site, building a comfort level that is critical to keeping visitors.

If you look at the structure of this book, you will see that each page has the same elements, all created by text elements. Imagine that you turn the page, and the page headers disappear, page numbers are moved to another location on the page, and the main font changes. Your instinct might be to look at the cover of the book again, to see if somehow, without realizing it, you have picked up the wrong book. Moving from page to page in a Web site is no different.

I included two pages from my Web site in Figure 13-1. The graphics help to provide consistency, but also note the page titles and the text layout. Even if the graphics on the left were not visible, these two pages form a set. The page title is in the same location with the same font. The body text is all the same, and the smaller right column with extra information is consistent in font, font color, and column width on both pages. As visitors click through the site, there are no surprises, the menu is always in the same location, and the text clues provide instant recognition for content and utility areas.

Adding visual interest and direction

So far I identified the responsibility of text for communication. Next, I held text up as an important part of the glue that binds individual pages into a cohesive site. But there is more. Text can also be used to break up the visual appearance of the page. In fact, as I became more experienced as a Web designer, I started to depend heavily on text as a design element, both in graphic and HTML text form. Today, I look for any opportunity to add text lists or even tiny menus within the structure of the page. The break in content provides a place for visitors to focus. Graphics can do the same job, but with text, you can put the visual clues to work with a real job.

In Figure 13-2, the first sample shows a page with plain text only. Compare that look to the second sample, which has had nothing added but text formatting. Adding headlines, creating a list, breaking some text out into an indented area, and slight adjustments to the menu area, change the entire look of the page. Observe what your eyes do as they look at each page. In the unformatted text example, your eyes wander lazily across the page, not finding anywhere to stop. The text formatting I did for the second sample provides a stop point for your eyes and breaks the page into manageable pieces.

Pay special attention to the menu area. The unformatted example was noticeable and would do the job. Breaking it into smaller chunks and using indenting for subcategories not only makes the menu easier to use, but also makes it visually more interesting.

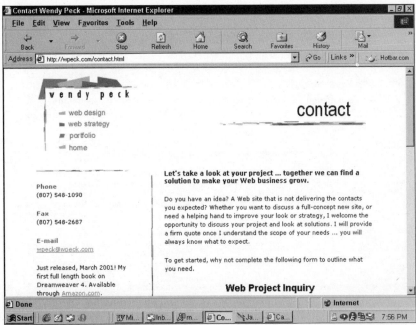

Figure 13-1: Two pages from my Web site, `http://wpeck.com`. Although the graphics help identify the pages as pages from the same site, the text layout and consistency also contribute to the connection between pages.

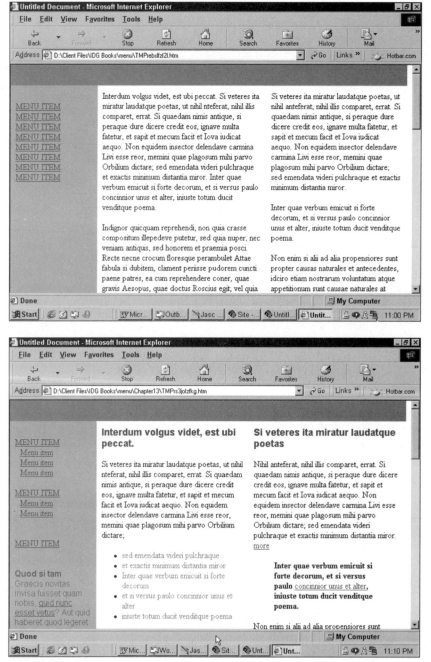

Figure 13-2: Simple text formatting changes a page from dull and difficult to use to visually interesting and breaks the page into manageable pieces for the visitor.

Contrast Counts

Have you noticed that when you arrive at some Web pages, your eye is drawn immediately to one area or another? A break in the visual flow of the page, as I mentioned in the previous section, is the most obvious reason for your eyes to settle in one particular place. Look at the difference between the two samples in Figure 13-2 again. It is not just a break in the flow of text that directs your eye around the page. Contrast is at play here, too.

A tiny red dot in the middle of a black and white page attracts attention every time. A large red menu in the middle of a very busy and colorful page may be missed completely. We can work with contrast to assign priority to our menu items through our site.

In Figure 13-3, I have the same block of text featured in different fonts and colors. In the block at the left, the small font color is light and the line spacing is loose. The sample at the right is in a heavier font, larger font size, default line spacing, and dark color. Both are legible, but look at the effect the gray bar at the top has with each sample. (It may help to cover one at a time and look at each sample alone.) With the lighter text, the darker bar jumps right off the page. However, with the heavier text, the bar nearly disappears. Find the black dot in the middle of the text. In the light sample, you find it instantly, and your eye remains there without conscious effort. In the middle of the dark text, your eye has to work to find the dot and continues working to remain there.

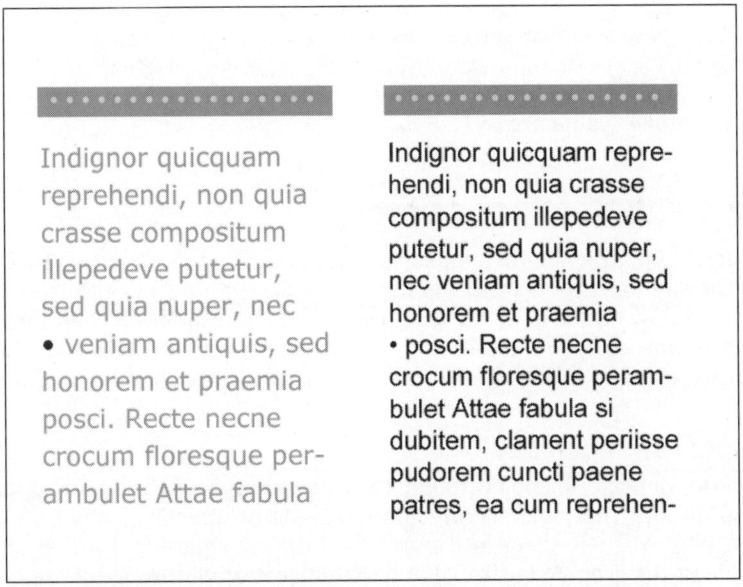

Indignor quicquam reprehendi, non quia crasse compositum illepedeve putetur, sed quia nuper, nec
• veniam antiquis, sed honorem et praemia posci. Recte necne crocum floresque perambulet Attae fabula

Indignor quicquam reprehendi, non quia crasse compositum illepedeve putetur, sed quia nuper, nec veniam antiquis, sed honorem et praemia
• posci. Recte necne crocum floresque perambulet Attae fabula si dubitem, clament periisse pudorem cuncti paene patres, ea cum reprehen-

Figure 13-3: The gray bar at the top and the black dot in the center of the passage jumps to your attention in the light text sample at the left. In the darker text sample, the attraction to your eye is almost lost.

Contrast is the most important design feature for attracting attention to a spot on the page, and there are as many ways to create contrast as designers in the world. White space (space around a design element), background color for menu areas, graphic enhancements, such as dots and lines, font color or weight changes, and placing items on an angle all are effective in providing the contrast you need to attract attention.

Tip   I do not have the space here to provide an entire lesson on contrast in design. The information is out there, though. If you do not have design training, I recommend that you find a few good sources of pure design information to increase your comfort with the subject. You can also absorb a great deal of intuition about contrast by keeping it in mind as you visit Web pages. If an area catches your attention, try to figure out why. Before long, your eye will become trained to watch for contrast, and you will be incorporating contrast area automatically into your design.

Power Tools for Making Text Pop

Design training and getting your brain in shape for design over years of observation are the most reliable ways to improve your design. However, isn't it nice when you can find a list of ideas that you can simply pick out and try on your page? I have design training and years of experience, and I still love to find design ideas neatly laid out for me. This section is devoted to jump starting your ideas to make the text, and specifically, text menus pop off your page for visitors.

Caution   Do not lose sight of your page as a whole and spend your contrast areas cautiously. Every new area that attracts attention on your page takes attention away from another. With too many areas on your page competing for attention, you lose all the benefit you set out to gain and are more likely to confuse your visitors than help them through your pages.

Creating a valuable set of tools

As soon as I have the direction for a site set, I automatically prepare a few tools to help me put the site together. As soon as the site colors and fonts are chosen, you can prepare the following items to have on hand as you put the pages together. Preparing these tools early in the process is important — deciding that you will add a design element after you have twenty pages or more already completed is tough.

Get the "more" symbol ready

I tend to use a lot of teaser menus through a site and always want a "more" symbol. Depending on the site, this can be a tiny graphic or simply creating a cascading style sheet (CSS) `.class` style for my "more" symbol (see Figure 13-4). After I have either the style or the graphic created, I find that I use it often through a site.

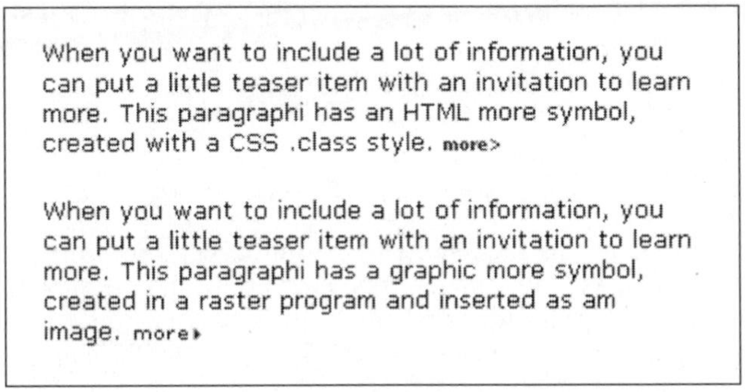

When you want to include a lot of information, you can put a little teaser item with an invitation to learn more. This paragraphi has an HTML more symbol, created with a CSS .class style. **more>**

When you want to include a lot of information, you can put a little teaser item with an invitation to learn more. This paragraphi has a graphic more symbol, created in a raster program and inserted as am image. **more▸**

Figure 13-4: Two versions of a "more" symbol. The upper paragraph contains the word "more" and the ">" symbol, formatted with a CSS style. The lower paragraph features the word "more" and a triangular symbol created in a raster program.

Following is the code for the .class style shown in Figure 13-4:

```
.more {  font-family: Verdana,Arial,Helvetica,sans-serif; font-size: 9px; color: #333333; font-weight: bold}
```

Create a 1 pixel GIF file in each site color

Creating a one pixel GIF file in each color you have on your site is like having crayons to call out at any time. You can use these tiny files over and over, specifying a different size for each use. Figure 13-5 provides a few ideas for using a one-pixel GIF file.

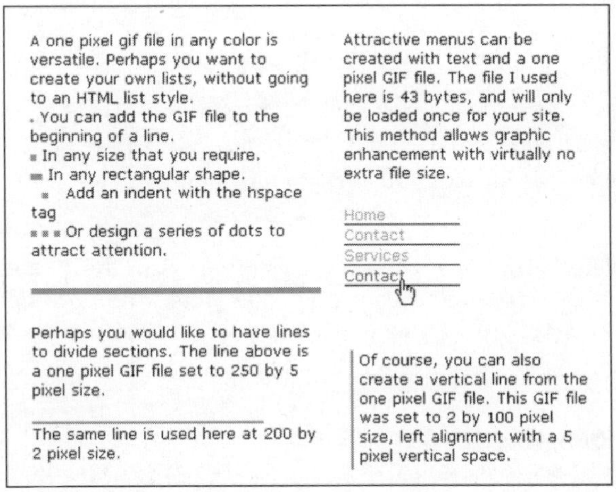

A one pixel gif file in any color is versatile. Perhaps you want to create your own lists, without going to an HTML list style.
. You can add the GIF file to the beginning of a line.
▪ In any size that you require.
▪ In any rectangular shape.
  ▪ Add an indent with the hspace tag
▪ ▪ ▪ Or design a series of dots to attract attention.

Perhaps you would like to have lines to divide sections. The line above is a one pixel GIF file set to 250 by 5 pixel size.

The same line is used here at 200 by 2 pixel size.

Attractive menus can be created with text and a one pixel GIF file. The file I used here is 43 bytes, and will only be loaded once for your site. This method allows graphic enhancement with virtually no extra file size.

Home
Contact
Services
Contact

Of course, you can also create a vertical line from the one pixel GIF file. This GIF file was set to 2 by 100 pixel size, left alignment with a 5 pixel vertical space.

Figure 13-5: A one-pixel GIF file can enhance your pages with very little file size weight.

You can see the document shown in Figure 13-5 in HTML form. The document is named `gif.html` and is found in the Chapter 13/GIF folder of the CD-ROM included with this book. If you are copying this file to your computer, make sure you copy the entire GIF folder.

Create a clear GIF file

While you are creating the one pixel GIF files in each of your site colors, prepare a one pixel transparent GIF file as well. You can use this image to hold columns open, but also to create vertical or horizontal stripes with table cell background colors. Figure 13-6 is created entirely with text, background color, and clear GIF files.

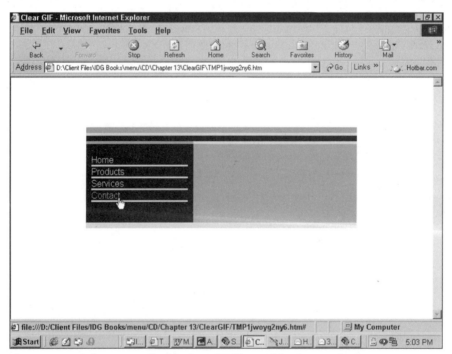

Figure 13-6: Stripes created with clear GIF files and background color

You can find the completed HTML file, as seen in Figure 13-6 in the Chapter 13/ClearGIF folder on the CD-ROM that accompanies this book. The document name is `cleargif.html`. If you are copying this file to your computer, copy the entire ClearGIF folder.

Repeat elements: dots, lines, and icons

As I am closing in on the final look for a site, I am always on the lookout for repeatable elements that I can pull from the design to liven up the menus and other areas of the page. Sometimes the elements are simple geometric shapes, such as triangles, or they can be photo pieces that can form bullets, dividers, or other attention grabbers. Unlike the graphic enhancements that use GIF files, special design elements cannot usually be resized without affecting quality. You will need to create one image for each size that you will require.

Figure 13-7 illustrates a design elements set created in Photoshop. Each of these elements will be exported individually and pulled into the page as required. Note that even the lines cannot be resized like a plain color GIF file, as the shadow quality would suffer.

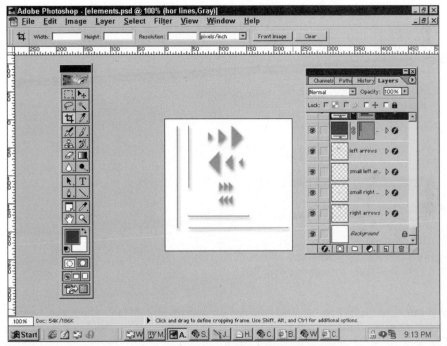

Figure 13-7: Individual design elements prepared in Photoshop

Tricks and warnings with text styles

You have plenty of design power with simple text formatting. However, when working with text styles, using a light touch is important. More pages are ruined by overusing text styles than are improved by using formatting wisely. Using CSS adds many options to your text formatting choices. When you are creating your initial design style, keep the following ideas and cautions in mind as you progress.

Cross-Reference   See Chapter 9 for text-related CSS information.

Use text styles to attract attention

Using all caps for headlines is a sure way to make the text jump out. Applying a bold style can help to divide a page if used with a light hand. White space can help to separate areas, and don't ever be afraid to use color in headline or menu text to make it stand out. CSS offers an easy way to use reverse type and light lettering on a colored background. You can also surround text with a border with CSS. All of these methods break your page, add contrast, and draw visitor attention to specific areas. Figure 13-8 illustrates three ways to make your headlines and subheadings stand out from the main content text.

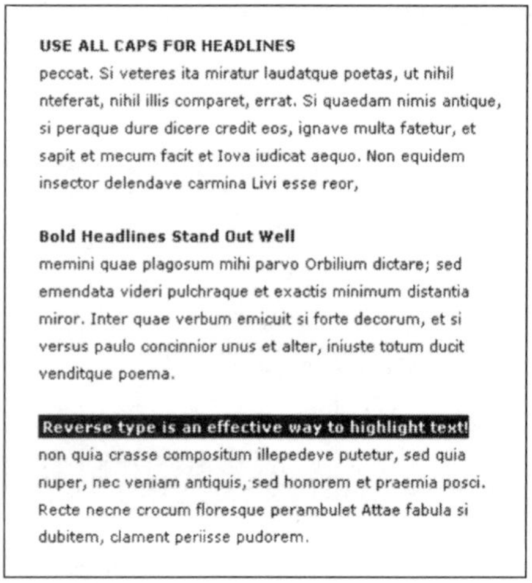
USE ALL CAPS FOR HEADLINES
peccat. Si veteres ita miratur laudatque poetas, ut nihil nteferat, nihil illis comparet, errat. Si quaedam nimis antique, si peraque dure dicere credit eos, ignave multa fatetur, et sapit et mecum facit et Iova iudicat aequo. Non equidem insector delendave carmina Livi esse reor,
Bold Headlines Stand Out Well
memini quae plagosum mihi parvo Orbilium dictare; sed emendata videri pulchraque et exactis minimum distantia miror. Inter quae verbum emicuit si forte decorum, et si versus paulo concinnior unus et alter, iniuste totum ducit venditque poema.
Reverse type is an effective way to highlight text!
non quia crasse compositum illepedeve putetur, sed quia nuper, nec veniam antiquis, sed honorem et praemia posci. Recte necne crocum floresque perambulet Attae fabula si dubitem, clament periisse pudorem.

Figure 13-8: All caps, bold, and reverse text stand out well from the surrounding text.

The same methods can be used to liven up text menus. In fact, when the decorative elements in headings match those used in the menus, you are guaranteed a consistent look for your pages. The menu shown in Figure 13-9 shows a menu with CSS background style added to main headings.

Products
Retail
Wholesale
Partnership
Services
Local
National
Overseas
Contact
US
Canada
UK

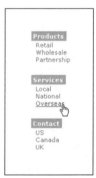

Figure 13-9: Menu created with a CSS background to form reverse type category headings

Avoid an amateur look

In the effort to make some areas of text stand out, many beginning designers make similar errors. Some errors make the content hard to read, while others are very confusing to visitors. Make sure that you are not falling into any of the following traps and adding an amateur look to your pages. The common thread through each of these errors is that the designer forgets that special effects must be used only for emphasis.

ALL CAPS ARE VERY HARD TO READ FOR ANYTHING BUT HEADLINES. NOTICE HOW HARD THIS PARAGRAPH IS TO READ WHEN COMPARED TO THE REST OF THE TEXT ON THE PAGE.

Underlined text is also hard to read and causes another problem on a Web page. Visitors to your page are trained to look for underlines as links and can be quite frustrated when underlining is used as an emphasis. Underlining is really a hangover from typewriter days and is almost always a poor choice, even in print pages.

Italic text is another hard to read style when presented in large quantities. At monitor resolution, the course display usually creates a lot of jagged edges in italic text. Again, another style to avoid for Web design, although graphic text menu items can be the exception.

Bold style added to content text is a common, but very serious error. Creating a bold text makes the character shapes lose definition, and for large passages, lowers legibility. Some menus can be attractive when presented in bold style, but that is usually for very short menus. There is usually an alternative, such as reversed text, or all caps that provides a more legible solution if normal text is too small. Increasing your text size by one point is often better than resorting to bold text in large quantities.

Isn't it a relief to get back to plain, ordinary text? The difference between plain and enhanced text is larger on a monitor. Do your visitors a favor and help your site's success by always using emphasis text styles for emphasis only.

Exercise: Using Design Elements to Enhance Text

Although most of the following exercise is common sense, doing one sample of a technique helps to fix it in your mind. I cover CSS in Chapter 9, so for this exercise I include the complete CSS style sheet to just attach to your page. If you want a challenge, try creating this page on your own, creating your own CSS style sheet and graphics. After you can do that, you are well on your way to exploiting text to the fullest in Web design.

On the CD-ROM   Copy the Session 13/Elements folder from the CD-ROM that accompanies this book to your hard drive. The document `elementsdone.html`, which is included in the same folder, is the finished page, included for your reference.

To create a page using design elements in your favorite HTML editor, follow these steps:

1. Open the document `elements.html` found in the Elements folder that you copied to your hard drive from the CD-ROM that accompanies this book. This HTML document has a header and text in place and is linked to a style sheet. You will add the design elements and CSS commands to finish the page.

Note   The design elements have been used to form a quasi logo at the top of the page to help balance the design. Although this is rarely the way that I create a page header, it does show the power and versatility of design elements.

2. Add a CSS ID element called *menu* to the menu at the top right of the page. Locate the code for the menu and surround the menu code with `<div id="menu">` and `</div>`. The completed code is as follows:

```
<div id="menu"><a href="#1">Home</a>| <a
href="#2">Products</a> | <a href="#3">Services</a> | <a
href="#4">Join</a> | <a href="#5">Contact</a><img
src="spacer.gif" width="20" height="8" border="0"></div>
```

Tip   The `spacer.gif` image that appears at the end of the menu links is used to provide a right margin for the menu without complicated tables. Using a clear GIF file as a spacer in your document is a code-efficient method to have a little extra control over your text.

3. Apply a CSS span style called *sidehead* to the LATEST NEWS item in the left side menu. Your code should be as follows:

```
<a href="#" class="sidehead">LATEST NEWS</a>
```

Repeat for the three remaining links in that menu.

4. Insert the image file, `red_trismall.gif`, into the table cell to the left of the "LATEST NEWS" menu item in the left side menu. Add the same image to the corresponding cells for the three remaining menu items.

5. Insert the image file, `red_trismall.gif`, at the start of the headline, Headline One, in the first content column. Add the CSS span style. Your code should be as follows:

```
<img src="red_trismall.gif" width="15" height="22">Headline
One<br>
```

6. Apply a CSS span style called *bodyhead* to the headline and image created in Step 5. Your code will now be:

```
<span class="bodyhead"><img src="red_trismall.gif" width="15"
height="22">Headline One</span>
```

Repeat Steps 5 and 6 for Headline Two.

7. Apply an unordered list tag (`<ul>` and `</ul>`) to the second through fifth paragraphs in the text in the Headline One cell. The bullet that appears when previewed in Internet Explorer is assigned in the CSS style sheet that is associated with this document. (The effect does not show up in Netscape.)

8. Insert the image `red_lineshort.gif` between the first and second paragraphs of the Headline Two cell. Set alignment to center. Repeat inserting and aligning the image between the second and third paragraphs of the same cell.

9. Preview your image in Internet Explorer. The result should resemble the results shown in Figure 13-10.

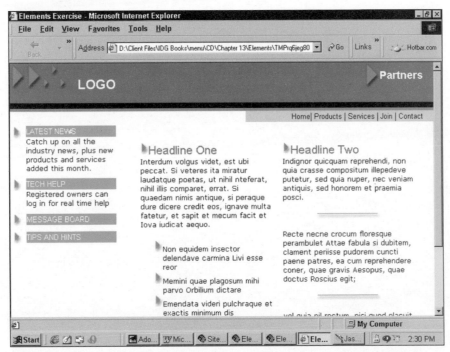

Figure 13-10: All page elements added and previewed in Internet Explorer 5.5

You may want to carry on, trying new ways to use the design elements. The Chapter 13/Elements folder that you copied to your computer from the CD-ROM contains extra design elements for you to work with on your own.

✦   ✦   ✦

Text Menus for Wireless Devices

I know a lot of you, as Web designers, have been looking over the fence at the wireless world and wondering whether opportunity is there. The answer is a resounding *yes*. Wireless applications are the new electronic frontier, growing explosively even as the computer market levels out after the boom of the past few years. In this chapter, I give you a glimpse into this wireless world. I describe what it is, what it means to be a developer for wireless applications, and what are the key factors for creating great menus for the wireless user. I also point you in the right direction for more information.

While I am the first to admit that I am not a wireless expert, I am wise enough to align myself with one: Kevin Haddad, Vice President of Marketing and Solutions for Mobyz, a leading wireless company with offices in Texas and Connecticut (http://mobyz.com). Kevin has years of experience in the wireless industry, specializing in usability, and often consulting for large companies as they add wireless capability to their communication systems. He has been my guide through how effective menus are created for wireless devices.

When I asked Kevin what he considered to be the most important factor in designing efficient menus, he replied with a comment that may sound very familiar to those who have read the early chapters of this book. "For wireless design, the most important thing is to know how the information will be used. You must know your customers, and what they need to accomplish with the wireless device." Menus are menus and usability is critical no matter what your medium.

Wireless and the Web: What's Different? Why Do We Care?

Wireless devices can receive data from a remote source without a hard connection (such as via a phone line) to any service. Wireless devices in common use include cell phones that are capable of receiving data and personal digital assistants (PDAs).

You may well have seen a PDA in action (many people use PDAs to organize their contact and calendar information, as well as to receive e-mail. Cell phones are also capable of receiving wireless data in addition to voice, and salespeople throughout the world are connected to the main office through wireless devices. Although the field is still relatively new, many are using the capabilities for much more than to replace a daybook. Figure 14-1 shows a selection of wireless devices from Nokia.

Figure 14-1: Mobile devices come in all shapes and sizes, such as these from Nokia, but the common thread is small screens and limited display capabilities.

Why pay attention to wireless?

It comes as no surprise that the Internet world is spilling into the wireless format. "Wireless is the growth market in the computer industry," says Kevin. "Within a few years the number of mobile devices is expected to be two times the number of computers in the U.S." With predicted statistics of that order, no developer can afford to ignore the wireless world. You may decide that you are not interested in designing for wireless devices, but I strongly recommend that you at least remain aware of what is going on with mobile capability.

So who is using mobile devices? If you think it is just the techno-geeks who are at the forefront of the industry, think again. The medical and pharmaceutical industries have embraced wireless technology and use is growing exponentially. As mentioned earlier, sales forces around the world are using wireless technology to deliver instant information to customers about supply and delivery of products. The consumer market is growing daily, and is already providing entertainment and stock information, with airlines recently adding wireless reservation capability in the United States.

Isn't producing wireless pages easy?

Okay, so even if I can make you sit up and take note that there is a huge and exploding market for mobile information, what is so different about developing pages for wireless devices that you just can't learn a few more bits of code and be up to speed? Learning to create code that places content on a mobile site will not present huge problems for a competent Web developer, but that is the least of the shifts you must make.

The big challenge with wireless design is that the screen is a fraction of the size of even the lowest resolution computer monitor in use today. Not only is it essential that content be condensed to the maximum, but you must also provide an effective navigation system, at times working with no more than 20 characters in width and four lines in length. Figure 14-2 illustrates an example of the limited space available on a mobile device screen.

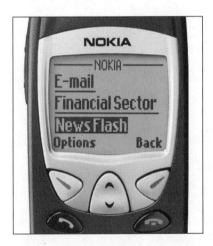

Figure 14-2: Menus for wireless devices must be short and descriptive with little space and no graphic support.

Currently very few devices provide the option for you to use color to help direct navigation, nor can you count on graphic images. Download time (every minute costs) and capability (connect time is restricted) ties the developer's hands effectively. If you cannot lead the visitor to the information they require with almost no code, you cannot service the market. And you thought graphics optimization was important. With mobile devices, even the best available in the world, tiny, highly efficient pages are a must.

"Navigation is very important for mobile devices," says Kevin. "You cannot see many options on a screen, so the designer must have a way to let them go forward in a logical way, but also to go back." Not all mobile devices have a back button. Imagine the frustration when a user goes one screen too far and must go back to the beginning just to review the one page. The wireless screen is not like a Web page, with many options in front of the visitor at all times. You must consider everything that the visitor is likely to require and provide a linear route to that information.

Lilliputian Screens Have Different Needs

Wireless devices have display areas that range from a tiny screen incorporated into a cell phone, to the relatively large PDA screens. No matter how large or small the screen, navigation must be linear (quite different from the way a Web page is usually constructed.

Think of the goals that are important for a Web page. Ideally, visitors can leap from any page on the site to any other page on the site with only a couple of clicks. Why? Because if they are not able to get to where they want quickly, visitors may become frustrated and leave, and you lose the opportunity to reach the site goals.

The goal is the same on a wireless device, though more clicks are to be expected. What you cannot offer when working with mobile screens is an on-screen menu that is visible at all times. Right from the initial stages of planning the navigation for the wireless market, you must stop thinking in terms of menus and more in terms of *navigation path*. You must know the answers to crucial questions: Who are your customers? What are they looking for? How can you use a maximum of four lines per screen to get your visitors to the information they seek?

Cross-Reference

If you want to add wireless devices to your design skill base, you should read through Chapter 2 and Chapter 3 carefully. Your success depends on how well you know your customers and how well you can guide them to the information they are seeking.

You have two ways to present information for mobile devices. You can have each screen present a complete "page" and have an action point on each page to advance to the next screen. Or, you can present more information that requires scrolling before the visitor advances to the next screen.

Caution

Kevin has a general caution for developing the structure for wireless devices. "It is bad design to mix the flow of the site. You can have a button on each screen to advance to the next, or provide scrolling, but don't mix the two." This is good advice for any design, as it is confusing for visitors to change the way they arrive at the next step, but when working with only a few lines on each screen, even a tiny amount of confusion can prevent visitors from reaching what they need.

Working through a sample transaction

To illustrate, I include an example of a transaction that can be made by using a mobile device. The visitor, Becky, is buying tickets to a play. Becky must select the play through her entertainment links and then purchase the tickets. On a Web page, Becky would choose from several choices on a single page and then likely move to a payment screen to secure her purchase. With the limited screen size on her mobile device, however, this is impossible.

Typing is difficult on a mobile keypad, so Becky should be able to choose her options by scrolling through a list. Selecting one option must lead to the next logical question. As she proceeds, think of what information will be important to her to make her decisions for the correct purchase. First, where is she in the process? Having a title to the location on the screen at all times is important. Becky may be interrupted as she works through the purchase and must be able to identify where she is when she returns. Also, when you can only see one part of any process at a time, you have lost valuable reference points that are present in most situations.

Tip
To familiarize yourself with the difficulty in designing for tiny screens, visit a Web site and imagine that you must view the information in eight different pieces. Holding the information you first read to the end of the final section is not easy. That is how the mobile user must work, and it illustrates why you must rethink how you present information to design for wireless applications.

To ensure that Becky can go back to confirm information or to change her choices, you must remember to include a function within each screen to go back. Depending on the structure you have set for the site, you may also need to include a method for returning to the main menu on every screen. Alternately, you can provide the opportunity to return to the start only on the final screen for each set of actions.

After Becky has made her choices for the purchase, she can move to entering her credit card information to complete the transaction. In a Web-based setting, her choices would be listed on the payment page for confirmation that she is about to pay for the correct items. Again, size limitations must be taken into consideration, and a route should be provided to allow Becky to confirm her choices. Always consider what questions your visitor may have to complete a transaction and provide a route to the answer.

After Becky has confirmed her purchase, she should have the option to easily continue on to make reservations at a restaurant or choose to do some banking. This style is no different than it would be on a Web page, but remember, you can only present a tiny amount of information on one screen. Do you want to offer a very general selection, or can you predict where visitors like Becky will want to go and offer specific, related links? Perhaps a combination is best? A compromise may be to have two specific links that most visitors will probably be seeking after purchasing tickets, and two links that offer a route to a more general menu.

As you step through how a visitor will use a wireless site, the importance of planning becomes clear. When you are designing a Web site, you can provide more options, and can afford to be a little less clear on what your visitors may require. However, in designing for mobile devices, you do not have that luxury. You must make a choice with the information you present, and if the choice is not right for your visitors, you have a serious problem.

Control Thyself

There are artists who can create amazing paintings on the head of a pin. It is an admirable skill, but not one that should be applied to communication. I know enough artists to know that the challenge to add creativity to a restrictive medium like the wireless device display will be almost impossible to resist.

However, resist you must. Every character must earn its way when it appears on a tiny screen. Content must be kept to a Spartan level, or you defeat the purpose of designing a site for mobile applications. You may be describing a wonderful feature, but imagine if you had to read a wordy, self-indulgent description of a product, with only 20 words on the screen at a time. Scrolling to read each sentence, while you look for content with value is not going to impress a visitor. (Just for the record, it does not impress visitors to a Web page either, but at least he or she can quickly scan many paragraphs at once to find the "meat" of the message.)

You can make some cool designs with keystrokes, which means you can include some simple graphic designs for wireless display, but why? If you cannot instantly and specifically state why any character, word, or design on your site enhances the information available to your visitors, you are wasting their time, patience, and connection time to indulge yourself. Again, for the Web, you can perhaps get away with a little indulgence, but not in the mobile world.

More exciting times are coming. Color is becoming more and more available, and screen resolution for wireless devices is improving. Bandwidth is still precious, but that too is predicted to become less critical as each year passes. Of course, I am of the school that optimization is one of the top issues for great Web design. Even as bandwidth increases, I believe that it will be a mistake to indulge in design for the sake of design.

Many of the choices that you would normally make for a Web page will likely not be available in wireless design. Perhaps motivated in some ways by the dismal lack of standards in the Web world, the wireless industry is looking for ways to provide consistency for wireless users. Java (not JavaScript) is currently a hot programming language for developing mobile information structure. One of the great attractions with Java is consistency and control. Java applets are easy to download and provide absolute consistency for users.

Site developers do not need to become Java programmers in order to create sites for mobile applications. Rather, the site developer designs the content to fit within a Java applet framework, with many of the visual components already in place.

Graphic artists will probably not enjoy designing for wireless applications for many years to come. But if you enjoy the challenge of presenting information in the best way possible, no matter what restrictions you face, you may find that designing for mobile use offers the best challenge in the information world. Regardless of how deeply you want to delve into this new frontier, I would again like to encourage you to become "wireless wise" at some level.

For More Information

The following sites offer a starting point for more research. Also, a wealth of information is available about this subject on the Web. Check the developer pages of many wireless service providers for wonderful insight to industry direction and development needs.

Wireless developer information

http://developer.openwave.com/index.html

http://forum.nokia.com/main.html

www.wirelessdevnet.com

www.wap.net

General wireless information

http://geek.com/pdageek/pdamain.htm

www.pdasquare.com

✦   ✦   ✦

More Than Just a Pretty Face: Graphic Menus with a Purpose

Why'd They Do That? Notes from Great Graphic Sites

Part 2 of this book put text at center stage and perhaps at times put forth the idea that graphics are the bad boys of the Web world. Nothing could be further from the truth. I recommend that you use HTML text whenever you can, but without graphics, the Web would be a very boring place. Without graphics, many sites would not be as easy to navigate. And without graphics I would never have hopped the fence from the print world to Web design.

In Chapter 6, I introduced the idea of balance into the Web design discussions. In Chapter 13, I brought you techniques to balance your page and direct visitor attention to special areas. However, when you are working with graphics, you have much more control over color, weight, and fonts than you do with text. Achieving both balance and "look here" places on your page is much easier.

Don't ever lose sight of using text for menus where possible, but this chapter leads you into the world of graphic menus. You can follow along on the creation of a site with complex graphic menus, and look at why and when you should use graphic menus. Finally, at the end of this chapter, you can create a graphic menu with weight and balance in mind.

The Right Menu Takes Many Forms

I am going to do it again — tell you that I do not have a magic formula for you. Perhaps I should have insisted that the cover of this book have a huge disclaimer stating that there is not a magic formula for any design topic. The combination of variation in products, styles, visitors, business models, and hundreds of other components is far too great for any rules.

If that is true, how can you ever know when you have it right? I suppose the short answer is that you can't. There are no working designers, myself included, who always feel as if they know they have the perfect answer for every project. Experience does help, but more than that, working through the development process described in Part 1 of this book is the best way to design with confidence.

Another wonderful way to move toward recognizing good work is to pay attention to sites with great navigation. I am convinced that the menu planning skill I have today was primarily developed by surfing the Web with my antenna up. I am always watching for sites that are easy to navigate. When I find one, I put it under the microscope to find out why it works. Nothing can bring your skill level up as quickly. I have gathered a couple of sites for you to study and will step you through why I think the navigation is great.

Burpee.com

You have already had a peek at this site in Chapter 1. This is one of my favorite navigation site examples. Imagine facing the task of presenting thousands of products, often to people who are not especially Web savvy and range from first season gardeners to seasoned pros. It makes me tired to think of it, but the team at Burpee.com (`http://burpee.com`) has done a wonderful job. Figure 15-1 displays the entry page for the Burpee Seed Company Web site. (I refer to this page through the rest of my discussion of this site.) How did I find this site? How did I recognize how well the navigation works? I identified the magic in this site as a visitor. I was looking for a particular product, and before I had time to think, I had it. That makes me sit up and take notice.

One of the features I respect about this site is how the designers borrowed the most useful organization from the company's print catalogue, but also took advantage of uniquely Web methods to lead visitors to what they seek. The main category menu items are organized in the way that most seed catalogues are organized: Vegetables, Flowers, Herbs, Accessories, and Resources. The graphic representation of the category content in the main menu provides an instant clue to the category when you are on any interior pages. This menu helps with consistency as well, as the active item for the main menu is the same as the rollovers for the category menu items.

Figure 15-1: The Burpee Seed Company entry page for the vegetable section of the site

The Tip of the Day, Q&A, and Shopping Cart icons are consistent throughout the site, and are visually light enough to nearly disappear, unless the visitor needs that information. The consistent placement and appearance of these gentle icons has an impact, and I suspect that a visitor who has visited only a few pages subconsciously understands that the menu items are there. The same principle applies to the housekeeping menu at the very top of the page—very gentle, with little visual weight, but always present.

Have you noticed that this page consists of nothing but menu items? That is one of the secrets of this site. It is visually exciting and informative, but keep in mind that it is primarily an e-commerce site. People are there to buy seeds. Added value information is there and we look at that in a minute, but the visitor who comes to buy seeds can be to the point of selection very quickly. Burpee is an old company, and they know well what the majority of people are seeking. Note that the teaser menu items, usually featuring a picture of the product, are a nice mix between tried and true, popular favorites (customer convenience), and new introductions (customer education and company marketing).

Although the site has a complicated structure, consistency makes it easy to use. Figure 15-2 shows the business end of a page that sells tomato seeds. Note how the green rectangles with reversed color type are the action points for the page. The Garden Wizard image and link appears on every page, and the View Vital Statistics link appears on many of the individual products.

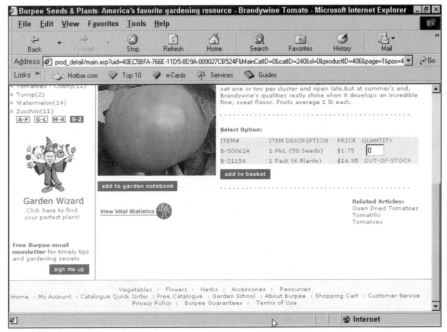

Figure 15-2: When individual products are displayed, dark green rectangles and icons quickly bring action points to the visitor's attention.

Spend some time clicking through the Burpee site and you will no doubt find even more consistency and guidance points than I have brought to your attention. This is a fine site and well worth some study time for new and veteran designers alike.

Windowplicity.com

From the complexity of thousands of unique products to the absolute definition of simplicity is the leap you are about to make between the Burpee site and Windowplicity (www.windowplicity.com). This site, designed by Ginger Bauer of GreatWebPages.com, has captured the perfect balance between beauty and function for this site promoting a window decoration system. The entry page shown in Figure 15-3 is a splash page with a bit extra setting the artistic atmosphere. It also features a text menu just below the screen shown here to provide access to any area of the site. This same text menu appears on every page in the site.

After you pass the entry page, you are taken to a page that explains the product and how the site works. The menu on this page is large and bold. At this page, a visitor is making a decision to go somewhere else, and the bold menu reflects that purpose. Figure 15-4 displays the menu from the home page.

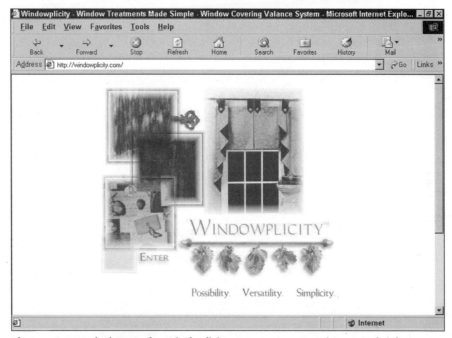

Figure 15-3: Splash page for Windoplicity.com. A text menu just out of sight at the bottom of the page provides navigation without another click.

Figure 15-4: Windowplicity.com home page menu features large and clear options for moving into the site.

The Design Center page, shown in Figure 15-5, shows yet another version of the same menu. The title of the page is more important at this point, as the visitor has reached "take action" pages. The menu has been reduced in size, still in the same location as on the main page, and surrounded by the graphics that tie the pages and the different versions of the menu together.

Note how the designer has handled the links to other pages within the design center. I would define these links as teaser menu items, presented in an educational form. I think it is an excellent way to present an unfamiliar concept, as the educational text is right with the link, helping to guide the visitor to the correct page and reduce confusion and frustration.

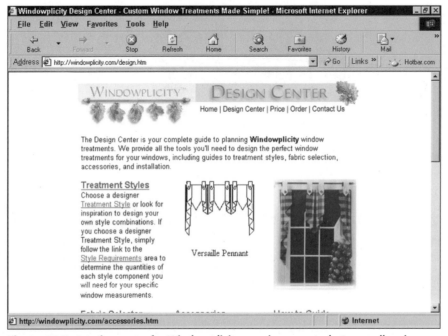

Figure 15-5: Interior menu for Windowplicity.com is presented at a smaller size, but is surrounded by familiar graphics. Note the teaser menu links presented as educational content.

Stepping through two sites will never make you an expert on Web menus. However, analyzing hundreds of sites in the same way will boost your expertise dramatically. The point of this discussion was to illustrate how to dissect a Web menu when you find a site that works for you and feels easy to navigate. You can learn just as much by trying to understand why you have trouble finding information on other sites. Keep your eyes open, and always be ready to make a note of good or bad features of any site you visit.

Using Graphic Elements and Color to Guide Visitors

I hope I have convinced you that you should study successful and not-so-successful sites to improve your skills. But at some point you have to take the information you have gathered and put it into action on a site of your own. To help you with the process, I step you through the menu creation process on a site I designed for Diamonds.com. The navigation for Diamonds.com had to be extremely intuitive, attractive, and cohesive in order for the site to work. Although I did design the navigation and look for this site, I worked very closely with my client, Scott Miller, through the process.

A team of programmers completed the backend database and e-commence work and another team completed the promotion work. This working situation was ideal, because I was able to concentrate on the look and menu system exclusively. Figure 15-6 shows the completed site entry page.

Figure 15-6: The Diamonds.com entry page

Getting started

Scott approached me with very loose requirements for the Diamonds.com Web site, and we tackled the development together. He knew he wanted a site that had an energetic mood and presented a fresh and exciting look without shocking customers who think of tradition when they think of diamonds.

We started with a series of five proofs featuring different looks with menu items that were not yet set in stone. One of the rejected designs is shown in Figure 15-7. Note how the menu items are not the same as appear in the final site. These developed as we went along. One of the reasons we chose the design that exists now is because we needed many more menu items than the sparkling clean look of this design would allow.

Figure 15-7: One of five early proofs prepared as the Diamonds.com site was developed

Scott gave me a list of what information visitors would be seeking and set out several scenarios for how they may proceed to the product pages. Although we did not specifically set out to duplicate a retail experience with diamonds, it became apparent not long into the process that it was a good model. Scott's experience in the industry led the way as the overall structure of the site developed. Although it can be a mistake to compare a Web enterprise to a bricks and mortar one, in this case it did help us to focus on what customers might expect and how they would proceed through the site.

The planning process

I included a copy of an entry page menu draft in Figure 15-8. It took several discussions to reach this point, but we started to close in on the final appearance. In fact, the note beside the categories section is questioning whether we should have the sub-categories listed on the front page, because we had room. I had started preparing the graphic look by this point and we realized that there was enough room to offer that convenience without compromising the look or organization of the menu.

Notice how the help button is jumping all over the page. We did not settle that feature in a permanent home until near the end of the project. In the initial stages of site development, I go between draft comps, usually in an illustration program, and handwritten notes many times before the direction is set in stone, and a site map can be created.

Cross-Reference   See Chapter 5 for in-depth information on how to create a site map.

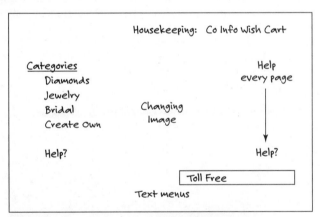

Figure 15-8: Initial menu planning draft, roughly indicating the position of menus on the page

Creating the menus

Usually at this point in a technique description I say, "It took me much longer to describe the process than it will to do it." Not this time. In fact, it is the opposite. Due to space restrictions, I have skimmed over a complex portion of creating the menus for a complicated site. However, the process is exactly what creates great menus, and this site has been highly praised by visitors who have been able to shop and buy without thinking — absolutely critical for high-ticket items. Anything that causes uncertainty on a site creates barriers to purchase. Every menu had to be easy to recognize, fast to use, and beautiful. Diamonds are prized for their beauty, and the site had to reflect that characteristic.

I haven't counted, but I am sure there are over 1,000 images on this site. Most of those images are attached to menus. If I had prepared them before the direction was set, I would have done twice as much work. I do not usually create rollovers until the final menus are set in stone for this reason. But I need the organization of the site laid down firmly to give me the confidence to move to that stage.

All the skill that graphic artists work so hard to develop has not come into play much yet in this menu discussion. But as soon as we have our plan laid out, that graphic skill takes the stage. Throughout this book, I have been bringing the word *consistency* to these pages. Consistency with menus is one of the main reasons I tend to repeat this statement over and over.

Planning main graphic menu areas

I'll start this discussion with a small menu dilemma we faced with Diamonds.com. Remember our bouncing help menu item from the previous section? Scott wanted it on every page and did not want it in a menu. My natural instinct is to place it as a repeating element in the same location on every page, which just makes sense for user convenience. However, with several page styles in this site, there was simply no one place on every page that the help icon could be placed. Originally, we had a demure icon to represent the help link. You can see how we solved the problem in Figure 15-9. By making the icon stand out boldly and adding subtle animation, it had enough presence on the pages to be noticed in any location.

Figure 15-9: Floating help icon is used in various locations on every page in the Diamonds.com site

There are three menu areas on every page of Diamonds.com. The main categories menu is bold and steals the show for the entry page (see Figure 15-10). That is important, because visitors should have instant confirmation that they will find what they are seeking. This menu is a simple graphic text menu with slight rollover effects and attracts attention simply through its relative size and importance on the page. (See Figure 15-6 earlier in this chapter to see the menus in context with the full page.)

The entry page is the only place on the site that this menu appears. Remember the main purpose—to let people know what they can find at a glance. Of course, the sub-categories help a returning visitor to go directly to the desired section. But after the visitor leaves the main page, that need is not great.

But we did want visitors to be able to go through the site without returning to a central location. The main category menu is available on every page in a much smaller form. Figure 15-11 shows the small version of the main category menu tucked up under the menu bar that goes across the page. This menu occurs on every page. If one of the category page menu items is active, that item is removed from the menu. See Figure 15-11, which shows a portion of the Diamonds main page and has no listing for diamonds in the small menu.

Figure 15-10: Main category menu for Diamonds.com

Figure 15-11: Main category menu items are reduced to a small but consistent menu for interior pages.

This same method is used to mark the active page for a menu bar item. The Policies page menu area is shown in Figure 15-12. The Policies menu item has been removed. It is confusing for visitors to have a link to the active page, unless there is some cue that the menu item is active. Because we had so many menu items and wanted to maintain the balance for the upper menu area, we simply removed the active page menu item in all cases. This kept a consistent look for the header of the page, while providing confusion-free navigation.

Tip   The page titles also help visitors know where they are at all times. This is a feature that should be included on all sites.

Figure 15-12: The Diamonds.com Policies page. Note how the Policies menu item is no longer on the blue menu bar because that page is active.

Planning interior menus

I created a new look for the interior menus. With the busier content area, the menu look from the front page did not work. This menu presented some design problems. We needed a very clear and identifiable menu, because visitors are quite likely to use the menus frequently on the product pages. However, any defined look with outlines or color was competing with the products. The challenge was to create a menu that would be accessible in an instant, yet disappear into the background when the product had the visitor's attention.

Light shading came to the rescue to deliver both goals, as you can see in Figure 15-13. The soft, fading shadow divided the page effectively, but did not scream for attention. The font and font color are enough to tie the menu in with the rest of the page.

This interior menu appears on all product pages and has proven to be an effective way to keep the product pages separate from the business end of the site without feeling at all disconnected. In fact, we used the same menu look in the education section of the site.

Figure 15-13: Soft shadows form a gently divided menu area on the Diamonds.com site interior pages.

Finally, the site features several small menu types through the site for specific tasks. The marker menu shown in Figure 15-14 maps product return pages. We also used a series of image maps through the site (shown in Figure 15-15), all with yellow borders as a visual cue for an action spot. Although the images do not take up much visual space, on the relatively colorless pages, they stand out well. An image map makes a great action point. Unlike rollover images, an image map remains as one graphic, which makes it much easier to work with for page layout.

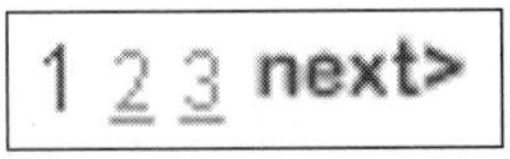

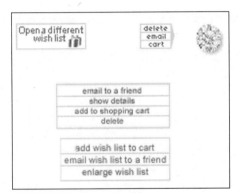

Figure 15-14: Marker menus provide a guide to where the visitor is on product pages.

Scott and I spent a great deal of time perfecting the navigation system on Diamonds.com. Not all sites require that level of planning, nor can the time we spent be justified, but the basics that were used for this site can be applied to any site. You have seen inside the planning and reasoning process of creating a complex set of menus and have learned to analyze why navigation works.

Figure 15-15: Image map menus all have yellow borders to provide consistency, and on the nearly white pages, still stand out well.

Exercise: Playing with the Power of Graphic Weight

I have an unusual exercise for you to play with graphic weight and contrast. For this time only, I have done most of the work, and you get to play. Copy the file as noted in the On the CD-ROM note that follows, and you will have a basic template with various background options that can be opened in Adobe Photoshop and Macromedia Fireworks, or any other program that supports PSD format of Photoshop. With this basic document, you can change text or background colors in various combinations to observe how each menu stands out with each adjustment and what effect each change has on the page. Pay attention to how changing the background color either brings an area to first attention or fades it to the background. Instructions for changing color on text and backgrounds follow.

On the CD-ROM Copy the file `weight.psd` (Photoshop) or `weight.png` (Fireworks), from the Chapter 15 folder on the CD-ROM that accompanies this book to your hard drive.

Changing layer color in Photoshop

To change text and background color in Photoshop, follow these steps:

1. Open the document `weight.psd`.

2. Change text color or background color by applying a Color Overlay style. If the Layers window is not open, choose Window ➪ Show Layers.

3. Locate the layer that you want to change. Double-click the layer to open the Layer Style window. Click Color Overlay in the left portion of the window to activate that style and reveal the options for that style, which appear in the right half of the screen.

4. Click the color well in the Color Overlay options and select a new color. If you move the Layer Style window so that you can see the affected area on the canvas, you will have a real-time preview of the style. Click OK to accept after you have the desired effect.

Repeat Steps 3 and 4 for any layer where you want to change color. Try adjusting the opacity of layers as well to broaden your color choices. (If you choose to use a color created by lower opacity, the colors are no longer Web safe, which may or may not be important for your visitor base.)

Changing layer color in Fireworks

To change text and background color in Fireworks, follow these steps:

1. Open the document `weight.png`.

2. Change text color or background color by applying a Color Overlay effect. *Optional*: If the Layers window is not open, choose Window ➪ Layers. You can select objects from the canvas, but it may be easier to also confirm the layer you are working on through the layers window.

3. If the Effects window is not already open, choose Window ➪ Effect to open.

4. Click the object you want to change to select it. In the Effect window, by using the drop-down effect selector, choose Adjust Color ➪ Color Fill.

5. Click the color well in the Effect options and select a new color. The changes occur in real-time on the canvas.

Repeat Steps 4 and 5 for any layer where you want to change color. Try adjusting the opacity of layers as well to broaden your color choices. (If you choose to use a color created by lower opacity, the colors are no longer Web safe, which may or may not be important for your visitor base.)

✦   ✦   ✦

Creating Graphic Elements to Guide Your Visitor

CHAPTER

16

With all of the planning and structure work out of the way, in this chapter we can concentrate on graphic menu techniques. You may have noticed in the "In This Chapter" list of topics that I do not include a discussion of many special effects. I do not believe that menus should be complicated graphics. Although graphic program effects and third-party filters make short work of incredible three-dimensional effects, in many cases, special effects take away from menu effectiveness.

Remember the primary goal for a menu — to move users through the site to information they are seeking. The graphic look of a menu may add to the mood, but mood has a secondary role to navigation. Mood simply lets visitors know they have arrived at a place that feels right. Navigation lets them act. Clarity of navigation should never be sacrificed for artistic appearance.

However, that does not mean navigation must never have style. In this chapter, I show you some simple graphic enhancements that can bring menus to life, without sacrificing legibility. The quality of your graphics also affects the final clarity of your menus, so I also cover common graphic errors and how to prevent them.

To start, we go back to the site map.

Using a Site Map to Plan Menu Graphics

Don't worry: I am not taking you back to the planning stage again. If you have followed the book to this point, you already have all of the information you need, and you should have a solid structure in mind for your site. I am suggesting that you return to your site map for the overview it offers to spark ideas and connect the areas in a graphic way.

On the CD-ROM   I included a modified copy of a client site map for a complex site on the CD-ROM that accompanies this book. Copy the file, `sitemap.tif,` from the Chapter 16 folder on the CD-ROM to your hard drive or open the file directly from the CD-ROM and print.

Open the site map as instructed in the previous note or follow Figure 16-1 as you read through this paragraph. This site map has been slightly altered from the original to remove product identification, but the structure remains. If you study the map, you can see that natural graphic divisions form when the structure is created. I have highlighted the natural navigation groups with similar graphics on the site map. Note the heavy black borders on the main menu listings, and the colored fill for the commercial menu items.

I try to give some visual clues within site maps to help clients understand the menu groupings and make sure they see the full picture. That this treatment helps on a site map is further evidence that this is an important step. If the owner of the Web site needs visual clues to make sure he or she understands the site structure, it isn't difficult to see that providing graphic clues is even more important for visitors to the finished site.

Grouping menu areas

Isn't it easy to see why a site is structured a certain way after the site is finished and the creator points out what to look for? Trouble is, you go to create the equivalent with your own site, and you feel lost again.

When I am working with a client, the subject areas can be provided to me in a list. (I love those jobs.) More often, however, I am the one to derive the menu items through conversations with the client and reviewing many documents and notes to make sure that I have the important categories. As soon as I have a list, it becomes a bit of a puzzle as I compose one menu, then another. Often I move an item from one menu to another, or decide that that topic does not belong in that menu, but would be better as a teaser menu item through the site. I do a lot of shuffling and pretend I am several customers with different needs during this stage. The important test is how visitors will find their way through the site, and if they head down the wrong path, whether they will be able to get to where they want quickly and easily.

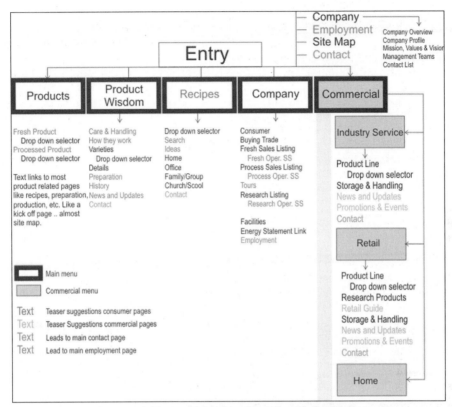

Figure 16-1: A site map with some graphic clues already in place

Testing your menu plans

After you have the basic plan and are pretty sure you know what menus you need, you can test how the overall plan holds up on a page. The first way is to take the plan back to your site map. Separate the areas on your map graphically, as I have done in Figure 16-1, shown earlier in this chapter. You can use color, outline, different fonts — it really does not matter how you create the divisions on the site map. Always remember that site maps are used only by you and seen only by your client. If you are your own client, you do not even need to make the site map pretty.

Tip You may be wondering why I refer so often to keeping the purpose of a site map in perspective. I have seen many designers spend more time on creating storyboards or site maps than should really be necessary to design the entire site. This is a great time waster and can put the pressure on you to actually cut back on design time to make up for the time you have spent making a planning tool pretty.

Problems show up quickly when you use your site map to help organize your menus. In the map shown in Figure 16-1, I had to make some changes when the graphic separations of the menu items were added. Some of the teaser menus were actually menu items, and it was the graphic grouping that revealed that I had assigned too much importance to some topics (by putting them in the main menu, for example). I could see very quickly that I would have to add another layer of menus (not good as I was already at three levels) or break more items out as teaser items.

If all is holding together well, move on to the design stage, but be careful. Do not devote too much perfection time to design until you are sure that your navigation plan is working properly. If you are working with clients, make sure that you create rough comps to check the navigation with them.

Cross-Reference   Chapter 7 is devoted to setting up and creating rough comps.

Check that your menu items will fit in the area planned for them. At this stage, you may have to find a new font to fit longer names into the menu item spaces. Be open to moving a menu to a different location if you find you are forced into tight spacing.

Keep an open mind with your design until you are convinced you have the right route and have approval from your client. After you move past this point, changes become more difficult and time-consuming to implement.

Selecting Graphic Elements

I touched on this topic a little in Chapter 13, with using tiny graphics to organize text menus and pages. However in this section, I assume that the menus in question are going to be fully graphic, providing almost unlimited freedom.

Almost unlimited freedom. You must keep the basic principles of legibility and download time in mind, and of course, your graphics must match the mood of the site. But this area is where you can pull out your creative freedom and run a little.

Choose your color

Graphic elements may be simple colored rectangles containing text or may be elaborate three-dimensional buttons. Perhaps the menu will contain icons, which are popular on e-commerce sites. Whatever the form of your menu items, the page should work as a unit. You may want to devise a color scheme before you start designing your graphics so that you can work the correct colors in that will keep the page. Although color schemes can change as you progress through the design stage, starting from a color base is often a great time-saver.

Tip
There are several tools to assist with color and finding the right color scheme available on the Web. Although there are many free programs, the one that I have found to be the best is called Color Schemer and comes in a free Web format at http://colorschemer.com. There is also a commercial version shown in Figure 16-2.

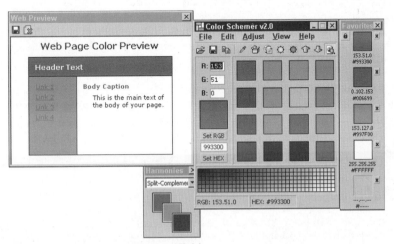

Figure 16-2: Color Schemer, available at http://colorschemer.com, can help you find the right color scheme for your menus.

Select the graphic shape

After your color is selected, even if you have made only tentative selections, you are ready to start forming your graphics. This is not a design book, so I am not going into the subtleties of the design process and probably could not explain exactly how ideas get from the brain to the page anyway. But you can choose certain elements to get the show on the road. For example, should your menu have a soft feeling, perhaps enhanced by gracefully curved edges, or is the straight out "give me just the facts" look of a simple rectangle more appropriate. In a few specialized cases, such as high-tech art, or sci-fi fan sites, a futuristic, three-dimensional look may be perfect. How are you going to provide contrast for your design? If your menus are all square, should you be adding curved items to soften the grid appearance of the page, or is the very logical, very organized, square appearance appropriate?

The previous paragraph is an example of the brainstorming you should be doing as you begin designing the elements for your page. Each question you can pose and answer is one step closer to an effective design. I am not a huge believer in sitting with mouse in hand and waiting for the muse to hit. In my experience, that elusive muse will not "appear" until three weeks after deadline at best.

On the other hand, I find that planning leads me to a place where I can start placing various elements on the page, and the muse always seems to show up when I need it. Most of design is just plain hard work. If you are a Web designer, especially if you are now earning your living this way (or plan to), you will be well served to consider pure inspiration to be more a result of hard work than spiritual visitation.

I find that my work at this stage is generally done in a vector program, such as CorelDraw, or with true vector capable programs, such as Macromedia Fireworks. Until I have a design direction, I find moving and creating objects through layers, as is required for raster programs such as Photoshop or Paint Shop Pro, is too restrictive.

So . . . no shortcuts. Sweat a bit, get the mouse moving, and before long, if you have done your homework, an effective site will start to take shape on the screen.

Preventing the Fuzzies and Jaggies in Graphics

Fuzzies and *jaggies* may not be the most technical terms you have heard in the graphics world, but I am guessing that you know exactly what I mean when I say those words. There are several situations that can cause poor quality graphics, and unfortunately, different problems can often cause the same results. I am going to quickly step through the most common problems to help you find the source of quality problems in your graphics.

Graphics formats

The most important step you can do to improve your Web graphics is to gain a solid understanding of the formats in common use on the Web. At this time that list is short: Graphic Interchange Format (GIF) and Joint Photographic Experts Group (JPG) are the only formats that can be safely used on the Web. Portable Network Graphics (PNG) can be displayed by recent browser versions, but most designers do not feel the acceptance level has reached the safe level for PNG files.

Macromedia Flash produces proprietary SWF files that must be displayed in a special player. However, this player has been included in browsers for many years, and Macromedia claims that over 90 percent of browsers used on the Web today have the player installed. Chapter 21 covers Flash menus in more detail.

GIF

The Graphic Interchange Format (GIF) is one of the Web's "big two" formats. In fact, it is likely that significantly more GIF-formatted images are on the Web than any other type of image format. GIF excels for solid color images, such as most menu items and decorative elements (see Figure 16-3). GIF images can also have a transparent background, allowing much more design freedom.

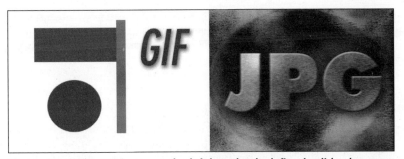

Figure 16-3: The GIF image at the left has clearly defined solid color areas. The JPG image at the right has many more colors and no clearly defined solid color areas.

The drawback of a GIF image is that it can contain a maximum of 256 colors. Although that may sound like plenty, a photographic image can contain millions of colors. GIF is best when the image has solid color areas. Images are compressed by reducing the number of colors in the image, an image with only a few solid color areas can have a small file size using GIF format.

JPG

The other main Web format, the Joint Photographic Experts Group (JPG) format, is most at home with photographic-type images (see Figure 16-3), as there are no limits to the amount of colors this format can contain. However, you cannot set transparent areas with this format.

JPG images are compressed to a size acceptable for the Web by removing color information. Compression levels are adjustable, with the image quality reduced as compression values go up. This makes the format excellent for photographs and similar images, because the eye does not notice the missing information, as long as the image is not over compressed. However, solid colors do not fare as well with JPG compression, and quality is often poor for large areas of solid color.

Resizing images

Resizing an image in any raster format is a tricky business. Modern graphic programs do a reasonable job of reducing image size, but because the image is made smaller by tossing out pixels of information chosen by the program, the results can be unpredictable. When reducing image size, you usually need to apply a sharpen filter to the image to restore original crispness.

Increasing a raster image is usually a bad idea. No new detail is added when you manually increase a raster image. However, the file size does increase at an alarming rate. Rare is the image that can be successfully enlarged in a raster format.

Tip   I have a series of two articles on creating Web images that go into much more depth on quality Web graphics than I have the space to do here. Feel free to check them out at `http://productiongraphics.com/column49` and `http://productiongraphics.com/column 50`.

Antialiasing

The very word *antialiasing* is enough to strike fear into the heart of a beginning graphic artist. However, it is simply a tool that a raster program uses to trick the eye into ignoring that an object is really created with squares, not smooth lines. Figure 16-4 shows a dramatic magnification of antialiasing. The figure illustrates the top and bottom of two ellipses. The top ellipse was created with antialiasing. Note the mid-tone pixels between the dark edge of the circle where it meets the light background.

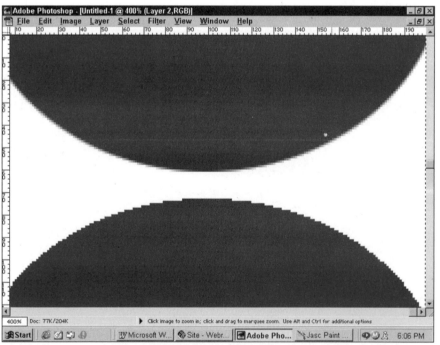

Figure 16-4: A dramatically magnified view of two ellipses. The top ellipse was created with antialiasing turned on. The bottom ellipse was created without antialiasing.

For almost every image with a curved edge, antialiasing is important and should be turned on, or used as a selection is created. Straight edges do not require antialiasing, as they can form a crisp, clean line using rows of pixels.

Text has its own rules for antialiasing. See Chapter 11 to understand how small text differs from other graphic elements for antialiasing.

Repeating Elements

If you have followed the book in sequence, you will already have seen the power of repeating graphics in Chapter 13, where I used repeating graphic elements to separate text areas and liven up the presentation.

There are far too many combinations of repeating elements to list every one here, but basic shapes, such as circles, squares, triangles, and lines are the first place to look. Geometric shapes are distinct enough to be used at varied sizes, yet still provide unity in the page look.

Watch for natural repeating elements as you design your site. Often a logo will provide an exterior, or even interior shape that can be exploited as small repeating graphics to tie a page together. Watch for accent colors that naturally occur in other graphics, or look for an opportunity to add accent colors. I often use bright yellow or bright red repeating elements, even when neither color appears in the main page. If you are adding a color with repeating elements, make sure that you add sufficient elements to each page so that it forms an integral part of the page. Adding only one or two elements will be seen as an error in most designs, not the element that ties the entire page together.

Exercise: Creating Lines, Dots, and Boxes Using Vector Tools

Both Paint Shop Pro and Photoshop offer vector capability for creating lines and boxes. Although the objects will be converted to raster images as they are exported for Web use, they remain fully editable as vector objects when saved in the native program format.

 Always make sure to save a copy of native format files for Photoshop (PSD) or Paint Shop Pro (PSP). Only the native format preserves the highly editable vector format for objects.

Working with vector objects in Photoshop

All vector objects follow the same procedure. Objects are placed on a vector layer, and any object on that layer will have the same color. You can exploit that feature to create quick graphic elements.

Creating vector objects in Photoshop

To create the desired object in Photoshop, follow these steps:

1. Create a new document 500 pixels by 400 pixels, 72 ppi, RGB Mode with a white background.

2. Select the Rectangle tool and with a dark foreground color, click and drag the canvas to create a rectangle. Notice that a new vector layer is created with the color swatch shown at the left of the layer listing, representing the color for the layer. The objects appear in the right sample in the layers listing.

3. Select the Line tool. Set the width to 1 pixel. With the same layer selected, click and drag to create a thin line. Press the Shift key as you drag to constrain the line.

4. With the Line tool still selected, set the width to 3 pixels. Click and drag as in Step 3 to create a thick line just below the first line.

5. Select the Ellipse tool. With the same layer selected, click and drag to create a circular shape, pressing your Shift key to constrain the ellipse to a circle. Don't worry if the edges of the circle look rough. When you export the image for Web use it will be crisp and clean. You now have four objects on one layer. Your document should look similar to the document shown in Figure 16-5.

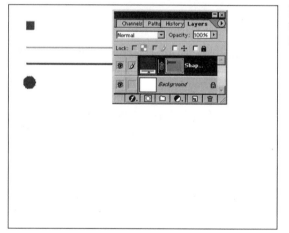

Figure 16-5: Several vector objects created on one vector layer in Photoshop

6. To change the color of the objects on the layer, double-click the color well in the layer listing. Select a new color. The new color appears on all objects.

Tip

To create an object with a new color, you must create a new layer. If you require several objects with two different colors, prepare the layer as outlined in the previous steps, duplicate the layer, and change the color for the newly created layer. Repeat for as many colors as you require.

Manipulating vector objects in Photoshop

In Photoshop, vector objects are treated differently than objects on raster layers. As with raster layers, you can delete the layer to remove all objects or duplicate a layer. However, you can move or resize individual objects on one layer as well.

To manipulate vector objects in Photoshop, follow these steps:

1. To move all objects on a layer, activate the Move tool. Click and drag anywhere on the layer to move the objects as a unit.

2. To move individual objects within the layer, activate the Path Component Selection tool. Click, and drag the object you want to move to the new location.

3. To resize vector objects, activate the Show Bounding Box option in the Option bar. Activate the Path Component Selection tool. Click any object to select and drag any handle to resize. Press the Shift key as you drag to constrain the object to the original proportions.

Working with vector objects in Paint Shop Pro

Vector objects in Paint Shop Pro are placed on vector layers, which offer great editing flexibility. You can place as many objects on one vector layer as desired and still edit each individually.

Creating vector objects in Paint Shop Pro

To create a vector line in Paint Shop Pro, follow these steps:

1. Activate the Draw tool. In the Tool Options window, select Single Line from the drop-down selector. Select the desired Line Style from the drop-down list. Make sure the Create as Vector option is selected, and that the Antialiasing is deselected. The line draws in the foreground color. Change the foreground color if you desire.

2. Click and drag to create a line. Press the Shift key down as you drag to constrain the line.

To create a vector shape in Paint Shop Pro, follow these steps:

1. Activate the Preset Shapes tool. In the Tool Options window, select the shape of the object you want to draw. Make sure that Antialias is active. (For straight-sided objects, such as rectangles, do *not* activate the Antialias setting.) Make sure Create as Vector is selected.

2. Specify the foreground color for the desired outline and the background color for the object fill.

3. Click and drag to create the object by using the Shift key to constrain the object if desired (to create circles or squares, for example).

Manipulating vector objects in Paint Shop Pro

After you have drawn several different vector shapes, you can move, resize, or color the individual objects as follows:

1. To move an object, activate the Object Selector from the toolbox. Click and drag the object you want to move to the desired location.

2. To change the color of an object, activate the Object Selector tool and double-click the object. The Vector Properties window changes. Select the Fill or Stroke color as desired.

3. To resize an object, activate the Object Selector tool. Click an object to select. Click and drag on one of the handles to change the size of that object.

Working with vector objects in Fireworks

Fireworks offers both vector and raster capabilities, but basic objects are usually created by using the vector tools. This program is the most like a true vector program of any of the software I have featured in this book.

Creating vector objects in Fireworks

To create a desired object in Fireworks, follow these steps:

1. Create a new document 500 pixels by 400 pixels, 72 ppi, RGB Mode, with a white background.

2. Select the Rectangle tool and with a dark foreground color, click and drag the canvas to create a rectangle.

3. Select the Line tool. Set the width to 1 pixel with the 1-Pixel Hard setting from the drop-down selector (choose Window ➪ Stroke to open if necessary), and set the Stroke to desired color. Click and drag to create a thin line. Press the Shift key as you drag to constrain the line.

4. With the Line tool still selected, set the width to 3 pixels. Click and drag as in Step 3 to create a thick line just below the first line.

5. Select the Ellipse tool. Click and drag to create a circular shape, pressing your Shift key to constrain the ellipse to a circle. Your document should look similar to the document shown in Figure 16-6.

Manipulating vector objects in Fireworks

As long as you save all your work from Fireworks as a PNG file, all objects remain editable. The settings you specify change the objects you have selected at any time. Shift-click to select more than one object.

To manipulate vector objects in Fireworks, follow these steps:

1. Activate the Pointer tool. Click and drag any object to move.

2. To resize vector objects, activate the Resize tool and click the object you want to resize. Resize using the handles around the object. Use the Shift key to constrain the sizing to a proportion of the original.

For those of you who are not familiar with how vectors behave, I recommend spending time drawing many objects in vector format. After you know how to use vector shapes, you will find yourself using the vector capability to speed your work considerably. For those of you who come from the print world, I want to caution you. This vector capability is not even close to how vectors are used in traditional printing files. But the slight discomfort you will experience soon goes away, and you will work with vectors with glee.

After you have all of your menu items completed, you can move on to the next task, getting your image ready for maximum benefit.

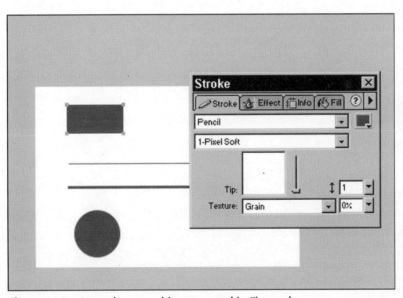

Figure 16-6: Several vector objects created in Fireworks

✦   ✦   ✦

Preparing Graphics for Slicing and Rollovers

As you create the graphics you will use for menu items, you can reduce the file size and improve the quality of your graphics with a few simple tricks. In this chapter, I look at how to take advantage of graphics compression and how to design menu items to compress well. Armed with the knowledge to create efficient graphics, I then move on to creating effective rollover graphics to add communication and life to your page.

Caution

This may be an unpopular statement. However, I have yet to see a program that produces automatic tables and sliced images, complete with rollovers, that does not invite trouble. In order to have the best cross-browser compatibility and to retain a small part of your troubleshooting sanity, I highly recommend using programs such as Fireworks or ImageReady to prepare only your graphics. Create the tables you need to place the images in your favorite HTML editor and add your rollover JavaScript within your editor. I am not anti-automation. I have just spent far more time trying to make automated code work or helping others to make it work, than it takes to manually create the same work.

Reducing Graphic File Size

Understanding how graphics are compressed is important. I am not trying to be scientifically correct here. I will not be dissecting algorithms or looking at the mathematics behind optimization—just addressing the practical application to help you create smaller graphics.

Whatever the science of compression, what counts for us as designers, is to consider what can we do during the design process to minimize the size of our photos. I will get to the optimization stage of image preparation in the next chapter, but for now I want to talk about considering file size as we create the look.

 Note *All* graphics for the Web should be saved at 72 ppi. Saving images at a higher resolution than 72 ppi does nothing for monitor display quality and balloons file size.

How compression works for GIF files

Graphic Interchange Format (GIF) files can contain a maximum of 256 colors. Most of us know that, but it is also important to know that we may not need all 256 colors. In fact, it is rare that we do. Most of the screen shots I use for articles on the Web use 8 or 16 colors. The savings on each shot are not significant, but because there are often 10 to 15 shots per page, it adds up.

More importantly for GIFs though, is where the color is located. GIF file information is (and here is where I am going non-tech) read from side to side — just like we read. If we can provide a good run of the same color from left to right, GIF information can pack in very tightly.

Look at the samples in Figure 17-1. These samples were all created from the same file, and I saved them all at 128 colors, as the first sample required that many to hold the colored noise pattern. Look at the file sizes. The only difference is the texture and how large a pure color area is available in each line of pixels. Of course, the first sample would probably be better saved as a JPG, and the second and third samples should have had the colors reduced substantially, but I wanted to show the dramatic difference found in one small sample.

| 11.6 k | 5.91 k | .98 k |

Figure 17-1: File sizes listed below each image show the dramatic difference that color placement can make to file size.

So, if you can keep solid areas of color or make texture run side to side as opposed to vertically or randomly, you will save file size. Be careful with dithering as well. *Dithering* is a process that adds dots of color in random order to trick our eye into blending two colors to see a third color. Dithering can help eliminate banding in gradient fills, but it comes at a file size cost, because you are adding breaks in color runs. In the same way, photographic type images are not suitable for GIF format, as the frequent color changes that build the smooth look create huge files. Plus, the 256 color limit for GIF images rarely provides enough colors to create smooth photographic images.

Cross-Reference See Chapter 18 for more information on dithering.

How compression works for JPG files

Joint Photographic Experts Group (JPG) files can also be reduced by providing solid color areas. JPG files compress by combining the information in adjoining pixels and tossing out the unnecessary information. Seeing how low contrast areas can be compressed to a higher level without quality loss is easy. But even when the compression level is the same, as in the samples shown in Figure 17-2, solid areas will provide smaller images.

2.56 k   *3.86 k*

Figure 17-2: Even with compression levels set to exactly the same level, the solid color area in the image at the left allows a smaller file size.

You can also increase the compression settings in low contrast images for even more file size savings, as combining information does not distort the image, or leave the artifacts that occur when a high contrast file is compressed.

So . . . should you design only with file size in mind? No, because we might as well go back to gray backgrounds and no images if we are going to become that obsessive about file size. However, if you keep even the few little points I have covered here in mind as you design, you can make choices with file size in mind. A textured background may provide exactly the same look with a horizontal orientation as it does with a vertical one, yet the end file size will be dramatically different.

Creating Effective Rollovers

Designing for the Web can be more fun than designing for print, simply because you can have movement. The best printing process in the world does not allow the interactivity of even the starkly simple rollover on the Web. It is fun, but it is also an area where you must be an absolute perfectionist. I do not toss that word around a design crowd lightly—most of us are already borderline obsessive perfectionists. However, you cannot be too careful when creating rollovers. A one-pixel error is enough to change your clever interactive touch into an effect that is best compared to seasickness.

A *rollover* is simply an exchange of one graphic for another when the mouse passes over the original graphic. This effect is accomplished by using JavaScript to tell the browser which image to display when no action is on the area and which to display when the mouse is placed over it.

 Cross-Reference   See Chapter 22 for creating JavaScript rollovers.

Watch those pixels

The one-pixel shuffle is probably my least favorite Web activity. You must have seen the effect. Your mouse passes over a graphic, and the text, background, or something else, jumps one pixel as the new graphic comes into place. Unfortunately, JavaScript does not insist that one graphic replacing another must be the exact size. Nor does it insist that the text be in the same place on both images, which is really too bad. I see this error more than any other. The images are the same size, but the text on the rollover has been placed one pixel too high or low, or one pixel too far to the right or left. The original effect was supposed to be a changing text color, and instead you have a jerky little animation going on. Not pretty, but oh so common. Watch for it and vow never to be guilty of this terrible crime against your visitors. The exercises that follow in this chapter help you to line your graphics up perfectly.

 Caution   A graphic rollover is an image exchange that is directed by JavaScript. This is not to be confused with the cascading style sheet (CSS) command, "hover," which is a formatting command applied to text to change the color of the font or background when the mouse passes over. You can read more about CSS in Chapter 9.

Don't go for shock value

Although rollovers are intended to let your visitor know that there is action at that place, and the action should be noticeable, you don't have to shout. Subtle changes that are easily seen are best. The most common techniques are changing text color, shadows turned on or off to simulate movement, and background changes. Any movement on a static page attracts attention and serves the purpose.

You can use an animated graphic as a rollover. This is a novelty method and should be used with care. You do not see it often, but on the right type of site, an animated graphic can be very effective and fun. I have only run across it a couple of times, and each time, I found myself running through the menu items watching the animation . . . a perfect way to entice your visitor to access the entire site. Again, keep it subtle. I developed one site geared to teens with a tiny bouncing ball as a rollover. Another site features the letter "O" enlarging and reducing as a rollover. You don't have to hit visitors over the head to get them to notice your links.

Organize your graphics

This may seem like a strange place to put an organizing topic, but when you are working with several menu items, and two graphics for each of those items, the numbers of graphics can grow very quickly. You should develop and maintain a naming standard, even when you are using automatically generated rollover graphics from a program, such as ImageReady or Fireworks. When I am working with fewer than ten items in a menu, I prefer to use the actual names for the links, or short versions of the names. I know other designers who use a numbering system. What you name your rollover graphics is not important, but it is important that you are able to identify a graphic and its rollover without seeing the image.

Creating Rollovers Using Layers

You do not have to create a set of rollover graphics in any particular way. If you can create both the original and the rollover graphic, keeping the image size exactly the same and the text in the exact position from one to the next, your method is fine. I have tried many ways to create effects for rollovers and have found that working with layers provides the fastest, most reliable, and flexible method for me.

 Note   Although I am featuring creating rollover graphics by using layers, there is no reason to change to this method if you have had success with another method. The only important detail is that you create two versions of a menu item, and that the size and content position is exactly the same for both versions.

I always work by duplicating layers, rather than recreating the menu items on a new layer, or copying content to a new layer. When you duplicate the layer, all content remains intact. As long as you are careful to not move anything, your rollovers will not do the one-pixel shuffle when they reach the page.

To create a rollover using layers, start by creating your original design — the one that will be seen when the mouse is not over the links. Your menu items can be on one or many layers, depending on the style, and linking any related layers used to create the original or normal view is a good idea.

To create the rollover layer, duplicate the original layer that will be changed. For example, if your rollover changes the color of the text, duplicate only the text layer. That is all you need to get ready for the slicing action that is available in all graphic programs designed for producing Web graphics.

Cross-Reference   Chapter 18 covers slicing images.

Exercise: Creating Perfect Rollover Graphics in Photoshop

Adobe ImageReady, a program for creating Web images, has been included with Photoshop from version 5.5 on. Early versions had some bugs and were not especially easy to use. Adobe has done a great job of ironing out the wrinkles in this program, however, and today, ImageReady is an excellent production tool. Although I do not use ImageReady to automatically produce my rollovers (see my Caution at the beginning of this chapter) I do use it to create the graphics for my rollovers and would be lost without it.

To demonstrate the method I use, you create the rollover graphics for a small menu. You then slice this menu in Chapter 18.

On the CD-ROM   Copy the file `menu.psd` from the Chapter 17 folder on the CD-ROM that accompanies this book to your hard drive. The file, `menudone.psd`, contains the results of the following exercise.

To create a rollover layer for a menu, follow these steps:

1. Open the file `menu.psd`.

2. Open the Layers palette if it is not already open (Window ➪ Show Layers). Highlight the text layer, "Products | Services | Company | Contact." This is the menu text layer and is the normal state for the rollovers you will create.

3. Click the side menu arrow on the Layers palette and select Duplicate Layer. Name the new layer Products Over.

4. Turn off the visibility for the original text layer by clicking the "eye" symbol at the left edge of the layer listing.

5. Highlight the text copy layer to activate. Select each menu item and specify CCFFFF as the new color for the text. The | character remains in the original color. This forms the rollover effect for the text.

6. To see the effect, toggle visibility between the original text and copy text layers. The entire menu changes, but each menu item is separated when this menu is sliced. See Figure 17-3 for the final layer setup.

And that's it. You are ready to move onto the next step, slicing your menu, which is described in Chapter 18.

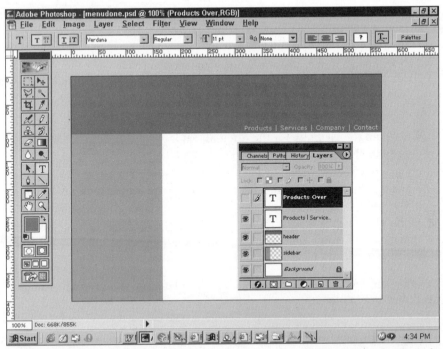

Figure 17-3: Final arrangement of layers for text menu rollover graphics in Photoshop

Exercise: Creating Perfect Rollover Graphics in Paint Shop Pro

Paint Shop Pro from JASC Software handles image creation in a similar way to Photoshop. Make sure that you are very careful with the placement of layers to avoid the one-pixel shuffle.

To demonstrate the method I use, you create the rollover graphics for a small menu. You then slice this menu in Chapter 18.

On the CD-ROM Copy the file, menu.pspd, from the Chapter 17 folder on the CD-ROM that accompanies this book to your hard drive. The file, menudone.psp, contains the results of the following exercise.

To create a rollover layer for a menu in Paint Shop Pro, follow these steps:

1. Open the file menu.psp.

2. Open the Layer palette if it is not already open (right-click the toolbar and select Layer Palette). Highlight the text layer, Text Normal. This is the menu text layer and is the normal state for the rollovers you will create.

3. Right-click the layer and select Duplicate. Name the new layer "Text Over."

4. Turn off the visibility for the original text layer by clicking the "eyeglass" symbol at the right edge of the layer listing.

5. Click the Text sublisting for the Text Over layer to select the text. Right-click the text in the canvas, and select Edit Text from the pop-up menu. Set the Fill color to CCFFFF.

6. To see the effect, toggle visibility between the original text and copy text layers. The entire menu changes, but each menu item will be separated when this menu is sliced. See Figure 17-4 for the final layer setup.

And that's it. You are ready to move onto the next step, slicing your menu, which is described in Chapter 18.

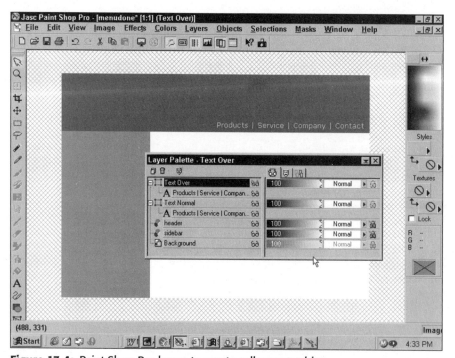

Figure 17-4: Paint Shop Pro layers to create rollover graphics

Exercise: Creating Perfect Rollover Graphics in Fireworks

Macromedia has been a leader in the field of preparing graphics for Web use. Fireworks is a program designed from the ground up for this purpose, and it does it very well, although in a slightly different way than other rollover creation programs. In Chapter 18, you move on to slicing the graphics for a menu, but in this exercise, you prepare the layers that you will use.

Copy the file, menu.png, from the Chapter 17 folder on the CD-ROM that accompanies this book to your hard drive. The file, menudone.png, contains the results of the following exercise.

To create a rollover layer for a menu in Fireworks, follow these steps:

1. Open the file menu.png.

2. In the Layers palette, double-click the Menu layer to open the Layer Name window. Check to make sure that the Share Across Layers is *not* selected. Highlight the Text object on the Menu layer.

3. Activate the Frames palette, which by default is in the same window as the Layers palette.

4. Click the arrow at the side of the palette, and select Duplicate Frame from the pop-up menu. Frame 2 appears. (See Figure 17-5.)

5. With Frame 2 highlighted, change the fill color for the individual menu items to CCFFFF. The | character should remain the same as on Frame 1. To see the effect, toggle back and forth between Frame 1 and Frame 2.

And that's it. You are ready to move onto the next step, slicing your menu, which is described in Chapter 18.

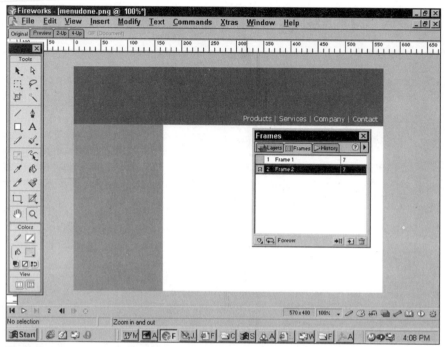

Figure 17-5: Frames form the rollover graphics in Fireworks

✦   ✦   ✦

Optimizing and Slicing Graphics for Menus

As soon as you have your menus planned and the design in place, you still have a crucial process to complete. How you slice and optimize your graphics can make the difference between building a rock-solid page that can be viewed on any browser, or a page that will take hours of troubleshooting and discourage visitors. In this chapter, I look at the important aspects of slicing and optimizing graphics, and step through the process in Photoshop and Fireworks.

The Zen of Graphics: Stripping File Size Without Mercy

The best site in the world is lost if a page takes too long to load. Optimizing your graphics is one of the most important details you can do to ensure the success of your page. You may have a cable modem or a DSL connection. Everybody you know may have high-speed connections. But not all of us do. I connect on a dial-up — usually at 21.6K. And believe me, this is not because I am cheap, technically challenged, or otherwise responsible for the sorry state of my connection. Quite simply, I have no other option. I live in an area that is far from the population base for this province, like millions of people in North America. I am in heaven when I am on the road and can connect from a hotel room at 56K!

Yes, much of North America has access to high-speed lines, but what about the rest of us? What about some areas of Europe and many other areas of the world? Many people still have slow connections, plus must pay for the local phone call in addition to hefty Web service charges.

We are far from the point where we can ignore slow connections. In fact, we will most likely go back before we go forward with all of the excitement over wireless devices, palm computers . . . the list of reasons to optimize can fill this page.

Does this sound like a rant? Perhaps it is. I have noticed a disturbing drop in discussion about optimization in the past while. In the newsgroups, tutorials, and Web developer forums, you hardly hear a peep. I am the self-appointed "tester of slow" on several newsgroups, because few can speak to download time with cable or DSL connection. But graphics size is still very important!

Tip I highly recommend that you read an article about optimizing Web graphics by Andy King of WebReference, found at `http://webreference.com/authoring/graphics`.

Graphic programs have done a great job of adding optimization features. Almost all will allow you to reduce GIF colors and preview the results of JPG compression as you save. But we can do more than just that. And it is important to understand how file size and compression works so that we can make good choices.

Cross-Reference You can read more about designing graphics with file size in mind in Chapter 17.

Use exact image size

A common mistake of beginners is to resize their images through HTML, whether hand coding or with an editor. Sure, the image shows at the right size, but the cost in download time is very high. Take a look at the image in Figure 18-1. The caption for this image lists original and reduced file size.

Many programs allow you to reduce the size as you export. For example, in Photoshop's Save for Web screen, you can click the Image Size tab and enter the desired size. The original image is not affected, just the exported image.

Tip Although many programs offer the opportunity to reduce file size on export, it is still a better idea to create a correct-sized file in the main graphics program. Images often require sharpening or increased contrast when they are reduced in size.

Also, consider cropping your images. I see many images on the Web that have so much "stuff" surrounding the subject. Try using white space to create the graphic break for the page. You can create the same impact without adding download time. For Web menus, check your design to see if you can crop away some of the graphic area from your menu items.

Cross-Reference In Chapter 20, you find out how to apply liquid design methods to tables, which can provide solid color and background images for your menus.

Figure 18-1: This image in original form was 485 by 446 pixels, with a file size of 31K. If this image was reduced to 200 by 183 for Web display in a graphics program, the file size drops to less than 6.5K. However, if the image size is reduced using HTML commands, the browser will download the original image size of 31K.

Optimize correctly

In Chapter 17, I provided a little insight as to how compression works, and how to design for small file sizes. However, there are some tricks to optimizing correctly. Not rules, of course, because graphics tend to defy rules, but guidelines for making the correct compromises between quality and file size.

Choose the correct format

The first and most obvious way to create great graphics is to choose the right format for each image in the first place. Your only choices for full compatibility now are JPG or GIF. JPG images are best for photographs and images that do not have clearly defined color areas. JPG does not allow a transparent background to be used. GIF is best for solid color images and is required for any image that requires a transparent background. Figure 18-2 shows representative images for each format.

> **Tip**
>
> I always strive to have any images that contain text saved as GIF format, even to the point where I will slightly adjust a design to fit within the format. JPG compression is not kind to text, and often you are not able to apply enough compression to make the image small enough for the Web.

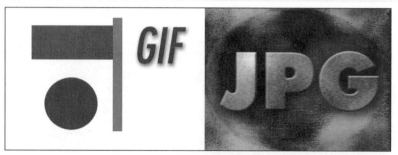

Figure 18-2: The GIF image at the left, which is also shown in Chapter 16, has clearly defined solid color areas. The JPG image at the right has many more colors and no clearly defined solid color areas.

Some images fall right on the dividing line for choosing GIF or JPG. If text is involved, I always choose GIF, but other than that, I simply use the generated file size as a guide. Most programs provide a real-time preview of the compression effects, so test both GIF and JPG. If they both look good, choose the format that produces the smaller size.

Use GIF's transparency feature

Minor color differences between graphics and HTML-specified can be a problem for creating a unified page, and many designers solve the problem by creating all design areas as graphics so that color is consistent.

There is a more elegant solution, however. If you create all of your GIF images with a transparent background, even for a solid color area, any color shifts will be impossible to detect. This method enables you to provide plenty of color areas on a page, but most will be HTML-specified color — nearly free for file size.

Use dithering or blur to "cheat"

Dithering, which is a process that adds dots of color in random order to trick our eye into blending two colors to see a third color, can help smooth color in GIF images, especially graduated color. You can specify how much dithering to apply when you are exporting a GIF format image in any graphics program. There are several forms of dithering patterns, but I have most often found that adding Noise provides the smoothest results.

Dithering has enabled me to use GIF format to keep the text clear, or allow a transparent background many times. However, it comes with a price tag . . . as you increase dithering, you increase file size.

Blurring is a feature you can add to JPG images to smooth some of the compression effects. As you increase JPG compression, information is discarded, often leaving visible "artifacts," areas where the color looks flawed, or dots and blurry sections. Applying a smoothing effect can help to smooth over some of these areas. In honesty,

I have used blurring only a few times to help. Most times it blurs the important content as well.

Tip   Adobe Photoshop contains a "lossy" feature that can be applied to GIF images. This adds JPG-like compression to GIF files, but as with JPG compression, quality is affected. In some cases, this feature can save file size, but watch the real-time results carefully when you use it.

Reduce colors in GIF files

GIF files are compressed simply by removing the number of colors used in the image. As colors are reduced, file size drops, because the file no longer carries the display information for the dropped colors.

As mentioned in previous chapters, you can have a maximum of 256 colors in a GIF file and a minimum of 2. Most images that I prepare for menus have no more than 16 colors. Always watch your real-time display when you are reducing color as quality can be seriously affected if you take the color number down too low.

Many programs also enable you to specify which colors will be included with the file. I find that this helps when I can reduce to a very low number of colors, except that one or two colors are lost at all but the highest settings.

Tip   Many of the high-end graphics programs are capable of excellent compression, but some programs still create files that are larger than necessary. Also, some images can be what I call "brat" images—images that refuse to reduce to a reasonable file size without excessive quality loss. A small, inexpensive program solves both of these problems: Image Optimizer from Xat.com. This program provides real-time display of compression and enables you to instantly compare JPG or GIF format for an image. The big feature of this program, however, is the ability to do *regional* compression. You can apply more compression to a plain area of an image, yet keep an area, such as a person's face at a lower compression level. You may want to download the demo version of Image Optimizer from www.xat.com and see if it can help you achieve smaller file size.

Slicing Graphics Is an Art

You may be a victim of marketing hype. Companies, such as Macromedia and Adobe have a full range of products, and they are both companies that listen to the pleas from customers. Each version of Web-based software that has been released included more automated features, plus increased interactivity between their graphics programs and HTML editors. Some of this is good and can save time. But for the most part, professional designers do not use much of the automation that is available. Automation is almost always equal to loss of control. In the Web design world, experienced designers know that the most important part of designing for every browser is to maintain as much control of code as you can. I find that using most automated features equates to loss of that vital control.

That is not to say that I don't use all of the programs that have been linked through automation. Quite the opposite. On the Adobe side, I use Photoshop and GoLive daily and for Macromedia products, would fight to the death to keep both Dreamweaver and Fireworks. I just use them as separate products, never mixing my graphics and code production. My practice is not for everyone, but works well for me in the constant browser compatibility battle.

Don't slice entire pages

If I seem to be on a soapbox throughout this entire chapter, please forgive me, but pay attention. I have seen many Web sites where the designer is just "not getting it." This is the Web. The Web is not print. If you insist on total control of the look of your pages, get into print. You can't achieve total control in Web design and still follow the important principles that make the Web work. I don't apologize for my hard line on this issue. Remember, I connect at a very slow speed and do not have reasonable access to most of the "beautiful" pages out there. A true artist is one who can make his or her art available to the public.

When the capability to cut one graphic into many separate images, or slicing, was added to most graphics programs, designers thought they had died and gone to heaven. No longer were they working with simple HTML, a markup language never designed to create pretty pages. We went through a stage where sites were designed mainly in graphics programs, such as Photoshop or Fireworks, and then simply sliced and transported wholesale into a blank HTML page. This slicing was so easy and allowed so much control.

Slicing was never a great idea, however. First, you are downloading a full screen of graphics. With my slow connection, you can imagine how much I enjoy the wait to see a page constructed this way. Also, the best time-savings come when you export the HTML and images and plop them into an HTML page. Trouble is, automatically generated code is rarely compliant with any standards that allow true cross-browser compatibility. I believe that responsible designers spend more time troubleshooting automatically generated code from a graphics program than they would spend to build the page from scratch.

Also, the great answer to varied monitor resolution, *liquid design* (see Chapter 20), is impossible with automatically generated code. Slice and go pages are pretty dumb and must fit into as tight a framework as they began life. If you have not experienced the total satisfaction of seeing your pages fill the screen with no horizontal scroll no matter what the resolution, you have been missing one of Web design's greatest accomplishments. I am convinced I will sell you on liquid design in Chapter 20, so listen up here. You will need to know how to create your graphics to create liquid pages.

So, what's the point in slicing? Don't get me wrong. I use slicing all the time, but only for graphics. I create my own tables following a very careful plan that assigns text and graphic areas very carefully, and use background color wherever possible.

Yup, planning is the key word again

If you have followed this book chapter by chapter, you may be at the stage where you roll your eyes whenever you see the word *plan*. But that is the secret of great Web design. Every last one of you probably came into this world with the promise of "it's so easy." That is the belief. Every last one of you probably believed it until you created your first "real" site. I don't mean the fill in the blanks site that abound. I mean the site that came into your mind as an original creation, and you set out to construct it. Web design is not easy. It is fun, but not easy. In fact, most of Web design is dog-hard work. That you bought this book tells me that you have recognized the intricacies and problems that can plague Web designers.

The largest part of that work is planning. An effective Web site is the result of piecing together an elaborate puzzle, and the graphics portion of that site is perhaps the biggest part of the puzzle-like work.

Planning is how you know what menu items to create. Planning is the reason that you know where to slice. Planning is the reason that you have a clearly laid out path to slicing that will fit within a table layout in an HTML page without stretching the limits of HTML past browser compatibility. (Netscape really hates multiple nested tables.)

How you plan your page is up to you. I tend to do mine in the graphics program, but that is after years of experience. In the beginning, I used pencil and paper to sketch the structure of my page to allow manageable slicing and placement in my HTML pages.

What's the ideal process?

Okay, if I present all of the problems, I had better be prepared to offer a solution. I step you through how I create my pages. You can adopt what seems right for your style, and adapt other techniques.

Ideally, while you most likely design your pages in a graphics editor (I don't know any designer who does not), the graphics that you use on your final HTML page will be a small portion of the initial, graphics-created design.

I prepare my page comps in a graphics program, and then export selected slices. I use the graphics automation to generate my rollover images, but put the rollover code together as I create the HTML page. I still have the benefit of automated changes for exported graphics, automatic naming of rollover images, no matter how many states are involved, and can optimize each graphic individually. Slicing is a wonderful function and saves me hours every day.

The exercises that follow are based on the method that I use to create my pages.

Exercise: Slicing and Optimizing a Menu in Photoshop and ImageReady

Adobe Photoshop is one of the most popular first-step graphics programs used by professional designers. ImageReady is bundled with any Photoshop program starting with version 5.5. Photoshop 6, on which this exercise is based, added no-save jumping between Photoshop and ImageReady. If you are using version 5.5, you will be prompted to save when you go between Photoshop and ImageReady.

Copy the file, `menuslice.psd`, from the Chapter 18 folder on the CD-ROM included with this book to your hard drive.

You extract the logo and menu area from this document and prepare an HTML page with the graphics by following these steps:

1. Open the document, `menuslice.psd` in Photoshop.

You could complete this exercise completely in ImageReady without opening Photoshop, but that is only because I provided the original document for you. In normal working conditions, you prepare the image in Photoshop and then jump to ImageReady, so I am following that route.

2. Click the Jump to ImageReady button at the bottom of the toolbar, as shown in Figure 18-3.

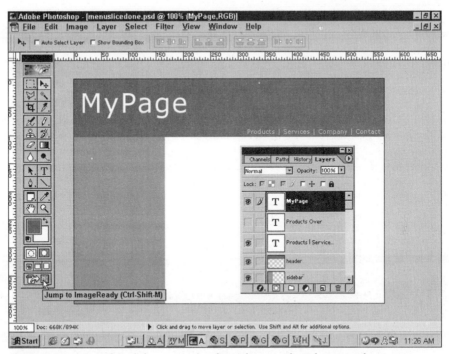

Figure 18-3: Completed document in Photoshop ready to be moved to ImageReady for slicing

3. To prepare the slices you will use, select the Slice tool from the toolbox. On this page, you are only going to extract graphics for the logo area and the four menu items. Click and drag to create a slice over the logo area, and each of the four menu items. Your document should look similar to the document shown in Figure 18-4.

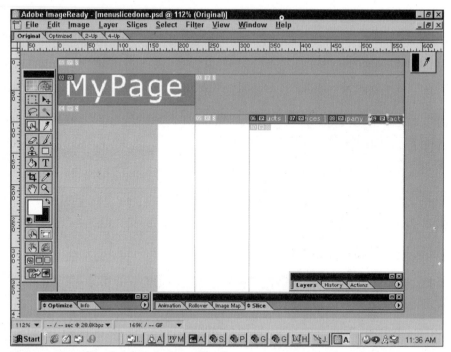

Figure 18-4: Slices in place in ImageReady

4. I prefer to name the slices, rather than let ImageReady assign names, as I find it much easier during the construction phase to work with file names that indicate the image. Select the Slice Select tool from the toolbox. Click the logo area slice, and a yellow bounding box appears around the slice. If it is not already open, open the Slice palette (Window ➪ Show Slice). Type **logo** in the Name field of the Slice palette, as shown in Figure 18-5. This slice will now create a file with the base name of "logo."

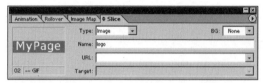

Figure 18-5: Enter the name to be used as the base file name for the logo slice.

5. Repeat Step 5 for each of the menu items, and using the title for each item (for example, type **products** for the Products menu item).

6. To apply optimization to each slice, first change to Optimize view. Click the Optimize tab at the top of the window. Don't worry if it looks terrible, as the

optimize settings are likely wrong, and you will fix that now. Make sure that your page is set to 100% view when you are optimizing. Choose View ⇨ Actual Size to set view to 100%.

7. Select the Eyedropper from the toolbox and click the dark teal color near the logo to set the Foreground color. You need that setting for the next step.

8. With the Slice Select tool selected, click the logo slice to select it. If it is not already open, open the Optimize palette (Window ⇨ Show Optimize). Select GIF, Adaptive, 8 colors, and No Dither. To set transparency for this image, activate the Transparency Option. The Matte setting tells ImageReady on what background the image is to be displayed and sets the appropriate antialiasing color at the edge of the text. Click the Matte drop-down menu and select Foreground Color. The dark teal color you selected with the eyedropper should appear in the Matte color well. Follow the image on the canvas to see the results of your settings. Your document should look like the document shown in Figure 18-6.

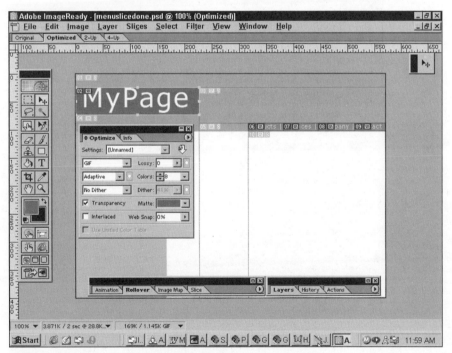

Figure 18-6: Optimize screen and settings for the logo area

9. Repeat Step 8 for each of the menu item slices.

10. Finally, you will create the rollover graphics for the menu items. If it is not already open, open the Rollover palette (Window ⇨ Show Rollover). Click the Create New Rollover State button at the bottom of the Rollover palette. A new

icon appears beside the Normal icon with the label "Over." At this point, the rollover state is a duplicate of the Normal state. In the next step, you create the rollover effect.

11. If it is not already open, open the Layers palette (Window ⇨ Show Layers). You create the rollover effect by turning off the visibility of the Products | Services layer and turning on the visibility of the Products Over layer. Make sure the Over icon is selected in the Rollover palette. Click the "eye" icon in the Layers palette next to the Product | Services layer to turn off that layer. Click the "eye" icon beside the Product Over layer to turn the visibility on. Note that the Over icon in the Rollover palette now shows white text, as shown in Figure 18-7.

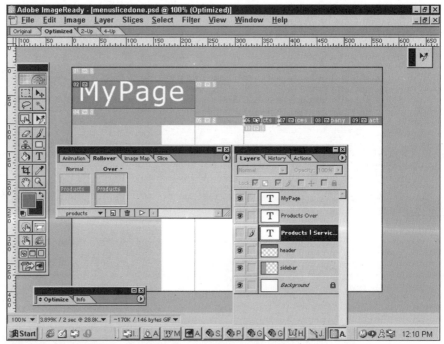

Figure 18-7: Rollover effect created by changing layers while the Over icon is selected in the Rollover palette

12. Repeat Steps 10 and 11 for the remaining three menu items. You are now ready to export your graphics.

Caution   Saving your document at this time is a good idea. Choose File ⇨ Save. The changes saved in ImageReady are automatically included after you return to Photoshop, whether or not the document has been saved (version 6 only), but periodic saving is always a good idea, and jumping back and forth from Photoshop to ImageReady, while much better than it was, can still cause the program to crash if you have been working for a long time.

Your rollover images are now prepared. To export the graphics you created, follow these steps:

1. With the Slice Select tool active, select all of the slices you want to export, which in this case are the logo area and four menu items. Use your Shift key to select multiple slices. Each of the selected slices have a yellow bounding box.

2. Choose File ⇨ Save Optimized As to open the Save Optimized As window. Browse to the folder where you would like to place your images.

3. The Filename field is only used if you are exporting the HTML. You are not, so it can remain as it is. Choose Images Only from the Save As Type drop-down menu.

4. Choose Selected Slices from the drop-down menu at the bottom of the screen.

5. Click the Output Settings button near the bottom of the screen to open the Output Settings window. You set how your file names are constructed on this screen.

6. I prefer to keep my file names very simple, with just the name I assigned the slice and the rollover state. To name your files in this fashion, use the drop-down selectors to select slice name, and then hyphen, and then rollover state. The next five selectors will say none, and the final selector is left at .ext (which places .gif or .jpg as the extension as appropriate, rather than .GIF or .JPG).

7. Uncheck the Copy Background Image when Saving and the Place Images in Folder settings. You may choose to leave the Include Copyright option active. Your screen should resemble the screen shown in Figure 18-8.

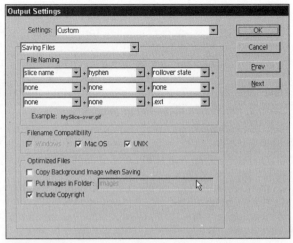

Figure 18-8: Settings for simple file naming in ImageReady

8. Click OK to return to the Save Optimized As window. Check to make sure that all settings are as you desire and click Save. Check the folder where you specified that files should be saved. You should have ten files. There will be eight files for the menu items, one file for the logo area, and one file called `spacer.gif`. This file is always saved and is simply a clear one-pixel image used for spacing in tables.

That's it. You have saved all of the files you need and will come back to these files in Chapter 19 and Chapter 23 as you create tables and rollovers.

Exercise: Slicing and Optimizing a Menu in Fireworks

Fireworks was one of the first graphics programs to offer automatic slicing and rollover capabilities, and the long experience shows.

Cross-Reference Because of the way that Fireworks creates rollovers, the exercise in Chapter 17 is the actual start of this exercise. If you want to have the full experience and have not completed the exercise in Chapter 17, please do so before you start here. You can also find a copy of the file, `menuslice.png`, in the Chapter 18 folder on the CD-ROM included with this book.

You extract the logo and menu area from this document and prepare an HTML page with the graphics by following these instructions:

1. Open the document, `menuslice.png`, which is found in the Chapter 18 folder on the CD-ROM that accompanies this book.

2. To prepare the slices you will use, select the Slice tool from the toolbox. Also, make sure that the Hide/Show Slices button at the bottom of the toolbox is depressed. On this page, you are only going to extract graphics for the logo area and the four menu items. Click and drag to create a slice over the logo area, and each of the four menu items. Your document should look similar to the document shown in Figure 18-9.

3. I prefer to name the slices, rather than let Fireworks assign names, as I find it much easier during the construction phase to work with file names that indicate the image. Select the Pointer tool from the toolbox. Click the logo area slice and a blue bounding box appears around the slice overlay. If it is not already open, open the Object window (Window ⇨ Object). Uncheck the Auto-Name Slices option. Type **logo** in the field that appears when you turn off auto-naming, as shown in Figure 18-10. This slice now creates a file with the base name of "logo."

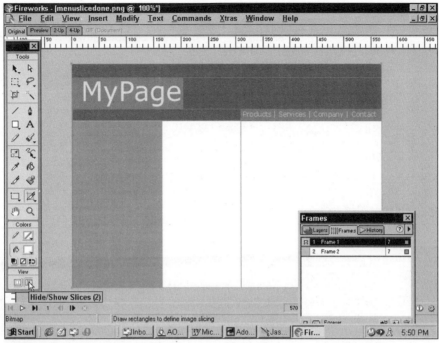

Figure 18-9: Slice tool selected and Hide/Show Slices button depressed in Fireworks

Figure 18-10: Entering the name to be used as the base file name for the logo slice

4. Repeat Step 3 for each of the menu items by using the title for each item (for example, type **products** for the Products menu item).

5. To apply optimization to each slice, first change to Preview view. Click the Preview tab at the top of the window. Don't worry if it looks terrible, as the optimize settings are likely wrong, and you will fix that now. Make sure that your page is set to 100% view when you are optimizing. Choose View ➪ Magnification ➪ 100%.

6. With the Pointer tool selected, click the logo slice to select. If it is not already open, open the Optimize palette (Window ⇨ Show Optimize). Select GIF, Adaptive, 8 colors, and No Dither. To set transparency for this image, select Index Transparency from the drop-down menu at the bottom of the Optimize window. To set the color that will be transparent, click the = icon below the transparency setting. An eyedropper appears. Click the eyedropper on the background color around the logo area to specify that color will be transparent.

7. The Matte setting tells Fireworks on what background the image will be displayed and will set the appropriate antialiasing color at the edge of the text. Click the Matte drop-down menu and an eyedropper appears. Click the eyedropper on the background color around the logo area. The dark teal color you selected with the eyedropper should appear in the Matte color well. Follow the image on the canvas to see the results of your settings. Your document should look like the document shown in Figure 18-11.

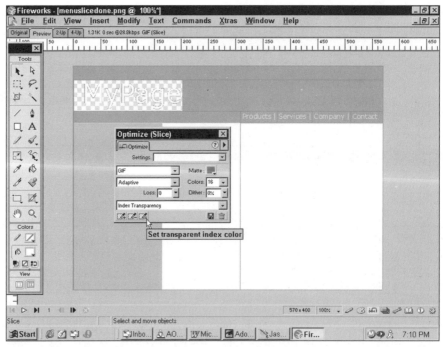

Figure 18-11: Optimize screen and settings for the logo area

8. Repeat Steps 5, 6, and 7 for each of the menu item slices.

Refer to the Fireworks exercise at the end of Chapter 17 to create rollovers if you have not yet done this exercise.

You are now ready to export your graphics.

Saving your document before you export the graphics is a good idea. Never neglect to save a native format copy of your menu items, as you may need to make small changes at a later time. Choose File ➪ Save.

Your rollover images are now prepared. To export the graphics you created, follow these steps:

1. With the Pointer tool active, select all of the slices you want to export, which in this case are the logo area and four menu items. Use your Shift key to select multiple slices. Each of the selected slices have a blue bounding box.

Technically, you should not export the logo area with the menu items, as an unnecessary rollover state image will be created for the logo area. However, I find it faster to delete an image or two than to do more than one export. If you prefer to do two exports, simply check Current Frame only in Step 2 when exporting the logo area image.

2. Choose File ➪ Export to open the Export window. Browse to the folder where you would like to place your images.

3. The File Name field is only used if you are exporting the HTML. You are not exporting to HTML so it can remain as it is. Choose Images Only from the Save As Type drop-down menu.

4. Check the Selected Slices Only option from the drop-down menu at the bottom of the screen.

5. Select Export Slices from the Slices drop-down menu. Make sure that Include Area without Slices is unchecked. Your screen should resemble the screen shown in Figure 18-12. Click Save.

6. Fireworks will create ten files in the location you specified. The file names will be the name of the slice, and the name of the slice plus "f2" for Frame 2, the location of the rollover image information. You do not need the image `logo_f2.gif` and should delete it. This is the extra image that can be avoided by following the instructions in the note early in this exercise.

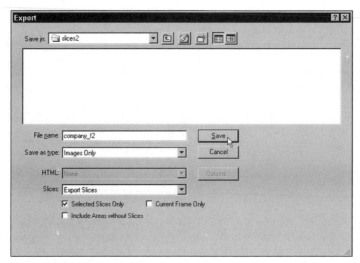

Figure 18-12: Settings for export in ImageReady

That's it. You have saved all the files you need and come back to these files in Chapter 19 and Chapter 23 as you create tables and rollovers.

Creating Tables that Stay Put in Any Browser

✦ ✦ ✦ ✦

In This Chapter

Why skipping automated tables is okay

Planning a table for sliced graphics

Working with table background color

Browser oddities that test your sanity

Exercise: Creating a table for sliced graphics

✦ ✦ ✦ ✦

Web design started toward its current state as the use of tables increased and expanded. In the beginning, HTML tables were designed to act like a spreadsheet program, providing cells for data to be displayed on a Web page. Artists, however, dismayed with the limited layout provided by HTML code, started to place graphics in cells as well as using cells to create columns. Amazing layouts have been created with tables that were never intended to be an artistic tool.

However, the very success of methods in common use today is what can undo a beginning designer. The standard for design has been raised so high that new designers are motivated to create the complex layouts they see as they surf. Unfortunately, creating an effective page is a long way from building a table and sticking some graphics in it, as new designers usually discover when they are holding handfuls of their own hair and cannot figure out why the page does not work in all browsers.

You can reach stable table status quickly though, as long as you are prepared to accept the limitations of HTML. This chapter focuses on the very basics of table creation, as well as liquid design. You won't find anything fancy here, just the methods I use to earn my living creating Web sites. And that's fancy enough for me.

Why You Should Skip Automated Tables

If you have been following along chapter by chapter, you probably know by now that I am not a fan of automatically generated tables from graphics programs. Tables form the structure for most Web pages — without solid tables your page falls apart.

There is a great irony with automatically generated tables. If you are an experienced designer, well versed in HTML code, and understand fully how a Web page works, you can probably slice and export automatically generated graphics and tables with success. You have the experience to structure the page correctly in the first place. You have the experience to watch for misplaced code or oddities in code that can cause problems in one or more browsers. But you are also the least likely to use the capability.

Unfortunately, automatically generated tables appear to answer many bewildering problems for a new designer. You are promised the ability to create a comp in a well-behaved graphics program, slice it up so that you can add rollovers for menus, click a few buttons, and have a perfect HTML page delivered to you. However, reality is never so simple, especially when you are not certain how HTML tables work. The program will generate the tables that you request. Trouble is, you don't realize that your "simple" design requires tables nested to three levels, with 27 columns, merged cells and rows throughout, and countless single pixel spacers to hold the shape you specified.

On the other hand, if you invest a little time to understanding how to create clean, efficient tables, you will have total design freedom (or as much freedom as HTML code allows), plus the ability to create pages with liquid or flexible design. Most importantly, when testing turns up a problem in your page, the chance you can spot the trouble and fix it quickly is much greater.

Working with automatically generated HTML table code is a serious challenge, even for experienced designers. I know a true design expert who devotes many hours to helping new designers on newsgroups. However, she will not help anyone with automatically generated tables. This is not an elitist policy, but the result of hours she has spent trying to unravel the code produced by people who do not understand the structure of a good HTML page.

Note   I do not intend to criticize the programs that create automatic tables or even the tables they create. If you know your stuff, the autogeneration works fine. If you really know your stuff, you can customize the code to meet any compatibility goals you must meet for your visitors.

Planning a Table for Sliced Graphics

Planning the tables that will hold your sliced graphics can certainly feel like a trial and error exercise. You have many details to consider. How many tables will form the page? Will the tables be nested or separate? Will there be cell padding or spacing added to the table? Does the same padding or spacing work for every cell you require?

In pages I design, I often find that I have one table created for the entire page with a secondary table nested in the main table. The reason? I do not need margin or padding for the main table so that the liquid elements can stretch from edge to edge, but require margins for the content areas so that the text does not go from edge to edge. In other cases, I create two tables, one for the head of the page that stretches from edge to edge, and one for the content with margins. You may find that your needs are completely different from mine, but chances are, you will discover a pattern of tables that work well with your style.

Merging cells and rows

Using tables for layout without turning to merged cells and rows to help place your page elements is hard. In fact, if you are not using these techniques for tables, you may not be adding as much life and energy to your pages as you could be. Creating a page with a pure three-column format may be easy, but, as much as I am against building convoluted tables to satisfy the designer's ego, I also believe that a page with well-planned tables and interesting layout are the best to direct visitors and hold their attention. Merging cells and rows helps to create energy and motion on your page.

Figure 19-1 is a simple table presentation with borders turned on and merged areas colored for clarity. The code that creates the merged effect is included in each colored cell. Looking at this simple table, seeing the visual interest that comes from varying the columns is easy.

Nesting tables

Nesting tables can be the answer to your quandary as you plan your pages. One table placed within a cell of another can help to add margins to one area or break a column format. Tables were designed for and can still be used to present information in tabular form. Using a nested table with many rows and cells is much better than merging many cells and rows to create open areas for the non-tabular areas of the page.

However, this comes with a warning. Many layers of nesting tables, as shown in Figure 19-2, slows download time and can cause serious display problems in some browsers. If you find yourself building layer upon layer of nested tables, stop! The layout you are trying to achieve can no doubt be accomplished with more creative planning or use of column and row merging. If you cannot create your look without many layers of nested tables, your layout is not a good one for the Web.

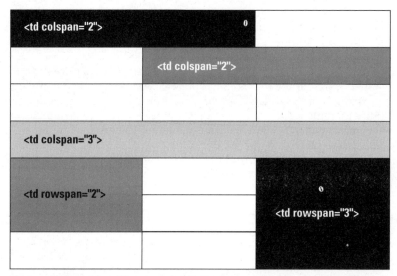

Figure 19-1: Table with merged cells and rows. This presentation is much more interesting than a plain three-column table would produce.

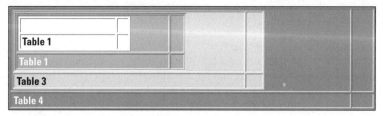

Figure 19-2: Four layers of nested tables — exactly how tables should *not* be used in Web design.

Planning the master table for your page

Some people like to start table planning on paper. However, that leads to a slight catch-22 for new designers. You really must understand tables well to be able to sketch potential tables on paper. If you are a beginner, you will probably move ahead faster if you "play" with various combinations of tables with merged rows and cells, plus nested tables until you have a solid idea of how tables work. If you are working with an editor that hides your code, such as Macromedia Dreamweaver or Front Page, get into the habit of watching the code that is produced as you work.

Caution I am a strong advocate for learning HTML, even if the editor you use creates pages without showing any code. When it comes to the subject of learning the code for tables, I become a raging maniac. Creating great tables (and therefore great pages) is almost impossible unless you understand table code.

I included a proposed table layout for a page in Figure 19-3. This page would do well with a single overall table, but the margin problem I mentioned earlier in this chapter appears. Note how close the menu items are to the bottom of the colored area. With cell spacing or padding added to the original table, that look would not be possible. The solution is to create a main table with no padding or spacing, and nest a table inside the content area that does have spacing applied.

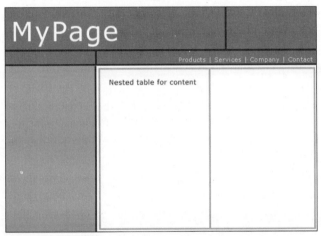

Figure 19-3: The nested table added to the content area allows cell spacing for just that area.

Working with Table and Background Color

When you add the power of merged cells and nested tables to a variety of background color options, you have a toolbox full of color tools without ever adding a graphic element. I have seen attractive pages that contain no graphics at all to form the layout. For most sites, abstinence from all graphics is probably overkill, but always watch how much plain color you are using in your graphics. If your image is surrounded by more than a border of color, take a look at table background tags to see if you can replace a portion of your graphic with simple HTML color.

Adding table background color

Backgrounds can be added to the full table as well as table rows or cells. (To create a background for a full column you must add a background to each cell in the column.) The code for each follows (CCCCCC is a light gray and can be changed for the desired color):

Table background:

```
<table bgcolor="#CCCCCC">
```

Row background:

```
<tr bgcolor="#CCCCCC">
```

Cell background:

```
<td bgcolor="#CCCCCC">
```

With these three tools, you can add color anywhere on your page with little file size cost. When you are planning the tables to hold your sliced images, check to see if you can use background color to replace some of the image size. The benefit stretches beyond file size, too. In Chapter 20 you discover how you can use tables and background color to create pages that will fill the screen no matter what monitor resolution displays your page.

Understanding cell padding and spacing

Cell padding and spacing can be confusing. *Padding* refers to the amount of margin within each cell, while *spacing* refers to the distance between cells. For separating text and images, the two commands do not differ much. However, as soon as you add color to backgrounds, they become fundamentally different.

The tables shown in Figure 19-4 illustrate the difference between cell padding and spacing. When cell spacing is applied, gaps appear between cell backgrounds. Cell padding allows a margin, but the color can still spread to the edge of the cell. For this reason, I tend to use only cell spacing when I am creating tables for Web content.

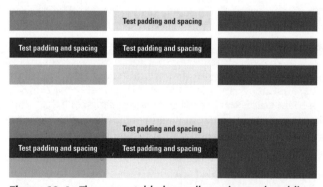

Figure 19-4: The upper table has cell spacing and padding set to 10. The lower table has the cell spacing set to zero, and the cell padding remains at 10.

Inserting table background images

Color is fun to work with and adds very little to file size, but you can also add a lot to your pages by using images as backgrounds for your tables. Technically, any image can be used as a background, but there are some limitations. First, any time you talk about graphics, you must consider download time. Technically, you could add a different background image to every cell in a table. However, each image would slow your page load. You must always walk a balance between appearance and load time.

But why would you use an image as a background rather than just placing an image? There are many reasons. First, a table background does not affect table size. Placing an image forces your column and row size. A background will not do this. The cells will shrink and grow, showing more or less of the background as determined by other content.

If you want to place other content, such as another image or text over your image, you must use a background. Table and table cell backgrounds are essential to liquid design, which I discuss in Chapter 20. Figure 19-5 shows a background image at work. This is an example of liquid design: the bar with a shadow stretches across the width of any resolution monitor by using a table cell background.

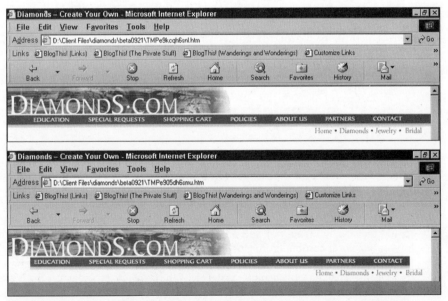

Figure 19-5: Table cell background in action on the Diamonds.com Web site. The top image is the final appearance. The lower image shows the same page without the table cell background in place.

The code for adding a background image is as follows:

Table background:

```
<table background="filename">
```

Row background:

```
<tr background="filename">
```

Cell background:

```
<td background="filename">
```

Caution   You can place an image as a table, row, or cell background. However, before your imagination runs too wild, I want to caution you. Netscape has a peculiar quirk with table backgrounds. If you specify a background for an entire table, Netscape will start the image over again with every cell, which can lead to some pretty unusual effects. In addition, Internet Explorer does not display a `<tr>` (table row) background.

Browser Oddities That Test Your Sanity

As powerful as table background image commands can be, browser variation shouts loudly on this issue. Take a look at Figure 19-6. Considering that these two previews came from the same HTML document, the differences are astounding.

Assessing browser interpretations of table backgrounds

Internet Explorer does a great job of displaying a unified background in the table and in the cells in the second example shown in Figure 19-6. But where is the table row background? Welcome to Web design.

Note   To protect myself, because I have been around this industry for a while, I am going to add a disclaimer. You *may* see a table row background with your platform and Internet Explorer combination. However, many combinations won't display it—in fact, I haven't found one that does. My disclaimer also tells a lot about this industry, because making an absolute statement about *every* browser on both platforms is almost impossible.

Now look at the Netscape preview in Figure 9-6. Netscape is not kind to table backgrounds, as you can see in the upper table. You can remove the gaps by specifying zero cell spacing, but the pattern starts over with every cell. Getting a seamless table background in Netscape by using a background for the entire table is almost impossible.

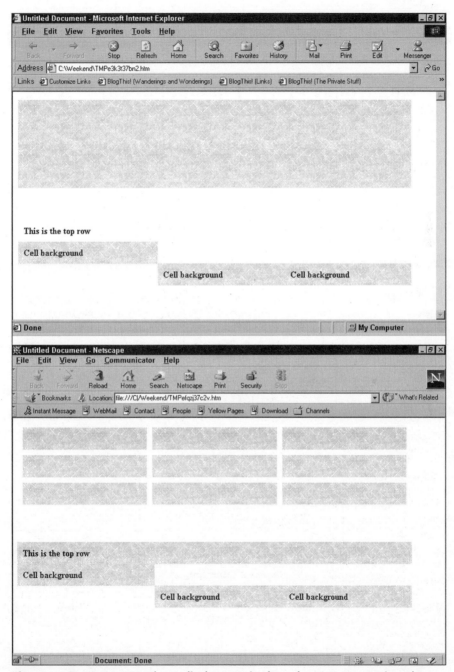

Figure 19-6: One page and two displays. Notice how the Netscape version places spaces between the table cells and that Internet Explorer does not display the row background.

But isn't that table row background working perfectly? Yes, it is. Well . . . almost. Look closely at the row and you can see a break in the pattern at each cell. The <tr> tag is recognized, but the background image starts over with each cell.

Working around browser interpretations of table backgrounds

Comparing what Internet Explorer and Netscape can do to your table backgrounds, it becomes clear fairly quickly that this is an area that takes great thought and planning. Often, the fix you would apply to correct a problem in Netscape creates a new and different problem in Internet Explorer.

First, if there is another way to accomplish the effect you desire, I recommend you use it. However, there is too much power in backgrounds — especially <td> backgrounds — when creating liquid design to dismiss them as too complicated or buggy.

One way around the problem with backgrounds is to use nested tables. You can create a JavaScript "sniffer," or code that will determine what browser and platform your visitor is using. The code then calls for the appropriate page, which has been custom designed for that browser and platform. This method is not popular, however, because you must create as many sites as the combinations of browsers and platforms you want to serve.

Tip   Never design your page for just one browser and then place a notice on your site that the visitor should use only that browser. It does not take much extra studying to learn how to create code that can be used by all browsers. If you are — or you plan to become — a professional designer, you *must* learn to create cross-browser-compatible code. That is your job!

I included this set of examples so that you can study what the effects are and make decisions based on what you have seen here. I never create a background for any table tag that has a horizontal repeat and usually only use the <td> tag to add a background image for liquid design.

Each design situation is different. You may come up with a very creative solution to use a background in your table that works for only one situation — the one you are working on. Watch for table and table cell backgrounds when you are surfing the Web. Study the code that has been used to create that effect. Before long, your table background color and image skill will increase, and you will enjoy design freedom while you create stable pages.

Exercise: Creating a Table for Sliced Images

In this exercise, you create a table to contain the slices that you created earlier in Chapter 18. If you did not do the exercise in Chapter 18, you can copy the image files you require from the CD-ROM that accompanies this book. Some of the techniques used to create this table will be fully explained in Chapter 20.

 On the CD-ROM   Copy the Slices folder from the Chapter 19 folder on the CD-ROM to your hard drive.

To create the table for slices, follow these steps:

1. Create a new HTML document in your favorite editor. Name it **slicepage.html**.

2. Create the page properties, including setting margins to zero with the following `<body>` tag attributes:

```
<body bgcolor="#FFFFFF" text="#000000" leftmargin="0"
topmargin="0" marginwidth="0" marginheight="0">
```

3. Create a table with three rows and three columns. Set table width to 100% and cell padding and spacing to 0.

4. Add a table row background to the first two rows of the table with the following code:

```
<tr bgcolor="#006666">
```

5. Merge the first two cells of the first row and insert the file, `logo.gif`, into the merged cell with the following code:

```
<td colspan="2"><img src="slices/logo.gif" width="226"
height="49"></td>
```

6. Merge the second and third cell of the second row, assign right alignment, and insert the four menu images as in the following code:

```
<td bgcolor="#006666" colspan="2" align="right"><img
src="slices/products.gif" width="64" height="14"><img
src="slices/services.gif" width="65" height="14"><img
src="slices/company.gif" width="68" height="14"><img
src="slices/contact.gif" width="57" height="14"></td>
```

Don't worry about creating rollovers at this point, as the point of the exercise is to be familiar with the table structure.

7. Merge the second and third cell of the third row and insert a table with the parameters as follows:

```
<td colspan="2">
   <table width="100%" border="0" cellspacing="0"
cellpadding="10">
     <tr>
      <td> </td>
      <td> </td>
     </tr>
   </table>
</td>
```

This table will be used to add content to the page — note that cell spacing is used to add margins for the content area.

Your table should now resemble the table shown in Figure 19-7. I turned table borders on for easy cell identification.

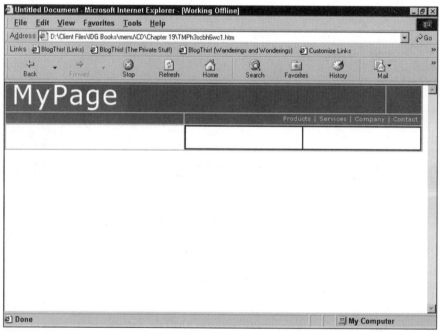

Figure 19-7: Grey borders on the table are turned on to illustrate the table structure. The black borders indicate the nested table.

This page is quite typical for liquid design using background color. Try to create a few of your own pages for practice. After you have done a few, you will understand why I believe that it is just as fast to create your own tables for sliced images, and the control you gain will take you far in the Web design world.

✦   ✦   ✦

Stretch Your Work: Liquid Design for Any Monitor Resolution

The pages you create will be viewed by visitors with monitors set to widely varied resolutions. Some visitors will have monitor resolution set as low as 640 pixels wide, while others will be sporting the latest 1600 pixel wide resolution. To complicate the matter further, some visitors will view your page with their browsers filling their monitor, others will surf with browser windows at a reduced size.

How can you make your pages look good no matter which monitor is used to see them? Creating a perfect display for all resolutions is nearly impossible, but you can reduce variation by creating your pages with content that stretches and shrinks according to the viewing resolution. In this chapter, I lead you through the few simple methods, commonly known as *liquid design* that can turn your pages from static to flexible.

Dressing Your Site in the Latest Style

There are styles in Web design. Although popular use of the Web is really just a few years old, we have already seen plain pages move to pages built with frames. Then backgrounds became all the rage, followed by the three-dimensional, console style of design. Tabs for menu items were a hot trend (and still popular).

Although I am not promoting following trends just to be cool, as a designer, keeping your eye on what is popular is a good idea. Popular trends often become popular because they work. The latest trend is simplified pages with stripped down graphics and content that fills the screen. Most professional designers work with liquid techniques.

What is liquid design?

What the heck is *liquid design*? The term has been around for a few years and came into popular use with two other terms: *ice* and *jelly*. Each describes a different method for creating page structure.

 I include a sample of each of the following page types in the Chapter 20 folder on the CD-ROM included with this book. The files are `icepage.html`, `jellypage.html`, and `liquidpage.html`.

Ice pages

Ice pages refer to pages that are designed with static tables forming fixed widths and the content located in the upper left hand corner of every monitor. In the days when 800 pixel wide display was the maximum visitors could be expected to have, ice pages were not too bad. Extra space is around the content, but not a serious amount. I will never forget the day I saw my ice site on a 1200 pixel wide display, when it was designed for 640 wide display, and looked fine at 800 pixels. Although that high a resolution was unusual at the time, it did not take away the shock of seeing my beautiful site displayed in a teeny corner of the monitor. I have closely followed the methods for liquid design since that day.

Jelly pages

Jelly pages are a simple variation of ice pages. The content is still contained in a fixed width format, but instead of being locked to the left, it is set to float in the middle. Although there is still the same amount of free space around the content, with jelly pages, the content is divided between the right and left margins and seems to be less. However, if you are designing for low-resolution monitors, and your site is seen on a high-resolution monitor, you still have a lot of empty space.

Both of these types of pages are still in use for a few very good reasons. First, many people are still generating sliced graphics and code. This method always produces static layout. Not all designers are aware of the techniques to do liquid design, so static design is easier for many. Finally, static design provides control to provide consistent display for visitors. In a world of unpredictable browsers, table width does remain constant no matter which browser or platform is used to view the page. You must give up almost all control of your page when you move to liquid design.

Liquid pages

Liquid pages are created with flexible width tables, usually with 85% to 100% as a specified width. If the color is to stretch from edge to edge, the main table must have a width of 100% and margins must be set to 0. Although liquid design solves the problem of too much space around content, it is the least predictable style of page. Designing for 640 pixel wide display and having your work potentially displayed at resolutions that are closing in on 1500 pixels wide can be a scary concept when you are working with liquid design. Most designers have now moved to 800 pixels as a minimum resolution to design for, and 1200 pixels wide is the highest resolution in common use. This range is manageable using the techniques in this chapter.

Note   Most sites are now designed so that users do not have to scroll for 800 pixel wide display, which means the few who still view pages at 640 pixels wide will have a horizontal scroll to see all the content on the page. However, keeping the least important content on a page at the right side is good practice. If any content is missed, and not everyone knows to scroll sideways, it will not be critical. The right column is an excellent place for teaser menus, for example.

Understanding the Principles of Liquid Design

When I first learned of liquid design, one of the hardest concepts I grappled with was what exactly had to be done to create a liquid page. I caught on pretty quickly that the content went from edge to edge, and figuring out that the tables had to be set to certain percentages to achieve that flexibility was not impossible. But what else was involved? It seemed much more complicated than that. What I discovered eventually was that nothing else was involved. Set your margins to 0, set your tables to a percentage width, and voila! . . . liquid design.

Tip   Page margins are set to 0 using the following code in your body tag:

```
<body leftmargin="0" topmargin="0" marginwidth="0"
marginheight="0">
```

You may note that the margin commands are stated twice. Netscape and Internet Explorer do not recognize the same tag for margins, so you must duplicate.

Is anything ever that simple in Web design? No! Of course not. However, flexible tables are the core of what is termed liquid design. Additional techniques you need to create liquid pages involve making flexible tables behave the way you require in all browsers. Liquid design depends heavily on carefully planned tables with specified cell widths, and often with a nested table or two.

Creating a table using percentage values

Jump into liquid design by creating a table that contains borders but no content. You create this table in exactly the same way as you create a fixed width table, but you specify different values.

To create a table using percentage values, follow these steps:

1. Create a new document. Name this document **liquidtable.html**.

2. Create a three-column, two-row table with a Cell Padding value of 10 and a Cell Spacing value of 0. Specify the width as 95% and the border as 1.

3. Before going any further, preview your document and reduce the size of your preview window. Increase it again. Note how the table becomes smaller as the window gets smaller. This element is the basic principle behind liquidity. Your results should be similar to those shown in Figure 20-1 and Figure 20-2.

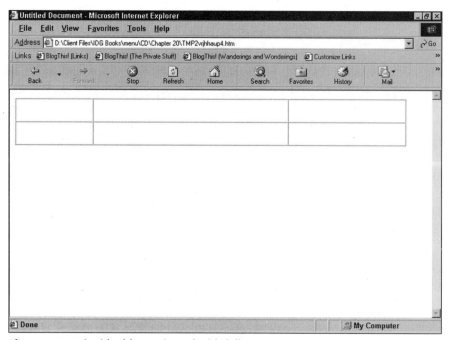

Figure 20-1: Liquid table previewed with full screen

4. Just to make sure you have the difference down solidly, edit your table to have a width that is approximately 100 pixels less than your own monitor resolution. For example, if your monitor resolution is set to 800 pixels wide, change the width of your table to 700 pixels (800 pixels – 100 pixels).

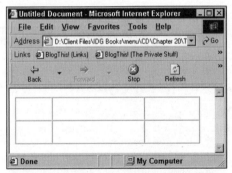

Figure 20-2: Liquid table previewed with reduced screen. Note how the table still covers 95% of the screen.

5. Reduce your window size and you see that the table stays the same size but creates a horizontal scroll. This is an example of a *non*-liquid design.

6. Return the table width to 95%.

Adjusting cell size with percentage values

Creating a table with percentage values is pretty cool, but what if you don't want equally sized columns? No problem. You can adjust the size of your table cells by using percentages values again.

Follow these steps to specify the size of your columns:

1. In the table you created in the previous exercise, specify the left cell in the first row of the column cell width as 20% (make sure you type the % sign; without the % sign, the 20 means 20 pixels).

2. Specify the cell width as 50% for the center cell in the first row of the table.

3. Specify the cell width as 30% for the right cell in the first row of the table.

> **Note**
>
> How's your math? Add the cell percentage widths of 20 degrees + 50 degrees + 30 degrees and you get 100%. But wait! Isn't your table 95% wide? Yes, it is, but the two numbers are *not* related. The table is taking up 95% of the available window. The cell widths must add up to 100% of the table width (in this example).

With a table set up as this one, the table width will range from approximately 570 pixels wide for a 640-pixel-wide resolution — 95% of approximately 600 (don't forget a few pixels are needed for window borders, scroll bars, and so on) — to over 1000 pixels for a 1200-pixel-wide resolution. The cell widths adjust according to the size of the table. For example, the left column, which is set for 20% of the table width, will range from approximately 114 pixels to over 200 pixels wide for the same resolutions previously described.

The completed document from the two previous exercises is included on the CD-ROM included with this book. Look for `liquidpage.html` file in the Chapter 20 folder.

Combining percentage and fixed column widths

But what if you need more control over your design than what the previous two examples illustrate? First, let me offer a caution. You can exhibit a reasonable amount of control over how your page displays, even with liquid design. However, when you are using percentage widths, you have to accept that, rather than designing exactly how your page will look, you are designing for a range of appearances. A page designed to be perfect at 800 pixels wide looks a little squished at 640 pixels. Your page is also likely to be a little more spread out than you would like at 1200 pixels wide. You are working to provide a great page to the majority of browsers, and an acceptable page that is easy to use for all who fall outside of your defined range.

What you can do is control at least part of the page so that menu columns and graphics display as they should. You most often accomplish this by combining fixed and percentage column widths in one table. The most reliable setup is to have the left columns fixed and to have the columns at the right expanding and contracting.

Creating a fixed width column

To begin, you make the left column of your table a fixed width. Insert the first menu item before you adjust the width, as you take the width value from the graphic.

Before starting the next exercise, copy the menuimages folder from the Chapter 20 folder on the CD-ROM included with this book to your hard drive.

1. Create a new HTML document and name it **liquidmenu.html**.

2. Create a three-column, one-row table with a Cell Padding value of 0 and a Cell Spacing value of 0. Specify the width as 95% and the border as 0.

3. Insert the image, `home.gif`, from the menuimages folder into the first cell of the table.

4. You need to know what width to set your left column, and you use the graphic width to tell you. You want this column to be consistent no matter what resolution the viewer is using. This image is 225 pixels wide.

   Set the first cell of the table to 225 pixels wide.

5. Insert the remaining menu items into the first cell, each separated from the previous menu item by a `<br>` tag.

What do you have now? You have a graphic inserted, which prevents that column from ever shrinking smaller than the image or 225 pixels. In addition, you specified that the cell is to be 225 pixels wide, which means that it will not be larger than it is now.

There are exceptions to this rule. Some browsers try to balance columns, regardless of the specified settings. You can use clear GIF images to protect your width settings.

Controlling percentage and fixed width column layouts

You have a decision to make at this point. The left column of your table is fixed. But what are you going to do with the other two columns? You have two choices for a liquid design. Assume that you will be placing text in the center column and menu items or news flashes in the right column.

You can set the columns so that both columns flex with the number of available pixels. The result is that your text has longer and shorter lines, depending on the page size. In addition, the column containing extras would expand and contract, not giving you much control over how the page appears.

Isn't it too bad that you can't set the outer column to be fixed and just let the text expand and contract to fill the window? The good news is that you can do that. The bad news is — you knew that was coming, didn't you? — that you do have to watch how far you ask your text to stretch. Good communication calls for short paragraphs, especially on the Web. When you are asking your text to do all the stretching to make a page liquid, you risk having one-line paragraphs at high resolutions, which look hideous and are very hard to read.

The answer? Add a little extra space to the extra column. That gives you very short lines of text on a 640-pixel-wide screen. Remember, though, that you are more concerned about your mid-range resolutions. Suppose the largest image that will be in your extras column is only 100 pixels wide, but you want to help reduce the center column width by setting the column to be 200 pixels. You must do more than just set the width of a column to add white space.

Using a transparent GIF to control layout

Most browsers won't observe your 200-pixel cell measurement. They do not respect white space and will push your text right over to the photos anyway. You have to convince the browser that you really want that space, and you use a neat little trick to do that. You insert a 1-pixel × 1-pixel image that has been created as a transparent graphic, which means it is completely invisible.

Follow these steps to place a transparent GIF image in the end cell:

1. Insert the image, `spacer.gif` from the menuimages folder into the third cell of the second row in the table.

2. The image size is 1-pixel × 1-pixel. Change the width value to 200. This will force the transparent image to 200 pixels and holds the column at that width.

3. Specify 200 for the cell width.

I always place transparent images that are holding a cell open in a blank row at the bottom of the table whenever possible.

I never recommend centering text, but the right column is a great candidate to be center justified. Centering the content in this column allows you to play with a few more pixels toward a liquid design. You can align to the left and have the content close to the text, but a wide white space would occur at the right because the 95% table width setting allows ever larger margins as the resolution is increased. Setting the alignment to the right aligns your content nicely along the edge, reducing that white space, but the content then appears too far from the main text for solid unity, and right justified text is hard to read (extras usually have some text content).

By using center alignment, you cheat both problems a little, and it may be worth considering adding a table in this column to hold the extras content. The overall content is centered in the column, but you can specify that the nested table have left justification. Liquid design is a series of compromises. You do get very good at spotting the opportunities before too long.

Caution   Adjust a transparent GIF to the size you require by using the image size command, but never resize a normal graphic using HTML code. The capability is there, but that does not mean you should use it. If you decrease the size of a graphic, you are forcing a visitor to download a larger file than is required. If you increase the size of a graphic, the quality will be poor. (You lose quality if you make an image with HTML, as well.) Graphic programs have better controls for retaining image quality as the size of the image is reduced. Often, I resize an image with HTML just to determine the required size, but I *always* take the image back into a graphics program to properly resize it.

Using 100% width for a column

The final step in setting the parameters for your table is to specify what your center column width should be. So far, you have a 225-pixel column containing the 225-pixel logo graphic. You have a 200-pixel column held open by a 200-pixel GIF file. Your table is 95% of the screen width. What are you going to do with the center column?

If you specify that the text column have a fixed width, you no longer have a flexible table. But how can you tell what percentage of the table remains available? Good point. You have fixed widths in a flexible table. I was not bad in math, but that is way past what I can calculate.

Luckily, the solution has nothing to do with calculated numbers. In fact, you can use 100% as a message to the browser to "use whatever is left for this column." It seems a bit strange, but think about it for a minute. You have a left column that cannot be less than 225 pixels because the graphic won't collapse. You have the same setting for the right column because you inserted a 200-pixel graphic — the transparent GIF. The table is going to cover 95% of the screen no matter what, as long as graphics do not override that width. By telling the center column that it is to take up 100% of the space, you are telling it to cover what is left.

Remember that browsers do not always respect the widths you specify. You have the two outer columns set so that they can be no smaller than the specified width. The 100% command tells the browser that you do not want it to decide that the left or right column deserves more space. See Figure 20-3 for the final appearance of the table.

Note   I added a black border to the table in Figure 20-3 to show the cell structure. You should not have borders in your sample.

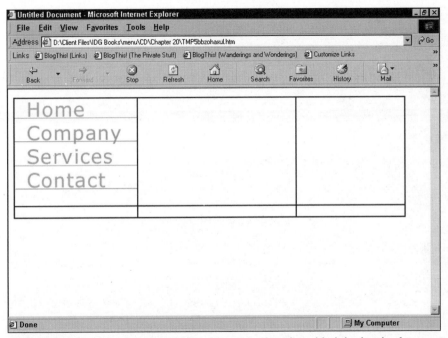

Figure 20-3: Menu items from this exercise are placed. I added the border for easy identification of the table structure.

Using Liquid Design for Table Backgrounds

You have the basics of liquid design now, but I would like to cover one more topic. It looks great when your content stretches from edge to edge on the screen. That's quite easy when you are working with solid color, but what do you do when you want a bar with a shadow to stretch from edge to edge? Insert a background image to stretch a graphic look from edge to edge.

Creating your graphic is easiest when you are creating your menu slices. The only criteria for a liquid design background is that it must be the same on each end of the graphic. The image repeats across the page, and any variation shows repeatedly across the page.

Figure 20-4 illustrates a menu prepared in a graphics program and sliced. The small slice of plain bar at the left edge of the slices creates the background image, which stretches the design across the page.

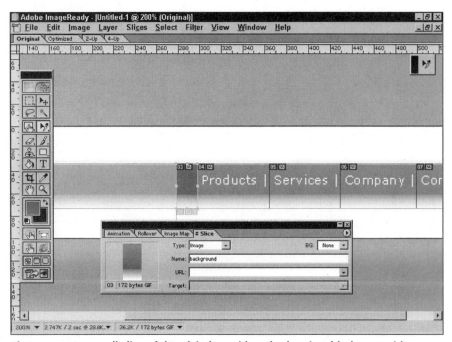

Figure 20-4: A small slice of the plain bar with a shadow is added to provide a background image.

Constructing the menu with a background image is almost identical to creating a plain bar. You simply specify a cell background image for each cell in the row as follows:

```
<tr>
    <td background="background.gif"> </td>
    <td align="right" background="background.gif"
width="50%"><img src="prod.gif" width="66" height="37"><img
src="serv.gif" width="65" height="37"><img src="comp.gif"
width="70" height="37"><img src="cont.gif" width="61"
height="37"></td>
  </tr>
```

This row contains two cells. The left cell has a placeholder non-breaking space, and the right cell contains the menu images.

The completed document for this menu bar, menuback.html, is in the Chapter 20/menuback folder on the CD-ROM. This document is an excellent reference as a sample for liquid design menus using background images.

Netscape reserves an area at the right of the screen for a scroll bar, even when there is not enough content to require a scroll bar. If you have a liquid design that won't extend to the right edge, add enough <p> tags to force a vertical scroll and the scroll bar will appear.

You now have all the tools that professional designers use to create liquid pages. Try it the next time you design a site. You may never go back to static design again.

✦   ✦   ✦

Special Techniques for Flash

Macromedia Flash, specifically designed for creating Web interactivity and animation, is a wonderful program that brought sophisticated animation capability into the mainstream design world. In addition to its powerful animation capability, Flash also offers a feature called *Action Scripting*, a quasi-programming capability that gives designers the power to add interactivity to the animations they create. Interactivity translates instantly into menus. When you can click a link and have an action happen, you have the ability to create a menu.

Note To display Flash animation on a Web page, visitors must have a plug-in, the Flash player, installed on their computers.

However, I value accessibility for Web navigation above all other considerations. Not that I am being profound or idealistic with that ideal. A menu is worth nothing if the visitor cannot see it. When I first came to know Flash a few years ago and as Action Scripting capability grew, making Flash menus very tempting, I was reluctant to even consider creating navigation using a technique that required a plug-in to work.

But, development does march on, and Macromedia has done a superb job of spreading the Flash player through the surfing community. The player has been distributed with Netscape Navigator and Internet Explorer for the last few versions. Today, Flash is as safe to use as most HTML and is probably safer than complex JavaScript or cascading style sheets (CSS). If drop-down menus are your goal, more visitors would likely see Flash than DHTML menus.

Of course, there is a learning curve involved with Flash. I assume that you have at least a rudimentary understanding of Flash, or you would not be reading this chapter. However, if you have just downloaded the trial version of Flash and want to get your feet wet, this is a pretty simple introduction to a complex subject. In order to focus on the *concept* of creating menus in Flash, I keep animation and fancy graphics out of the picture completely.

Tip   If you are looking for basic techniques for Flash, I cover some elementary construction with Flash as part of several tutorials at `http://productiongraphics.com`.

The Wow! and the Catch of Creating Menus with Flash

If you have produced a few Flash movies, I don't have to sell the Wow! of the program very hard. If you have focused on animation, however, you may be surprised by the power Flash brings to menus.

Flash offers one of the few ways in which designers can actually have some control over their results, no matter which browser is used to view their movies. There are a few problems with Flash and Internet Explorer on the Macintosh platform, but for the most part, what the designer sees, so sees the visitor. That alone is a refreshing change.

Plus, as mentioned earlier, Flash players have nearly fully saturated the market, so it is rare to have a visitor that cannot see the movie, even with older browsers. If the visitor does not have the Flash player, he or she will be invited to download the player if their browser will not display a Flash movie. When you consider that you can create drop-down menus with Flash, the darlings of the DHTML world (see Chapter 23 and Chapter 24), but that Flash has much better compatibility across browsers, you will wonder why every menu on the Web has not been created with Flash. Yet few are.

Why is Flash still on the fringe?

There are several reasons for the small number of menus being created with Flash. It is not long since Flash became an accepted format for banner ads, the first and most obvious commercial use for Flash movies. Designers have not yet adopted Flash as a way to create the structure of a site. My opinion is that we will see more sites created completely in Flash as the acceptance grows, though I can't say I expect to see it take over the mainstream Web market, replacing the HTML family any time soon.

First, Flash is a tough program to learn. Those who have used it for a while will loudly proclaim that it is easy. Memory is short. Flash does work in a different way from all other programs in common use for Web development and features the added mystery of working mainly with vector format graphics. Many Web developers have lost a lot of hair on the way to mastering Flash. I don't mean this as a criticism of the program. Animation is like thinking on another plane, and Flash has brought a powerful tool for creating movies into the graphic design world. At one time, motion was only created with exceptionally expensive and complicated programs.

Flash also has limitations when combined with other Web design tools, because it cannot be integrated. Flash gets along very well with other scripts, but a Flash movie is . . . well, simply a Flash movie: solid and square with no way to overlap or slice.

Why is Flash so popular?

However, after you hop over the front-end learning curve and understand the limitations that Flash has in Web design, you start to realize where the strengths of this program lie. If anyone ever did put it off as a fluffy program intended only for creating cute animations, I am sure their attitudes have changed by now. Macromedia has worked hard to increase the Action Scripting capabilities in Flash, which is probably a major reason for the phenomenal success it has enjoyed over the past few years.

Action Scripting is the function that combines graphics with JavaScript to create almost unlimited effects, including interactive elements, such as menus. That is the only area of Flash I cover in this book, and even the material covered here is just a teaser for the full capabilities Flash offers for menus. If you choose to dive deeply into creating movie clips and directing the action with creative JavaScript, there is nothing that could not be done.

The real catch for creating Flash menus

If I am not careful, I will earn the nickname "Queen of the Buts." I love Flash. I love the potential, even if I do not have the time to pursue as much as I can imagine with it. However, someone who spends a good percentage of a book on menus discussing type quality, and even dares to wander into typography, is by definition, pretty fussy about her type. And Flash stumbles a little here.

One of the ways I gave you to create crisp, clear text at small sizes (don't we usually want our menus to be as compact as possible?) was to use a special font that was designed to be used without antialiasing. Flash, however, aliases all text. You can't turn it off for small sizes. You can work around the problem by using a field entry text, but that robs many of the best controls Flash offers for design, and I find it awkward. Although it is a little more work, as long as you are exporting a movie that is a fixed size, I prefer to create my menu items in a graphics program and import them into Flash as a GIF file. If you optimize the colors used in a GIF file, the file size will be miniscule for small text. However, if you are creating a scaleable movie, GIF files will lose quality as the image is enlarged or reduced.

Tip   Joe Gillespie, of Web Page Design for Designers, has an excellent typography section on his Web page that provides a very good explanation of Flash text limitations (www.wpdfd.com).

Working with Buttons for Menu Items

If you have created even a few simple movies with Flash, you have likely discovered that the secret to production and download size is working with symbols. (If not, immediately break out the help files and start using symbols.) Buttons are nothing more than symbols that can have mouse actions applied to them.

The word *button* conjures up a vision of a three-dimensional look and may not be appealing considering some of the horrible buttons that still prevail on the Web. But fear not, as there is nothing that says you must create a graphical, three-dimensional button. In fact, a button can be any object created in Flash or imported from a graphic program. Here, a *button* simply refers to an automated function that does much of the work for you to create various button states.

Buttons are created with imported images or constructed in Flash and activated with Action Scripting to form a button that shows a rollover effect and leads to a link. Creating your first button may be confusing, but after it all clicks into place, and you have wrapped your thinking around the individual pieces of the puzzle, it is instantly simple. (Flash is like that for most new techniques. That may be why those who get good have a hard time remembering how tough it was.)

Exercise: Creating Rollover Buttons in Flash

I kept this sample very simple so that you can focus on the concept of creating the rollover buttons. As you work along, though, remember that any graphic or text can be placed in the same way that you are using the simple elements. Don't stop with this sample. I strongly advise that you create several samples to establish the method and concept firmly in your mind. As soon as you have the concept and construction feeling like it is automatic, you have it forever.

On the CD-ROM Copy the `rollimages` folder from the Chapter 21 folder on the CD-ROM included with this book. A finished copy of the Flash file is also in the Chapter 21 folder, called `menutrial.fla`. As well, I include an HTML page with the menu placed. The file is called `rollhtml.html` and is also in the Chapter 21 folder. The Flash movie file, `menutrial.swf` is required to view the HTML page, so copy it to your computer with the `rollhtml.html` file.

Creating and placing buttons

To create rollover buttons in Flash, follow these steps:

1. Create a canvas, called a "stage" in Flash, that is 400 pixels by 200 pixels in size. You reduce the size of the canvas later, but it is easier to work with a large canvas. Save the file as **menutrial**.

2. Double-click on Layer 1 in the Timeline to activate the name-editing capability. Rename Layer 1 to **Base**. You place the background for the menu on this layer.

3. With the Base layer active, draw a rectangle with no stroke, filled with color #330033. This rectangle should be narrow, at least 20 pixels high, and stretching across the canvas. Don't worry about exact size right now, as you can resize the rectangle after you have placed your buttons.

   The next step is to create a button. When you elect to create a new button, you are taken to the button edit screen, which is blank. The button is created using this screen, and when you return to editing the movie, the completed button appears in the Library list. The next steps take you through the process, but I wanted you to know what you were doing as you proceed through the construction.

4. To set up a button, choose Insert ➪ New Symbol. The Symbol Properties window appears. Select Button for the Behavior and enter **Products button** in the Name field. This name will be the title for your button in the Library list when complete. Click OK to complete.

   You are now in the button-editing screen. Note that your rectangle is not visible and that the timeline at the top of the screen has changed to contain Layer 1 with space for Up, Over, Down, and Hit versions of the button. (See Figure 21-1.) The various button states are created using the timeline screen. *Up* is for your original image. *Over* will contain the view of the button that is shown when a mouse is passed over the button. *Down* is the view that will show when the button is clicked. *Hit* represents the area of the button that is active as a link. Normally, you have the full shape of the button included in this area. Hit is never shown as part of the rollover, and only the outer edges of the object contained in this frame are used to define the hit area.

   Tip The crosshairs in the center of the screen represent the center of the button and can be used to help you align the objects for each button state.

5. Choose File ➪ Import and select `products` from the `rollimages` folder that you copied from the CD-ROM at the beginning of this exercise. The image is automatically placed at the center of the button screen. Do not move the image from this location, as we will use that placement for the over image to ensure that the two images are aligned. You now have the Up state of your button in place.

6. If your Library panel is not already open, choose Window ➪ Library to open. You should have a products symbol, which was automatically placed into the Library as a symbol when you imported the image and a Products button entry (the button you are creating) in the list. Your screen should closely resemble the screen shown in Figure 21-1.

7. To place the image that forms the Over state for your button, highlight the Over frame in the timeline. Choose Insert ➪ Blank Keyframe *or* right-click the frame and select Insert Blank Keyframe *or* press F7 to insert a keyframe to contain your Over state. The canvas should be blank except for the positioning crosshairs.

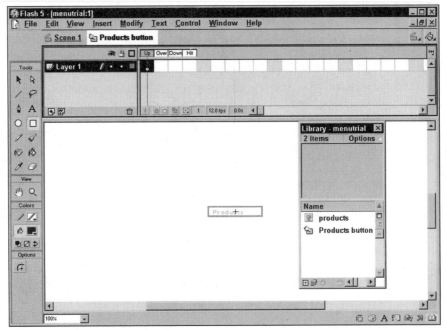

Figure 21-1: Up state for a Flash button in place. Note the button and symbol listing in the Library panel.

8. Choose File ➪ Import and choose `products-over` from the `rollimages` folder. This places the rollover version of your menu item in the button.

9. For the Down state, you duplicate the frame you created for the Over state. Highlight the Down frame in the timeline and choose Insert ➪ Keyframe *or* right-click the frame and select Insert Keyframe from the drop-down menu *or* press F6 to duplicate the previous frame.

10. Repeat Step 9, but highlight the Hit frame instead of the Down frame. This setting tells Flash that the active area for this button is the size of the image placed in this frame.

11. Choose Edit ➪ Movie, or Ctrl + E (Windows) or Command + E (Mac) to exit from the button-editing screen and return to the main canvas. Note that the Library now contains one button and two symbols.

12. To place the button on the rectangle, simply click and drag the Products button from the Library panel to the canvas. Position the button at the left edge of the rectangle, leaving a little margin as shown in Figure 21-2.

13. To quickly test your button, choose Control ➪ Enable Simple Buttons. The mouseover effect is displayed, as you can see in Figure 21-2. To return to editing your canvas, choose Control ➪ Enable Simple Buttons again to toggle the test setting off.

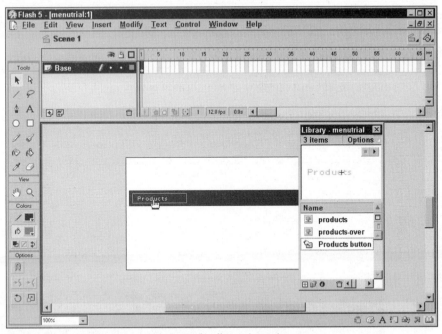

Figure 21-2: First button in place and rollover in action

Adding links to your menu

So far, you have created a great looking menu, complete with rollover action, but clicking the buttons will not lead anywhere. You must add the links to the buttons in order for the menu to work.

Note

The following instructions are for use in Macromedia Flash 5. You can choose the same commands in previous versions, but the route is a little different. Check your manual or download a trial version of Flash 5 at http://macromedia.com. This is a great upgrade from an interface standpoint, especially on the Action Scripting.

To add a link by using Action Scripting, follow these steps:

1. Open the Object Actions panel if it is not already open by choosing Window ➪ Action. With the Arrow tool, select the first button so that you can add the link action to it.

2. Click the + (plus) symbol at the top left of the Object Actions panel and choose Basic Actions ➪ On Mouse Event. The following code appears in the right window:

```
on (release) {
}
```

This code specifies that the action to follow should be invoked as the mouse is released after pressing. You still have one more step so don't leave this spot.

Tip   You can also choose to have the action (in this case, changing to the link page) occur with different mouse actions by deselecting the Release field at the bottom of the screen and choosing another mouse action.

3. Click the + (plus) symbol again and choose Basic Actions ➪ Get URL. Type **http://wpeck.com** (or any other URL) in the URL field at the bottom of the Object Actions panel. The right window should now contain the following code (wpeck.com is replaced by your own URL if you used another):

```
on (release) {
    getURL ("http://wpeck.com");
}
```

To translate: After the mouse is released, the browser is instructed to load http://wpeck.com into the browser window. (See Figure 21-3.)

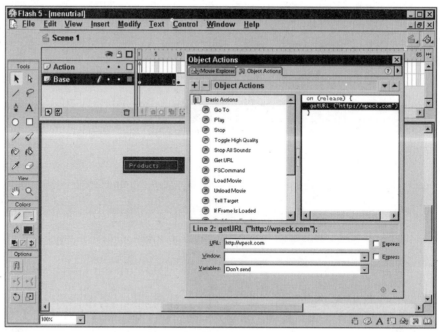

Figure 21-3: Adding a URL link to the button in Flash 5

4. Repeat Steps 2 through 4 for each of the four buttons, starting with the button you want to add the action to. You, of course, can use any URL.

5. You must also add a command to stop the menu from playing as if it is a menu. Insert a layer above the menu and label it **Action**. Highlight the first frame of the layer. In the Object Actions panel, click the + (plus) symbol and choose Basic Actions ⇨ Stop.

Testing and finishing your menu

Your menu is now functional. In order to use it in an HTML page, do the following:

1. To test your menu, choose Control ⇨ Test Movie. Your links should be active and load the specified URL into a browser window.

2. Reduce the size of the canvas to match the menu.

3. To finish, publish the Flash movie specifying Flash only in the settings. Place the Flash movie in your HTML document, and you have a fully functioning menu.

Tip

After you have the method mastered, specifying the desired final size of the menu as the movie size and using background color instead of a rectangle to set the color is much easier. You can then add your buttons in the same way as described on the smaller canvas. I find when I am learning Flash techniques that I like a lot of "breathing room," which is why I had you build this first menu on a larger canvas.

I can hear a few of you wondering why we worked so hard to create a look that you could get with HTML for a fraction of the effort. While that may be true, this menu would be right at home in a full-page Flash movie. Although this sample is plain, the concept behind it can be used to create effects you could never achieve with HTML and JavaScript. This is just the start.

One more attribute: This menu is very light in file size, even though we used images for the menu to overcome the small text weakness in Flash. And it is consistent. If the visitor can see the movie, you know that they will be seeing exactly what you created. There is some comfort in that.

However, this is just the start. Carry on to discover how you can stretch this technique to create menus that drop-down when the mouse passes over.

Exercise: Creating a Drop-down Menu in Flash

The menu you create in this exercise is a very simple example to introduce you to the concept of creating pieces of menus that disappear. The entire goal is to have an extension to the menu pop down when the mouse is rolled over a link and pop down over any other content that is in the area. Your visitors can then choose the most appropriate selection from the exposed list.

With this method, you cannot have the menus pop down over HTML content, because the movie must be large enough to contain the dropped areas as well as the initial menu. However, you can enter content in the area of the movie that will be used for the expanded menu. Of course, if you are building a full-screen Flash movie, the expanded menus can drop down over any content.

I want to stop and discuss how this sample is constructed before I move to the instructions. The visible part of the menu is built in a similar way to the rollover buttons created in the previous section. In addition, an extra layer is included to contain the content that is hidden until the mouse is passed over the visible content. Each button is controlled by a separate action in the timeline.

It may help to stop thinking about the timeline as you do when you are creating an animation. For this sample, time means nothing, and separation between frames is inserted only to simplify construction.

Creating buttons for a drop-down menu

To make the workload a little less daunting, you reuse the buttons that you created for the previous exercise.

Copy the folder dropimages from the Chapter 21 folder on the CD-ROM included with this book to your hard drive. If you have not already done so, copy the folder rollimages to your computer. If you did not do the previous exercise, or if you are not confident that the buttons are perfect, copy the file menutrial.fla to your hard drive.

To create a drop-down menu in Flash, follow these steps:

1. Create a new movie that is 400 pixels by 200 pixels in size. Save the file with the name **dropdown**.

2. To reuse the buttons from another document, choose File ➪ Open as Library and select menutrial.fla. This opens the Library panel with the symbols from the selected file.

3. Rename layer one as **Menu Background**. With the first frame in this layer active, draw a rectangle and fill it with color #330033.

4. Highlight frame 50 and select Insert Keyframe to place the menu background for the entire movie. (See Figure 21-4.)

5. Create a new layer and name it **Visible**. This layer holds the images for the main portion of the menu, the part that is always seen.

6. Create a new layer and name it **Hidden**. This layer holds the images for the drop-down portion of the menu.

7. Create a new layer and name it **Action/Label**. This layer holds the menu area labels, which you use to direct the action.

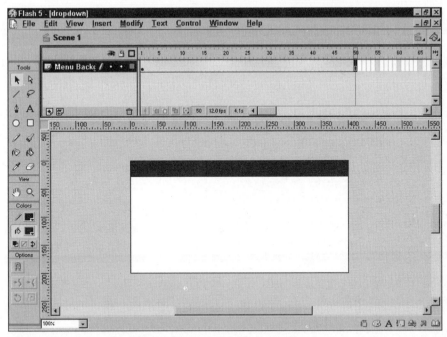

Figure 21-4: Menu background is set for the new movie.

8. With the layer Visible active, insert a blank keyframe in Frames 10, 20, 30, 40, and 50. Remember, do not think of elapsed time as you are creating this menu. You are simply creating areas to hold the individual menu button. Repeat for the layers Hidden and Action/Label.

9. With the Action/Label layer active, highlight the first frame. If the Frame panel is not open, choose Window ⇨ Frame to open. Type **Normal** in the Label field.

10. Repeat Step 9 to name frames 10, 20, 30, and 40, entering **Products**, **Services**, **Company**, and **Contact** respectively for the Label field.

11. To complete the work on this layer, highlight the first frame again. If the Frame Actions panel is not open, choose Window ⇨ Actions to open. Click the + (plus) symbol at the top left of the screen and choose Basic Actions ⇨ Stop. Repeat for frames 10, 20, 30, and 40. This entry is a safety element. Although the actions that you apply to the menu items should stop the movie from playing (remember, this menu is not run like a movie), it does not always. Your timeline should look like Figure 21-5.

12. With the layer Visible active, Highlight Frame 1 and drag the Product button from the Library panel to the canvas. Position it close to the left edge of the menu background. Repeat for Services button, Company button, and Contact button, arranging the buttons in the positions you desire.

Tip

Positioning the buttons for this exercise is much easier with guides. To use guides, choose View ⇨ Rulers and View ⇨ Guides (if a check mark is beside Guides, the Guides are already turned on). Click in the side ruler and drag to the location for a vertical guide. Click and drag in the top ruler to place a horizontal guide. To turn guides off, choose View ⇨ Guides again.

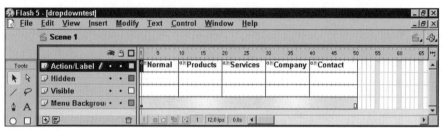

Figure 21-5: Labels and actions in place on the Label/Action layer

13. The images you placed in Step 12 must be placed at Frames 10, 20, 30, and 40 as well. Select all of the buttons with the arrow tool, and choose Edit ⇨ Copy *or* Ctrl + C (Windows)/Command + C (Mac). Highlight Frame 10 in the Visible layer, and choose Edit ⇨ Paste in Place. Repeat for Frames 20, 30, and 40. This completes the main menu positioning.

14. Following the instructions in Steps 5 through 12 of the previous exercise ("Creating Rollover Buttons in Flash/Creating and placing buttons"), create buttons with images listed as follows:

Note

All images are located in the `downimages` folder and are GIF files.

Button name	Up image	Over/Down/Hit image
Products 1 button	products1	products1-over
Products 2 button	products2	products2-over
Services 1 button	services1	services1-over
Services 2 button	services2	services2-over
Company 1 button	company1	company1-over
Company 2 button	company2	company2-over
Company 3 button	company3	company3-over
Contact 1 button	contact1	contact1-over
Contact 2 button	contact 2	contact2-over

The elements for your menu are now complete, and you move to placing the menu items that are hidden into the menu.

Caution

Pay close attention to the active layer and frame position as you create the hidden layer. The content must match up with the labels as we use the labels to invoke the correct images to drop down when the main menu item is clicked.

15. With the Hidden layer active, highlight Frame 10. Drag Products button 1 from the Library panel and position it directly below the Products menu item. Repeat for Products button 2, placing it below Product button 1.

16. Highlight Frame 20 and position the Services submenu items. Repeat for the Company and Contact menu items, placing them in Frames 30 and 40, respectively.

You have now completed the construction phase of the menu.

Adding action to your menu

The final phase of this exercise is to add the show and hide action for the content on the Hidden layer of the menu. You do this by adding action to the main menu buttons, action that sends the visitor to the correct place on the timeline to present the requested information. The following actions set the menu buttons to display the correct submenu after the button is clicked, and if the button is clicked again, to collapse the submenu.

To add action to your menu buttons, use the following method. The names I refer to are the labels from the Label/Actions layer.

1. Click in the Normal area of the Visible layer. On the canvas, deselect the selection by clicking in another area of the canvas and select the Products button.

2. If the Actions panel is not open, choose Window ➪ Actions to open. In the Actions panel, click the + (plus) symbol at the upper left of the panel, choose Basic Actions ➪ On Mouse Event, and make sure that Release is checked at the bottom of the panel.

3. Click the + (plus) symbol again and select Go To. At the bottom of the panel, click the Type field to open a selection menu and choose Frame Label. Type **Products** in the Frame field. Click Go To and play to uncheck. The code in the right side of the panel should be as follows:

```
on (release) {
    gotoAndStop ("Products");
}
```

4. Repeat Steps 1 through 3, but activate the Products area of the Visible layer and in the Actions panel, type **Normal** for the Frame field.

5. Repeat Steps 1 through 3 for the Services, Company, and Contact areas of the Visible layer. Type Products for the Frame field in the Actions panel for each area.

6. Continue adding the action to each button in each area with the following pattern. In the frame labeled with the same name as the button you are adding action to, use **Normal** as the Frame field value. In all other entries for that button, use the label that matches the button. For example, the Contact button will have gotoAndStop ("Contact") in all areas but the Contact frame label area, which will have gotoAndStop ("Normal").

7. Finally, you must add the link to each of the submenu items. Click the Products 1 button and click the + (plus) symbol in the Actions panel. Select On Mouse Action. Click the + (plus) symbol again and select Get URL. Type the URL you want to include or use http://wpeck.com in the URL field in the lower section of the panel. The code in the right window of the panel is as follows (the URL is different if you have used your own address):

```
on (release) {
    getURL ("http://wpeck.com");
}
```

8. Repeat Step 7 for each submenu item, changing the URL to the desired link for each button.

9. Reduce the movie size as much as possible, but making sure that the lowest part of the menu when expanded is included. Your screen should now look similar to the screen shown in Figure 21-6.

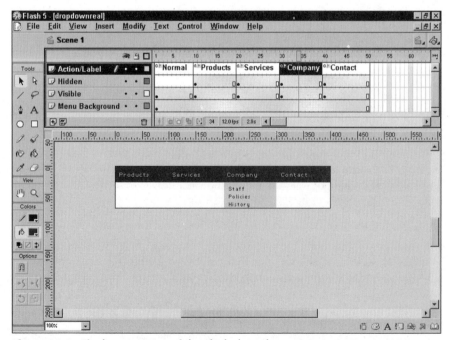

Figure 21-6: Final appearance of the Flash drop-down menu screen

10. To test your movie, choose Control ➭ Test Movie. Check to make sure that all links work and that the menu opens and collapses as you click the main menu items.

11. As soon as you are satisfied with your menu, publish it and place in an HTML file.

On the CD-ROM

A finished copy of the Flash document and an HTML page with the menu included is in the Chapter 21 folder on the CD-ROM that accompanies this book. The Flash document is named `dropdown.fla` and the HTML document is `dropdown.html`. The file `dropdown.swf`, in the same folder, is required for the HTML document to display the menu.

Using Flash to create menus may be a little confusing in the beginning, but after you have the menu working, go over each area and absorb what is happening. Click each button and check the Object Action panel to see the code that makes it work. If you can grasp the concept, there is no limit to the variety of menus you can create. You can include animation as a menu item, or make the layers slide in and out rather than just drop down. The secret is to grasp the concept and let your imagination go to discover unique ways to create exciting menus. Don't stop here!

Final Notes on Flash Menus

If Flash menus could drop menus over HTML content, designers the world over would probably be flocking to use the program, if only for menus. However, that is not the case, so any content savings must happen in Flash. With a little planning, however, you can incorporate some content in the movie, as shown in Figure 21-7. Note how the menu is dropping over the slogan in this example. The slogan is entered as a separate layer in Flash.

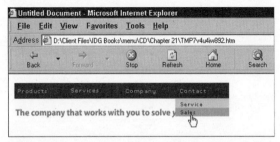

Figure 21-7: Content added to the Flash movie before publishing. The menus drop over any content in the Flash movie, saving space if you plan carefully.

Of course, if you are working within Flash exclusively, as with a full-page Flash presentation, you can have your menus drop over any content, making for very efficient menus.

If you are careful with your type and use a graphics program to create small type, Flash menus look as good as other menu types and provide an extra option for menus, especially if you want to include any animation (such as a glowing light bulb as one example).

I recommend that you have a good grasp on publishing and HTML inclusion code for Flash if you are going to be creating Flash menus for HTML pages. Don't ever forget that you are creating the backbone of your site when you build a menu. If your menu does not work, or does not work properly and consistently, you have wasted every bit of time you put into your site.

✦   ✦   ✦

Lights, Camera, Action! Time to Create the Show

Mouse Moves: Creating Simple and Complex Rollovers and Image Maps

In this chapter, you add some motion clues for the visitors to your Web pages: rollovers and image maps. While rollovers and image maps provide links to follow, they also add visual clues as an action spot on the page. Bells and whistles have come and gone, but the ones that improve visitor experience tend to linger. Navigation clues earn their download time many times over, and you look at three types in this chapter: simple rollovers, complex rollovers, and image maps. All three techniques can help to guide your visitors in different situations.

Showing 'Em You're Alive

When you think of action on a page, I bet that you do not even consider rollovers to be part of that class. They are, however. When a visitor holds his or her mouse over a menu item, what's the clue that it is a link and not just a pretty picture delivering words? The clue is that the image changes and that change has become a universal symbol for action on the Web. As designers, we are smart to capitalize on that common knowledge and provide the action clue. However, as for all facets in Web design, you have many issues to consider before you can create great rollovers.

What is a rollover?

A *rollover* is a simple exchange of images. Simple JavaScript is used to tell the browser to display one image when the page is loaded and also to load an image that is not yet visible. The script reacts when a mouse is passed over the original image and flips the preloaded image onto the screen, creating what we call a rollover (also known as a *mouseover*). Most scripts also bring the original image back to the screen if the mouse is removed. If the image is not preloaded, many visitors will never see the effect, as the browser would have to load the image and then display it while the mouse was in place. The original image is returned to prevent confusion as to which link the visitor is about to activate. All navigational rollovers also have a link added, so that when visitors click the link, they are taken to the page represented by that menu item. Figure 22-1 shows a color change rollover effect on the Web site, Diamonds.com (`www.diamonds.com`).

Figure 22-1: Holding the mouse over an image changes the color of the menu item and tells visitors that the area is a link.

Caution   Occasionally, Web designers use rollovers as a novelty to illustrate a process, or just to add a cool effect. I do not recommend doing this though, as it is confusing to visitors. When visitors see a change on a mouseover, they expect a link.

Designing Rollovers

Rollovers are often seen as a design element, but — here I go again, the graphic artist abandoning the design focus for communication — rollovers are primarily used for navigation, not a major part of the page design. Of course, it is always best if effective navigation looks great, but the important factor is that your visitors know instantly that they are holding their mouse over a link.

File size is vitally important for rollover images. Generally the original, or normal state of a link, and the rollover state are similar in regard to the size of the files. Increase the file size of one image and the added size is doubled, because you require two similar images to create the effect. In some cases, there are three or four states to a rollover, with all images preloaded for effective action on the page. Suppose you have six menu items with three states on a page. That totals 18 images for the menu alone. It makes a big difference if each image is 10K as opposed to 5K.

Note   Although there are no "official" Web standards, it is generally accepted that the ideal Web page does not exceed 45K.

So, you want to make the rollovers look good and keep the file size down, but the most important aspect of a rollover is that the visitor "gets it." This is not the place for a subtle one-shade shift in color or a light drop shadow effect on a dark background. The power of rollovers comes in guiding your visitor to where they are going without making them think. Make your rollover image stand out so that there is absolutely no doubt what will happen if they click in that spot.

Caution   Please don't play hide the menu. Yes, a page with nothing but design elements is very pretty and clean, but unless you are offering a page that demands mystery, leave the "guess where the menu is" game to personal sites. I am talking about a site where the visitor does not know there is a link anywhere until they set their mouse on a mission, seeking the "magic" spot. I have left sites when I encounter this type of navigation. In my opinion, if the designer does not respect my time enough to provide obvious links through the site, I am not at all motivated to find out what is there.

On the other hand, you don't have to scream at your visitor. As long as there is a noticeable shift in color, dimension, or some other parameter, the effect works.

Tip   Keep your code clean. Rollovers, pre-loading, and returning original images when the mouse is removed take a lot of code to complete, even when it is perfect. When you make changes, especially if using an editor, such as Macromedia Dreamweaver or Adobe GoLive, leaving redundant code behind is easy. Being vigilant and keeping your code clean is always important, but when you are working with a lot of code, especially when it is on every single page in your site, perfection is in order.

Using Special Effects for Rollovers

Occasionally, you may want to add extra impact to your rollovers. Instead of using a static image to static image rollover, you can use an animated GIF file for one or both of the rollover states. You may also want to have the rollover effect show in a different spot than the rollover. These special effects can add a lot to the page, but should be used judiciously.

Using animated GIF files for rollovers

An animated GIF file can be used anywhere a GIF or JPG file is used, including as rollover elements. You can use an animated GIF file as the normal state, the over state, or both. Email Beyond features a gentle animated rollover on the interior pages (`http://emailbeyond.com/faq.html`). When the mouse is passed over the link, a small ball bounces above that menu item.

Keep in mind, however, that this effect is appropriate for a site directed to young people, and it reflects the fun nature of the site. Always be cautious when adding special effects to any commercial page. A bouncing ball may not inspire confidence on a financial site. Also, some animated GIF files are large. This simple little ball image adds very little to the size of the page.

To add this effect to your pages, simply specify an animated GIF file as the desired image for the normal or rollover image.

Creating complex rollovers

In the previous section you learned about *simple rollovers*: when one image changes for another in the same place. You can also use JavaScript to change both the original image in the original location, plus change an image somewhere else on the page. I have seen this technique called a *double rollover* or a *disjointed rollover*. The most common term I have seen and the one I use is *complex rollover*.

Complex rollovers can be used for extra communication with your visitors. The change in the original image lets the visitor know that there is a link, but an extra image change can guide them to more information about that link. One of the most common setups for a complex rollover is to have a blank or common image change to text or another image that provides an extra guide to the contents.

The cautions and methods described for simple rollovers all hold for complex rollovers, but multiplied. Because you have two images changing at the same time, you certainly do not want to overload your visitor's senses and you want to be especially careful with file size. You are now loading two original images and pre-loading at least two images for every link. It is easy to see how page size can balloon if you are not careful.

Image Maps: Simple and Well-Behaved

Image maps are created from a single image. Action is added to the image by specifying that certain areas, defined by coordinates, contain links. Although image maps are not used as much as rollovers, there are places where they can provide valuable links without the extra download time and page structure required for individual rollovers.

An image map is simply added to an image, so anywhere an image can be placed, an image map can be added. Image maps are also the most browser compatible of all graphic links, working well in all browsers as far back as Netscape and Internet Explorer version 3.

You can create menus from image maps. However, unless you have a compatibility or high download time issue to address, main menus are best with rollover clues for visitors. Image maps are perfect for auxiliary menus, such as the one shown in Figure 22-2. Image maps are also the method you require to present a graphic link choice, such as clicking an area of a map to see information for that area.

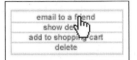

Figure 22-2: Image maps do not have a rollover clue for the visitor, but the hand symbol, as shown here on an image map from Diamonds.com, is usually enough indication that a link exists.

You will probably find that you do not use image maps as often as you use rollover images, but when you are looking for a simple graphic link to help direct visitors in a visual way, keep image maps in mind. They are simple to create, light on download weight, and display reliably no matter what browser displays your pages.

Exercise: Creating a JavaScript Rollover in Dreamweaver

The entire subject of JavaScript, much of which is used to create a rollover effect, is beyond the scope of this book. If you are not familiar with this powerful scripting tool, I recommend that you pick up a basic book to at least gain a working knowledge of how JavaScript operates. Several Web sites provide excellent basic and advanced JavaScript tutorials. You may want to check out Doc JavaScript at WebReference.com (http://webreference.com/js) or JavaScript.com (http://javascript.com).

Note HTML editors, such as Dreamweaver, can make short work of rollovers. The following instructions are specifically for Dreamweaver.

To create a rollover, Dreamweaver generates three sections of code, placing JavaScript into the document head, into the <body> tag, and also into the document body where the rollover is to be placed. Check your code before you place the rollover so that you can view the change.

On the CD-ROM Copy the images folder from the Chapter 22 folder on the CD-ROM to your hard drive.

To create a JavaScript rollover in Dreamweaver, follow these steps:

1. Create a new document in Dreamweaver and name it **rollover.html**.

2. Insert your cursor in the document. Choose Insert ⇨ Interactive Images ⇨ Rollover Image and the Insert Rollover Image window opens.

3. Type **home** for the Image Name value.

4. Click the Browse button next to the Original Image field. Select the file, home.gif, from the images folder. The image that you specify in this field is seen before the mouse is passed over it.

5. Click the Browse button next to the Rollover Image field. Select the file, home-over.gif, from the images folder.

Caution Never use images of different sizes for rollover images. The original and the rollover image must be the same size. Also, be careful that the elements in your original and rollover graphics line up when preparing rollovers. A 1-pixel difference when positioning the two images can cause a distinct jump as the images change, an effect that can be quite disturbing.

6. Verify that the Preload Rollover Image option is checked. This prompts the browser to load the rollover image into the browser cache when the page is viewed. When the mouse is passed over the rollover image, a preloaded image displays instantly.

7. Add the link for this menu item. You can browse for a file to link to this page, or enter a URL. If you do not have a link to add, type **http://wpeck.com**. This creates a link to my Web site.

8. Click OK to return to the document. Press Shift and your Enter key to place a <br> tag to separate this menu item from the next.

   The menu item continues to resemble a simple graphic link, even when you roll your mouse over the item. Dreamweaver does not display live JavaScript. To see the results, preview your document in a browser.

9. Preview the document in your primary browser. Move your mouse over the top menu item and the image should change. Preview the document again in your secondary browser to ensure that your rollover is working in both.

10. Repeat Steps 2 through 9 for the other menu items on the page, changing the details for each menu item, placing menu items in the following order: Company, Services, and Contact. The rollover images have the same name as the original with the addition of the word "over." For example, if company.gif is the original file, then company-over.gif is the rollover image. Your completed page should closely resemble the previewed image shown in Figure 22-3.

That's all there is to creating a simple rollover. It is almost as quick and easy as creating a simple graphic menu link, but it does add a lot to your page.

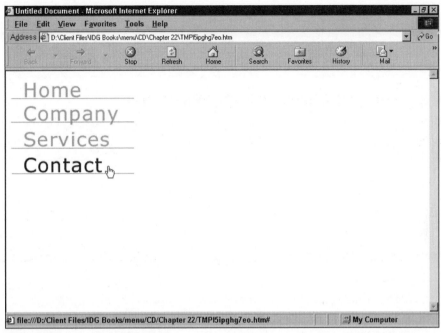

Figure 22-3: Completed rollover menu created in Dreamweaver and previewed in Internet Explorer 5.5

Exercise: Creating a Complex Rollover in Dreamweaver

The rollover is becoming increasingly popular and with good reason. When you roll your mouse over one image, another image in a different location appears. When used properly, a lot of visual information is presented in a small space.

Using the Behaviors palette in Dreamweaver accomplishes this task. Instructing Dreamweaver to write the code step-by-step is more involved than placing code from another source, or using the menu to create a simple rollover.

This process can be very confusing, but as soon as you get the concept, it is easy. I designed a very simple menu for simple explanation and construction. The menu items have names to help you track what is happening and grasp the concept. You can view the finished menu, `complex.html`, located in the Chapter 22/images2 folder on the CD-ROM that accompanies this book.

On the CD-ROM For this exercise, copy the Chapter 22/images2 folder to your hard drive. Even if you do not use Dreamweaver, you can still follow the code used to create this effect. The completed document for this exercise is in the Chapter 22/images2 folder and is named `complex.html`.

Preparing to create a complex rollover

This exercise is divided into two parts. First, you prepare the initial menu by placing images and naming the images you place. This step is very important. After you prepared the entire menu, you add the behaviors that run your rollovers.

To prepare your menu for a complex rollover, follow these steps:

1. Create a new document in Dreamweaver and save it as **complexrollover.html**.

2. Create a table with one row and two columns and the following parameters: Cellpadding 10, Cellspacing 0, 500 pixels wide, and Border 0. You place your menu titles in the cells in the left column with your extra rollover image in the right column.

3. Place the image, `wine.gif`, in the left column.

4. Name your images so that JavaScript understands which images to change. Click the image you just placed to select it. In the Properties Inspector, type **wine** in the Name field of the Property Inspector.

5. Create a "dummy" or, more precisely, a "null" link, because the behavior must be attached to a link. Type **#** into the Link field in the Properties Inspector.

Note If you are creating a rollover that links to another page, as you would expect for this menu, you can create the correct link now or return at a later time to enter the correct link. Because you are just doing an exercise here, you need not worry about creating the links. When you create the menu for the next site you build, you can create complex rollovers with working links.

6. Repeat Steps 3, 4, and 5 to place the three remaining menu images. Each is separated by a `<br>` tag. The second menu image is `salad.gif` and should be named **salad**. The next menu image is named `entree.gif` and should be named **entree**. The bottom menu image is named `dessert.gif` and should be named **dessert**.

7. You also need to place an image in the right column. When the mouse does not activate menu items, the original image in this column is displayed. In this case, place a blank image to hold the place for the rollovers. Place the image `blank.gif` in the right column and type **blank** in the Name field.

Tip Although the images in this exercise are very close to one another, an image can be placed anywhere on your page. However, ensure that images affected by the mouse action are noticed. If you place them too far from where the visitor is focused, the effect may be lost.

Attaching behaviors to the images

You are now ready to add the JavaScript to this image and create a double rollover. Each of the menu items on the left has two separate rollovers added to them. The image you just placed in the right column is used only to receive the images called with the menu images when the mouse rolls over it.

To add behaviors to our images follow these steps:

1. Open the Behaviors palette, if it is not already open.

2. Select the wine menu image you created in the first part of this exercise. Now add behaviors to change the menu item image and also place an image where the blank image currently resides. Both actions are included in one behavior.

3. Click + (add) in the Behaviors palette to add a behavior. Choose Swap Image from the menu that appears. The Swap Image window opens.

4. Add a behavior to change your menu item to a different image when the mouse is held over the image. In the Images section of the Swap Image window, the entry image "wine" should be highlighted. Remember that "wine" was the name of the first menu item. Click the Set Source To "browse" button. Select the file, `wine-over.gif` from the listing in the Select Image Source window. Click Select to close this window and accept the file. *Do not click OK in the Swap Image window yet.* You have only completed half of the rollover so far.

5. Complete this behavior by replacing the blank image with the image that should display with the top menu item. In the Images listing of the Swap Image window, select "blank."

Note   Don't worry—the changes you made to "wine" are still there, even though you cannot see them. To confirm, simply click that image name again in the list to view the Set Source To field that contains the instructions you just completed.

6. With "blank" selected, browse for the image, `wineimage.jpg`. Highlight the file, and click Select to return to the Swap Image window. Now click OK, because you have done what you needed with that image.

7. Preview your rollover in your browser. When the mouse passes over the top menu item, the words turn to black, and an image appears to the right. If you are getting that result, you have created the behavior correctly and can move to the next menu item.

8. Repeat Steps 2 through 7 to complete the menu. The over and extra rollover images all follow the same naming pattern. One view of the finished document is shown in Figure 22-4.

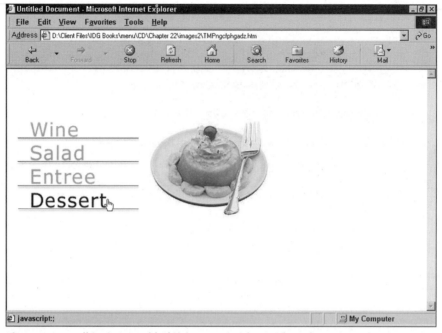

Figure 22-4: All images and behaviors are in place. When the mouse passes over the dessert menu item, the title is replaced with black characters and the blank image changes to the placed dessert image.

Note   Your document is exploding with code. See if you can trace which section of the code is performing which part of the action. It is all there for you to view, and if you follow it bit by bit, much of it makes sense.

If you are still a little uncertain about how to do this exercise, I recommend you start again from scratch. This technique may seem confusing until you have a "Eureka! I get it" moment. As soon as you understand how this menu works, you are well set to create your own and to apply other behaviors.

✦   ✦   ✦

Building DHTML Drop-Down Menus with Text and Graphics

Dynamic Hypertext Markup Language (DHTML) is a lofty term for a simple markup language used to facilitate movement on Web pages. After you understand HTML and how it works, DHTML is not much more complicated. Yet, DHTML has a reputation as an "experts only" technique. Some of the reputation is deserved, as DHTML is often combined with JavaScript to create special effects, such as drop-down menus and animation. However, when approached in a step-by-step manner, the construction of DHTML pages is quite logical. The tough part of DHTML is the lack of standards in the way that browsers display DHTML effects.

In this chapter, I offer an overview of how DHTML works, information about where it can be applied, and hopefully give you a clear picture of its basic principles. I also look at common browser compatibility problems. However, if you are interested in using DHTML for menus, I strongly advise that you use the information in this chapter only as a base for further learning. (If you are working on intranets, for example, you should look seriously at learning DHTML methods.) This is a complex subject that I cannot do justice in only a few pages.

In order to cover the most popular use of DHTML (creating drop-down menus (in the most productive way, I guide you through setting up a brilliant script produced and perfected by my fellow columnist at WebReference.com, Peter Belesis. This script has been developed and perfected for over a year.

If you are curious about DHTML menus, working with this script can get you up and running quickly. If you are deadly serious about learning DTHML from the ground up, I can think of no better training ground than this script and the series of in-depth tutorials that go along with it.

What Is DHTML?

Most basic HTML pages are created using tables for layout. If you require a three-column layout for the page, you create a three-column table and place content in the appropriate table column and row.

DHTML, however, offers an entirely new way to work. By placing content on named layers and adding CSS (cascading style sheets) positioning, you position content on independent sections. This method of placing content allows great flexibility in page design. Adding JavaScript to the mix allows you to move layers when a mouse action takes place. To understand the concept, you must first understand DHTML components and what each does.

DHTML components

DHTML is not actually one scripting language. It is used to describe the method when HTML, CSS, and JavaScript are used together to create a page with layers and movement. I can remember being very confused as I was searching for a primer for DHTML, or a tag chart as I had for HTML. As soon as it clicked in my brain that DHTML was a combination of many techniques, the way was clear to understand how DHTML works, which led to understanding how to create pages using this powerful method. To help you separate the pieces, I will step through each component separately.

Layers

Pages created with layers work in a totally different way from table-based layouts. The content at the right of the page can be completely separated from the content at the left of the page if the content for each section is created on a layer. Picture a piece of paper with a square drawn on it, and another with a circle. Now imagine moving the two pictures around a table. Moving one does not affect the other, and you can place either of them anywhere you want to have them. Layers can be positioned in much the same way as two separate pieces of paper and overcome many of the restrictions that HTML places on page design.

Layers work much the same in DHTML as they do in graphics programs. Content that is stored on one layer does not affect content on any other layer. You can move layers in front or behind one another and place more than one object on each layer. In fact, each layer behaves much like an independent HTML page. You can see the power of layers in Figure 23-1 and Figure 23-2.

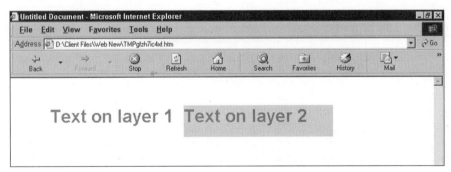

Figure 23-1: This is a typical layout for Web content, easily accomplished with a table-based layout.

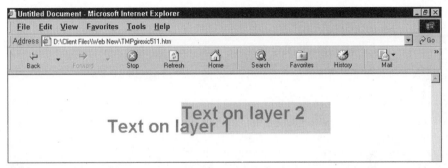

Figure 23-2: Using layers, you can position content in any place including overlapping another layer.

Caution When I use the word *layer*, there is a good chance that it can be mistaken for the Netscape Navigator specific tag, `<layer>`. However, as that tag is rarely used and the word layer is the perfect description for how DHTML content is organized, I am using the term layer in its generic form. The `<div>` tag is a much more flexible way to define layers for DHTML.

What good are layers?

Layers and DHTML can be buggy. How can they be so popular if they are so hard to control? Intranets offer one clue. You see the Web, and you can understand the growth in this world, but intranets also have become extremely popular tools for large businesses and organizations to share information and resources. Intranets are a controlled environment. The designer often knows which browsers or platform site visitors will use. If I were working in a controlled intranet environment, I would work exclusively with layers.

Others working with an HTML editor, such as Macromedia Dreamweaver, use layers to create a layout and then convert the layers into tables. The construction method is easy, usually a matter of clicking and dragging an area, as shown in Figure 23-3.

I would like to offer an extra caution on this method, however. Tables will display, even in older browsers. However, you must construct tables very carefully to avoid surprises in many browsers. Creating your page in layers does not remove that requirement. After you convert layers to tables, you still must have very clean work and a layout that fits into the table format, which takes away many of the benefits of working with layers.

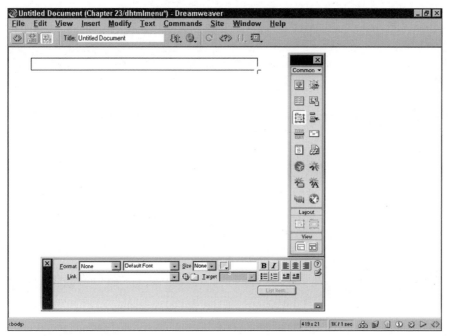

Figure 23-3: Creating a layer in Dreamweaver is a click and drag operation.

So why teach — and more importantly to you — why learn layers? You may be interested in intranet design. That is reason enough. Some people are just more comfortable with the layers concept for construction. That is reason enough, as long as the work is done with tables in mind while you work. But the biggest reason of all is that the day will come when you can freely use layers. Every month that passes takes us closer to the day when there are few disadvantages and many advantages to working with layers. You may already be designing for a target group that is likely to have only the most modern browsers, and you may be willing to go through the extensive debugging process required even for a specific Web group. Layers should not be ignored.

CSS

Alone, a layer has no power. The browser must know where to display the content that is included on a layer. CSS positioning is used to arrange the layers on the page. Although a lot of code is required to set the position, it is all quite logical.

Take a look at the code that follows, and you can no doubt follow the coordinates setting the position for the layers.

```
<div id="Layer1" style="position:absolute; left:182px;
top:73px; width:235px; height:45px; z-index:2">
  <h1><font face="Arial, Helvetica, sans-serif"
color="#666666">Text on layer 1</font></h1>
</div>
```

This code produced the text with no background color shown previously in Figure 23-2. The code starting with `<div>` and ending with `</div>` is the full layer code. The portion of this sample starting with `<h1>` and ending with `</h1>` is the content code. (The reference to z-index is the layering position of the layer in relation to other layers, in other words, in front of or behind other layers.)

Caution   CSS is powerful, but remember the warnings you heard about using CSS for text only (see Chapter 9). It is no better for positioning. Not all browsers support every command. *Buggy* is the word you often hear associated with layers and CSS. You can create a document using layers and CSS, and it will go together very quickly. In addition, layers offer routes around much of what frustrates us when working with tables. The tricky part is getting it to display on a variety of browsers.

JavaScript

With your layer created and positioned, you have the basic tools to make your content move on the page. Add a little JavaScript to tell a specific layer to behave in a certain way when the mouse passes over or is clicked, and you have DHTML on your page. DHTML can be used to create animation and special effects, but for this book, we are only concerned with the most menu friendly application for DHTML: drop-down menus.

I'm sure you've seen the menus that are nice and tidy, tucked into a small space . . . until you pass your mouse over one of the links. This mouse action causes more menu choices to drop down over the content on the page. From a screen real estate and effective navigation standpoint, there is no better way to create a menu.

JavaScript is used to make layers visible and invisible when creating menus. When the mouse passes over a link, JavaScript instructs the original layer, usually with nothing on it, to change to a layer with menu options listed. When the mouse moves off the link, the original, blank layer is returned to the screen.

Such a simple concept, yet addressing display issues in every browser is so complex. Again, at the risk of sounding like a broken record, I have to caution you that this chapter will not give you the tools to be fully functional for any aspect of DHTML menus. This discussion should be treated as an introduction and explanation of the techniques so that you can decide if you want to explore more in this field. Hopefully, working through the example later in the chapter will inspire you to learn more.

How Safe Is DHTML?

As powerful as DHTML drop-down menus are, always keep in mind that DHTML does not work in any browser before version 3, is unpredictable at best for version 4 browsers, and requires plenty of troubleshooting to guarantee display in every current browser version.

I recently asked a well-respected designer, who makes her living almost exclusively designing with DHTML, whether we had reached the point that we could use DHTML safely for the general population. Her response was: "Use DHTML only for tasks that are not mission critical."

That leaves us with a terrible dilemma. A major goal for any site is to provide easy access to any page on the site. DHTML drop-down menus are the absolute best answer. But menus are the most "mission critical" portion of any site, so according to the most knowledgeable expert I know, menus are a risky use for DHTML methods.

There are compromises. You can create an elaborate browser sniffer and create separate JavaScript files for each browser. As a simple solution, ensure that visitors can click on the original link, even if the drop-down portion does not work. They then go to a special page that presents the options in a more compatible form. Most of your visitors will be able to use the advanced capability, but those who cannot use them will still be able to navigate your site.

Cross-browser issues with DHTML

I guess by now you are getting the idea that I am a little nervous about DHTML for the general Web population. I admit that I am a stickler for creating pages that are available to whomever may visit your pages. But even those who are less adamant about the subject will agree that DHTML brings out the worst in our current lack of standards.

Not only are there Netscape versus Internet Explorer issues, but there are also many between different versions of Explorer and dramatic variations between Mac and PC display for the same browser and version. You saw just a glimpse of the differences in Chapter 9 when Netscape and Explorer displayed different bullets and Netscape failed to recognize CSS commands for mouseovers.

Tip   One of the best resources on the Web for DHTML and browser issues is the DHTML Lab at WebReference.com (http://webreference.com/dhtml). Peter Belesis has worked for over a year creating a truly cross-browser compatible drop-down menu, and he has shared his knowledge and research every step of the way. If you want the freedom to build truly functional, compatible menus using DHTML, you owe it to yourself to follow along the building of this menu. This site will not give you cut-and-paste solutions, but if you want to learn to do your own menus, there is no better site.

You have a choice with DHTML for menus and browser compatibility. Menus that will work in Internet Explorer are extremely easy to create. However, unless you are designing for a very controlled intranet site, this is not a good solution. Menus can be created using DHTML that are very compatible with most modern browsers, but you are pushing into advanced CSS and JavaScript functions in order to create the menus. The latter choice is obviously the best overall, as you learn the techniques as you create the menus. And while the learning curve is steep, the reward is a menu you can use with confidence.

Caution

Always remember that a menu is the heart of your site. If you are using menus that even a few visitors cannot see, make sure that you provide another option for them. You should always add text menus to the bottom of your page. For smaller sites, consider adding JavaScript to your page to detect the visitor's browser, and direct those who cannot access the more complex menus to another set of pages with simple rollovers or text menus. You will have to create a second version of your page, but by using SSI (see Chapter 10) to automate changes, you can make the double system manageable.

As an in-between measure, there are scripts now available, both free and as a paid product that can be cut and pasted into your documents and customized with your information. These scripts can be a great way to add the drop-down menus to your site, but I strongly recommend that you do not blindly cut and paste. Testing is exceptionally important for any DHTML function, especially when you are placing code you do not understand.

Exercise: Creating a Simple DHTML Menu in Dreamweaver for IE 4+

The exercise I feature here creates a menu that works only in Internet Explorer, version 4 and above, which severely restricts where you can use this method. It is an excellent way to understand the basics of how layers are created, shown and hidden. After you understand the basics of this method, you will be better prepared to move ahead to methods that are more compatible across browsers, but using more complicated coding to turn layer visibility on and off.

To create a simple menu in Dreamweaver, you must first create the menu elements in layers.

On the CD-ROM

Copy the file menucss.css from the Chapter 23 folder on the CD-ROM that accompanies this book to your hard drive. A copy of the completed document for this exercise is also in the same folder. The file name is dhtmlmenudone.html.

1. Create a new document and name it **dhtmlmenu.html**.

2. If it is not already open, open the Objects panel by choosing Window ➪ Objects. Activate the Draw Layer tool.

3. Drag over a rectangular area to create a new layer, as shown earlier in Figure 23-3. In the Properties Inspector, type **menu** into the Layer ID field.

4. Using the Properties Inspector with the layer you just drew active, select color #CCCCCC for the background color.

5. Attach the CSS file to the document. Choose Text ⇨ CSS Styles ⇨ Attach Style Sheet. Select the file `menucss.css`, the file that you copied from the CD-ROM and click Select.

Note

This CSS file contains margin specifications that place margins between the layer edges and the text.

6. Insert your cursor into the new layer and type **menu 1 | menu 2 | menu 3 | menu 4**. Add a null link (#) to each individual menu item, being careful not to include the | character in the links.

Note

The null link is necessary to add behaviors to the menu. Specify center justification for the text.

7. Create a new layer directly below the first menu item, as shown in Figure 23-4. Name the layer **sub1**, and assign a background color of #CCCCCC. Type the following in the layer, and assign a link to each entry:

sub 1a

sub 1b

sub 1c

I use a link to `http://wpeck.com` for these links instead of a null link. You can use any URL for this link or simply assign a null link.

Test your document in Internet Explorer and you will see that the layer with the submenu is overlapping the main menu. You can set the submenu layer to display behind the main menu layer by adjusting the z value for each layer. The z value sets the order the layers will display with the highest numbers representing the layer at the top of the stack.

8. Select the submenu layer (sub1) and specify 2 for the Z-index value. Select the main menu layer (menu) and specify 3 for the Z-index value. The main menu layer now always displays on top of the submenu layer, and both layers display on top of any layer with a lower number.

9. Repeat Step 7 to create a new layer directly under the second menu item and each of the remaining two menu items. Label the layers **sub2**, **sub3**, and **sub4**, respectively. Set the background color to #CCCCCC. Type and create links as for the first submenu layers, substituting the correct number to match the submenu to the correct main menu item. Assign a Z-index value of 3 to each of the new submenu layers. (The submenus are never seen at the same time, so overlaps won't show.) Your screen should resemble the screen shown in Figure 23-5.

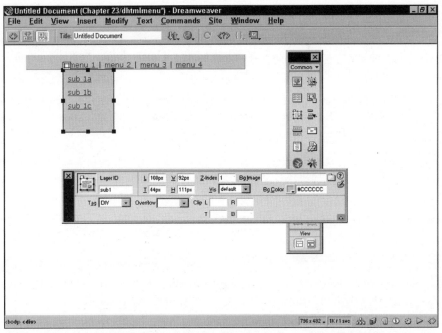

Figure 23-4: The selected layer forms the first drop-down menu element.

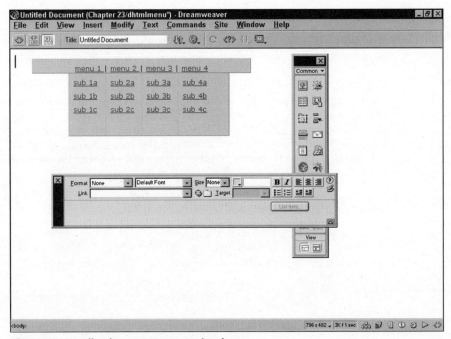

Figure 23-5: All submenus are now in place.

Tip   Use the W (width) and H (height) value in the Properties Inspector to create all submenus with an identical size. You can type the size values right into the Properties Inspector rather than trying to draw precise sizing. You may also find it easier to create each layer away from the main menu and to move it into place after it is perfect.

With your layers all in place, you can move on to adding the scripts that will make your layers behave like a drop-down menu. Make sure your layers are as you want them to be, because you are about to hide the layers, which makes editing cumbersome.

You add the JavaScript to your main menu items using Dreamweaver behaviors as follows:

1. Highlight the "menu1" menu item from the main menu. The JavaScript command is added to this link to make the sub1 layer drop down when the link is clicked.

2. If it is not already open, open the Behaviors panel by choosing Window ➪ Behaviors. Click the + symbol, and choose Show Hide Layers from the drop-down menu. The Show/Hide Layers window opens.

3. Select layer "sub1" from the list and click the Show button. This command tells the browser that after the link is clicked, it is to show the layer called sub1.

Note   If you are thinking ahead, you will have noticed that the submenu layers are currently visible and are confused that we are stating that the JavaScript should make the layer visible. You turn off the visibility for the sub-layers after you have added all of the Behaviors. With the sub-layers invisible, the JavaScript makes sense.

You want the visible sub-layer to become invisible again if the visitor clicks elsewhere on the page. If you did not add another command, the menus would remain visible after they were clicked. You make the layer invisible by using the onBlur event handler, which is not a default option in the Dreamweaver behavior list. To keep this lesson simple and focussed on hiding and showing the layers, I have chosen to use the onMouseOver event handler as a placeholder and substitute onBlur by hand.

4. In the Behaviors panel, click the + symbol and select Show/Hide Layers. Select layer "sub1" from the list, and click the Hide button.

5. With the new entry still selected, click the arrow between the Events and Actions columns in the Behaviors panel, and select OnMouseOver from the drop-down menu. The Behaviors panel should look like the panel shown in Figure 23-6.

Figure 23-6: JavaScript is added to show the submenu when the link is clicked. The onMouseOver entry is a placeholder that is changed in the next step.

6. Change to a code view and locate the following code:

```
onMouseOver="MM_showHideLayers('sub1','','hide')
```

Change `onMouseOver` to `onBlur`. Your code now looks like this:

```
onBlur="MM_showHideLayers('sub1','','hide')
```

Your Behaviors panel should look like the panel shown in Figure 23-7.

Figure 23-7: The `onMouseOver` entry is replaced by `onBlur`, which makes the submenu layer invisible as soon as the mouse is clicked anywhere outside the link.

7. Repeat Steps 1-6 for each of the remaining menu links, selecting to show or hide the respective sub-layers, respectively.

Although the layers that should be invisible are still visible, you can test your menu before committing to making the normal state for the sub-menus invisible. Preview the document in Internet Explorer, click each of the main menu links, and then click off. Clicking off should make the layer hidden, and after all sub-layers are invisible, the menu behaves exactly as it will on completion.

8. As soon as you are satisfied that your menu is working correctly, you can hide the sub-layers for the normal view. Click the sub1 layer and select Hidden from the drop-down selector. The layer disappears from the screen. Repeat for each submenu layer.

And that's it. Test your menu in Internet Explorer. You can add another layer with any content in the same area as the drop-down submenus, and the menus will drop down over that content as long as the layer has a Z-index value lower than the submenu values. The completed document, with the extra content layer added to illustrate the drop-down effect, is shown in Figure 23-8.

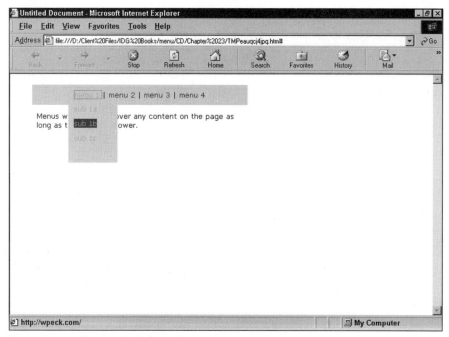

Figure 23-8: The finished drop-down menu in action.

Don't stop here. Remember this menu works only in Internet Explorer. But when you consider that you can place text or images and use percentages for layer sizes if you prefer, the possibilities are endless. Now that you have a grasp of the idea behind layers appearing and disappearing, the more complicated methods that provide cross-browser compatibility will not seem overwhelming. DHTML is well worth the time required to learn.

> **Tip**   An excellent series of basic DHTML tutorials is at Webmonkey, a well-known developer site. The tutorial contains five lessons and ends with a DHTML menu tutorial. (`http://hotwired.lycos.com/webmonkey/authoring/dynamic_html/ tutorials/tutorial1.html`.) You can also find a wealth of browser specific information straight from the browser creators. (Netscape: `http://developer. netscape.com`. Internet Explorer: `http://msdn.microsoft.com`.)

✦   ✦   ✦

Creating Jump Menus and Customized Forms

*J*ump menus are often also called *drop-down menus*, just to keep us all confused. In this book, I chose to refer to DHTML (dynamic HTML) menus that drop over content from a main menu as *drop-down menus* and have borrowed the Dreamweaver term of *jump menu* to describe the menus that drop down from a selector box. Commonly seen in forms, jump menus are also highly valued as navigation aids.

In this chapter, you will learn where and how to use a jump menu, as well as make it match the look of your site. Because I want to show you the customization, while we are on the subject, I digress a tiny bit to teach you how to customize forms as well. Although not strictly on the menu topic, forms do contribute with visitor interactivity and feedback, so I believe are a forgivable topic into which to wander. Customized forms are fun for designers, too. You deserve a little dessert in the midst of all the meat and potatoes I have been dishing out in this book!

Using Jump Menus

Most large commercial sites feature a jump menu as part of every page and for good reason. Creating navigation that gets visitors to where they want to go in the site from any page they happen to be on is a tough job. Getting them from any page on a site to any other page on a site is darn near impossible . . . unless you use jump menus.

Jump menus take up very little space on a page when they are not active. One click presents the hidden menu. In Figure 24-1, you can see the jump menu items covering the content but not disturbing it while the menu is active.

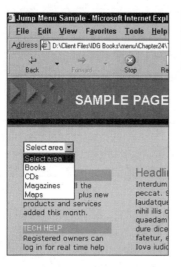

Figure 24-1: Jump menu items are hidden until the menu is activated. You can fit many menu items into a tiny space on the page using this method.

Jump menu selections are exposed after the arrow at the right of the menu is clicked. After the visitor makes a choice, you can set the menu to jump immediately to the new page or allow the visitor to make a second click on a "Go" button. The result is the same, and the visitor can quickly get to another spot on the page, another page entirely, or even another site through the jump menu.

Where to use a jump menu

I have seen many creative applications for jump menus. It is common to see a jump menu included to provide a site-map-like navigation option for visitors on every page, but they are also used very efficiently to provide navigation within each major section of a site. Multiple jump menus can be used on the same page to further streamline and organize options for navigation. Creative designers have used jump menus to present final options, such as articles or samples of work by title.

Tip   Whenever you are presented with a challenge to present many choices to a visitor and want to accomplish the task in a very efficient manner, keep jump menus in mind.

However, jump menus do not have a sexy reputation. They are small and, well, maybe a little ugly (although you can improve the look of them as you see how to do later in this chapter). But sexy or not, visitors will thank you for the navigation ease if you can grasp where jump menus shine and use them effectively. After all, isn't that what a superior designer can do — make a site work well *and* look great?

Exercise: Creating a basic jump menu

Time to roll up your sleeves and create a basic jump menu. This sample is as basic as jump menus can be in order to emphasize just how easy it is to add this function to your pages. Jump menus are really forms with JavaScript action added to a button and as such, must be placed between the <form> and </form> tags.

On the CD-ROM

The completed jump menu from the following exercise, jumpmenudone.html, is available in the Chapter 24 folder on the CD-ROM that accompanies this book.

To create a jump menu, follow these steps:

1. Create a new document in your HTML editor. Name the file **jumpmenu.html**.

2. Enter the following code in the body of your document to create the structure of your menu. You can change the URL values if you prefer. The form name and select name values were names I selected and are used in the JavaScript that adds the function to the menu.

```
<form name="dropdown">
  <select name="choices">
    <option>Select</option>
    <option value="http://wpeck.com">Option 1</option>
    <option value="http://productiongraphics.com">Option
2</option>
    <option value="http://webreference.com">Option 3</option>
  </select>
  <input type="button" value="Go" >
</form>
```

This code completes the physical structure of your menu. In order to have the menu work however, you must add JavaScript.

3. In the head of your document, place the following code:

```
<SCRIPT LANGUAGE="JavaScript">
function menuselect()
{var number = document.dropdown.choices.selectedIndex;
location.href =
document.dropdown.choices.options[number].value;
}
</SCRIPT>
```

The code placed in the head of the document directs the action when it is called at specific places on the page, in this case, when the Go button is clicked. The term *menuselect* is simply the created name for this function. The var number reference creates a variable named "number," and provides a map for how the variable is to be defined. In this case, the selectedIndex reference defines the variable as the menu choice that is selected by the visitor. Finally, the location.href entry completes the action, telling the browser to link to the specified location as stated in the selected option's value.

4. To apply the action to the button in your menu, insert `onClick=`
   `"menuselect()"` into the input type tag. The full tag is as follows:

   ```
   <input type="button" value="Go" onClick="menuselect()">
   ```

   This code simply tells the browser to start the actions contained in the
   "menuselect" JavaScript, which is stored in the head of the document.

5. Test the menu by previewing in any browser.

This example is as simple as a jump menu can be. More sophisticated JavaScript
can be used to remove the Go button, and have the links jump immediately on
selection to the new link, or to have fixed-size windows open instead of loading a
new page. Make sure that fancy techniques actually add to the visitor experience.
As a visitor, I prefer to have the Go button on the menu because I like the option to
change my mind before I commit to the new link.

> **Tip**   Jump menus are a wonderful learning ground for JavaScript. The form elements
> are simple and are easy to separate from the JavaScript. If you are looking for prac-
> tice, consider building jump menus with many JavaScript additions to hone your
> skills.

Exercise: Creating a jump menu in Dreamweaver

Macromedia Dreamweaver has taken much of the work out of creating jump menus.
You can quickly create the menu structure and add the JavaScript necessary to run
the menu with just a few clicks.

To create a jump menu in Dreamweaver, follow these steps:

1. Create a new document and name it **dwjump.html**.

2. Choose Insert ⇨ Form Elements ⇨ Jump Menu. The Insert Jump Menu window
   opens.

3. Make sure that the text in the Text field is highlighted, and type **Select** to
   replace the text. Note how Select now appears in the Menu Items list.
   Important: Do not close this window just yet.

4. To add a menu item, click the + symbol, and type **Option 1** in the Text field.
   Type **http://wpeck.com** in the When Selected, Go to URL field. Alternately, you
   can use any other URL or browse for a file within the site for this link.

5. Repeat Step 4 to add two more options, naming them **Option 2** and **Option 3**,
   and adding a link to each. Your screen should be similar to the screen shown
   in Figure 24-2. The links for this menu jump automatically to the new link on
   selection.

6. Click OK and your menu is complete.

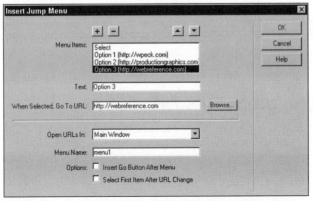

Figure 24-2: The completed Dreamweaver jump menu before accepting the settings

Creating Custom Forms and Jump Menus

I alluded to the less-than-exciting appearance of jump menus. The function of jump menus is so good that you really must use them in your pages, but you do not have to accept the default settings for style.

Changing a little code can give your jump menus an entirely different look, which can really dress up your pages. Be careful as you work through this process though. Don't forget that visitors must be able to instantly recognize the form items, so do not become so creative that the interaction you were adding is lost.

Changing button styles

Okay, the worst ugly offender in the world of jump menus is the HTML default button. Big, gray, uninspired, and oh so easy to fix. In a regular form, you can easily substitute an image for the Submit button that controls a form.

On the CD-ROM A file named go.gif is in the Chapter 24 folder on the CD-ROM that accompanies this book. This image can be used to test the following code substitution if you do not have an image you want to use.

To use a graphic of your own design as a form button, simply replace the form button code with the code:

```
<INPUT TYPE="image" NAME="submit" SRC="yourfilename.gif/jpg"
BORDER="0" ALT="button">
```

The result of this code substitution is shown in Figure 24-3.

Figure 24-3: The image on the left is the default submit button for HTML forms. The image on the right does the same job, but can be accomplished with any image.

Changing form properties with CSS

Substituting a button in a simple HTML form is quick and easy, but when you add more complicating factors, such as JavaScript to create action for page elements, you must be more careful. Cascading style sheets (CSS) comes to the rescue for customizing forms and jump menus.

If you have not read Chapter 9 in this book, which covers CSS in detail, you may want to before moving on through the rest of this chapter.

Changing form element properties

Text fields are often a large part of any form and to fit the look of the page, designers often look for the option to change parameters, such as the background colors and text properties. With CSS, inserting a style tag into the form tag accomplishes the job.

A text field is added to a form with the following code:

```
<input type="text" name="name">
```

However, adding CSS commands to the same tag gives you the option to match any background or style on a page. The same tag appears as follows, but with font style, color, and background color added:

```
<input type="text" name="name" style="font-family: Arial,
Helvetica, sans-serif; font-size: 12px; color: #FFFFFF;
background-color: #666666">
```

See Figure 24-4 to compare the results between the two code samples.

Figure 24-4: The top entry is a text field in a form with no enhancement. The bottom entry has CSS styles added to the text field form element.

Using CSS .class files for form items

You can also use a class style to assign properties to a form item, which reduces typing and code considerably. The .class code is shown here:

```
.form {
font-family: Arial,Helvetica,sans-serif; font-size: 12px;
color: #FFFFFF; background-color: #666666
}
```

After defined, the style `.form` can be applied to the form items, as shown in this next code.

```
<input type="text" name="email" class="form">
```

Figure 24-5 shows the result of adjusting text field appearance with CSS `.class` styles. Each of the text area form item contain only a `class="form"` entry to direct the appearance.

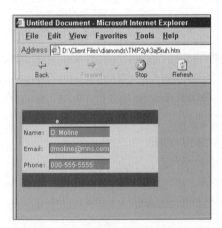

Figure 24-5: Three text fields have background and text controlled by one `.class` CSS style.

Changing button properties with CSS

Finally, you may want to use the default button in a form, but change the appearance. CSS once again comes to the rescue.

The default submit button code for an HTML form is shown here:

```
<input type="submit" name="Submit" value="Submit">
```

Adding a style to the tag produces the change in results that you can see in Figure 24-6. The code for a style to be added to the button is shown here:

```
<input type="submit" name="Submit" value="Submit" style="color:
#FFFFFF; background-color: #666666">
```

If you are controlling many buttons with this code, you can also create a `.class` style as with the previous example, and add it to each tag. Using the same `.class` style as the previous form, you obtain the same results as with the direct style entry.

The code for a button using a .class file is as follows:

```
<input type="submit" name="Submit" value="Submit" class="form">
```

Figure 24-6: Default HTML form submit button on the left with CSS styles applied at the right

Caution

Most of the techniques for customizing forms work well in Internet Explorer, but do not work in Netscape 4. However, they do degrade to default values very well. As long as you are careful to test your forms with Netscape to ensure that you have not placed white type on a white background, your forms will be cross-browser compatible. They won't look as good in Netscape, but if they are useable and look okay, I think including this technique for Internet Explorer users is fine.

Building a Form to Match Your Page

To give you hands-on practice with manipulating your form items, I include a short exercise, and even give you the CSS code to start you off. As soon as you are familiar with where the code goes and what effect it has, you can start experimenting with all the CSS controls that you have in your toolbox.

On the CD-ROM

Copy the file `cssform.html` from the Chapter 24 folder on the CD-ROM that accompanies this book to your hard drive.

To create a document with a customized form, follow these steps:

1. Open the document `cssform.html`. This document has a CSS style sheet in place, as well as a table and form ready to receive your form elements.

2. Insert a text form element in each of the right columns, opposite the titles of the fields in the left column.

3. Insert the following CSS styles into the style sheet in the head of the document and within the `<style>` tag:

```
.form {
font-family: Arial, Helvetica, sans-serif; font-size: 12px;
color: #000066; background-color: #CCCC99
}
```

4. Add the code `class="form"` to each text field. The final code for each field is as follows. The name value is different for each entry.

```
<input type="text" name="email" class="form">
```

5. Add a submit button below the table and apply the same class style to the button.

6. Preview your form in Internet Explorer. Your results should be similar to those shown in Figure 24-7.

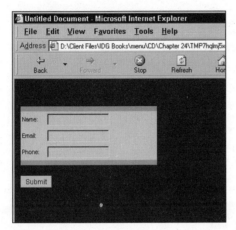

Figure 24-7: Final results of form elements with class styles applied

A copy of this exercise in finished form is on the CD-ROM that accompanies this book. The file is named `formcssdone.html` and is in the Chapter 24 folder. Make sure that you copy the graphic file `space.gif` from the same folder if you copy the HTML file to your computer.

Always keep CSS in mind as you create forms. You can often make the page much easier to navigate by adding color to your form elements. If you create a linked CSS file, you can apply the same styles to many pages with only the code that is needed to specify which style is to be used. (See Chapter 9 for more information about CSS styles.)

Have some fun with this idea. This is one simple enhancement that is still not well used, so does attract attention. Nothing feels better for a designer than to improve the function of a page at the same time as you improve the look. Using CSS styles in forms falls into that class.

✦ ✦ ✦

Automation and Template Tricks

Just because you have worked through all of the techniques you need to create great menus doesn't mean your
job is done. If you are going to take the time to create effective
menus for your visitors, you should also take the few extra
steps to implement an efficient and accurate work pattern.

In this chapter, I present ideas for how to streamline your
work through automation and template tricks. In Web design,
production techniques are not used just to save time, so don't
think you are off the hook if you are a hobby designer who is
not concerned whether every hour is productive. You have two
other reasons to duplicate work: accuracy and consistency.

This chapter helps you to put some tools into place so that
your site remains consistent from the first to the last page.
How many times have you worked on a project and found that
you had to return to work early to update pages that were
done before you developed the site idea fully or perhaps
before you learned a better way to accomplish a task? The
danger with this common scenario is not the lost time so
much as the potential lack of consistency.

Accuracy can take a beating when you are constantly editing.
Perfecting a technique before moving on is always best. As
soon as the code is perfect, you can place the complete code
into a template or copy and paste it into your other pages.

Why Do It a Hundred Times When Once Will Do?

This book focuses on menus, but the techniques in this chapter apply to all Web design. Creating reusable templates and
code snippets makes especially good sense for menus, however. Think of the issues that can cause problems on a Web
page. Most often trouble spots are menu-related. Whether it is

making sure a table holds together for an elaborate graphic layout or getting the CSS (cascading style sheets) code to display similar results in all browsers, menus eat up a high proportion of both design and troubleshooting time.

When you create any menu, consider whether that style or method of creating a navigational system is one that may work well for sites you will do in the future, or perhaps have already done. If the answer is yes, then it is worth spending extra time to make sure that the components of the menu are modular.

You can create repeatable content several ways. Of course, every Web site is different, so I am not implying that you can create a few pieces and then pull the pieces into place for an instant new site. That would be wonderful, but not at all realistic. I just want you to be aware of what pieces *can* be used again and again. As you read through the methods for saving "pieces," look for ways to apply the techniques to your style.

Designing effective reusable content

As a beginning designer, I could not have created many repeatable elements. Not unlike many who are new to Web design, I worked very hard to come up with an original look that would be different from anything else on the Web. In my own defense, the Web design world was pretty awkward when I started. Hardly anyone could be called an honest-to-goodness expert, and style was all over the map. But as the World Wide Web developed, some classic styles started to appear, much like we have seen for decades in printed materials.

Now that I have a few years' experience behind me and have focused much of my learning time on navigation and usability, creating repeating elements is much easier. I reuse my own ideas, layouts, and menus that work *because* they work. Of course, I do try to use interesting color and graphic treatments, but if you have noticed a startling similarity to many of the top commercial Web sites, perhaps you should heed the message.

I included a copy of a reusable template that I use for simple liquid design sites. Figure 25-1 shows the document open in Dreamweaver. Although the colors are not relevant and the borders are still turned on, you can see a fairly classic layout in this file. If this layout is close to what is required by another site you are designing, it is a simple matter to change background colors, turn off the borders, place images, and enter content. This file allows me to put together a site for personal use in almost no time at all.

You can find the file illustrated in Figure 25-1, basic_liquid.html, in the Chapter 25 folder on the CD-ROM included with this book.

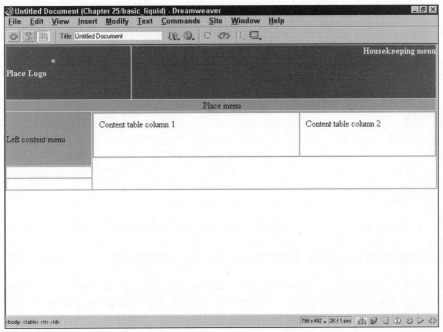

Figure 25-1: Basic template for a simple liquid design page

Using the copy and paste method

Any code can be copied from one document to another. When I was new to this field, I would often copy the table structure from one site to another. My table knowledge was weak enough that once I had a perfect table, I wanted to use it again. As I became better at constructing tables, that became more work than it was worth.

If you are reading this book, it is likely that you know how to copy code from one document to another. In every program from the simplest text editor to full-function editors, such as Dreamweaver, you simply highlight the code you want to move and choose Edit ➪ Copy or use the keyboard shortcuts, Ctrl + C (Windows) and Command + C (Macintosh). To place the code into the new page, position your cursor where you want to place the content, and choose Edit ➪ Paste or use the keyboard shortcuts, Ctrl + V (Windows) and Command + V (Macintosh).

Caution Be careful when you are copying code from a full-paged document, as is usually the case. Leaving behind a start or end tag is easy, and picking up an extra tag is even more common. Copy and paste only saves time when you work very carefully with the code.

Copy and paste is such a simple action for experienced computer operators that we tend to treat it casually. That attitude can be a very bad thing when you are transferring code from one document to another. (Yes that is the bitter voice of cocky, code-copying experience talking!)

Create a snippets folder

If you want to take the copy and paste idea a little further and always have code snippets at your fingertips, create a folder to contain nothing but snippets of code that work well for you. To create a code snippet, copy the code you want to store and create a new document. Paste the code into the empty document and save it with a meaningful name. The next time you want to use that particular code, simply go to the snippets folder you created, open the document, copy the code, and paste it into place in the new document.

Tip   Dreamweaver offers a great time-saver for saving snippets of code. Click the Quick Tag Editor, found in the upper-right corner of the Properties Inspector, and the code from the selected object appears as shown in Figure 25-2. Select and copy the code and then paste it to the new location. Although you can only display a limited amount of code with the Quick Tag Editor, I like that only the selected tag is presented when I am copying. You can also edit any tag through the Quick Tag Editor.

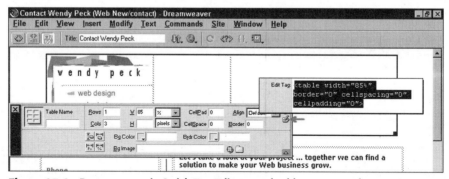

Figure 25-2: Dreamweaver's Quick Tag Editor, marked by an arrow here, presents the code for any selected object.

The time you spend setting up a folder and creating snippet documents will pay you back many times over. If you do Web design professionally, you should consider setting up subfolders for code snippets, such as menus, JavaScript, CSS, and so on. After you are in the habit of creating these files, you will be amazed at how quickly your folder grows. Saving code snippets only works if you can get to them very quickly.

Reward Yourself for Automating Tasks

Professional Web designers are always looking for ways to save time and automate the process of creating a site. Don't sell yourself short, however. If you have spent time creating an automated process, by all means, use it on client sites, but don't simply charge an hourly rate for the time you have spent without considering the development time you have invested.

Although I rarely work under an hourly contract, I always estimate the hours for every job to come up with the contract amount and allow an extra charge over my hours if I will be using my automated methods. Most of my stored code took me hours of unbilled work, through many projects, to perfect. The results have value to my clients that is far beyond the time it takes me to place the code in their pages. The client benefits from tested and true code, but the automation benefit should remain with the developer.

Start from an existing document

If you are copying most of the items on a page to a new page, it often makes sense to duplicate the existing page, either by choosing File ⇨ Save As or copying and renaming the file, to create the new page. You can then remove or change items as necessary on the new page. This method can be used to create new pages in the same site, or to create a page for a new site when the basic structure is similar. In effect, you are using the existing, tested, working page as a template for the new page.

As an example of how this method can be put to use, I often design the look and navigational system for client sites, but do not compile the pages or place them on the server. Many of my clients have highly knowledgeable backend Web developers on staff who may not have graphic or interface skills. They take my work and create the necessary pages on the site. If they do not use Dreamweaver or Adobe GoLive, I will prepare HTML templates that they then use to create pages.

I use a different version of starting from an existing page when I create my biweekly columns for WebReference.com. I have a standard "look" for each page. In addition, a lot of code is on the page that delivers the WebReference.com content, such as ad code and copyright notices. Only the center of the page changes with each new article I write. In fact, I start from an entire folder to keep page numbering and navigational objects in place, as each page advances to the next, requiring a different link.

To start a new column, I copy every page from the previous column, create a new folder, and paste the new files into the new folder. See the view from the Dreamweaver Site window in Figure 25-3. I copied the files from the Column50 folder to the Column51 folder. Note that I did not copy the art folder, as that folder contains only the unique images for each column. The images for the constant portion of each page are stored in an art directory one level above the column folders. This type of organization allows automation.

Figure 25-3: Files are copied from the previous column folder and pasted into the new column folder. The "art" folder is not copied.

In Figure 25-4, you can see a page from the new folder. Note that the image is not showing, because the images are all in the art folder in another folder. From this point, I delete the table rows that include the content and add new rows for the new content. I also use the powerful Find and Replace feature in Dreamweaver to change page titles, headlines, and update the column number in the top menu, replacing content in the entire folder in one step.

Figure 25-4: One of the copied files from Figure 25-3 is opened. There is no image for the page to show as the "art" folder was not copied. The content from this page will be removed and replaced with new content.

This is an efficient way for me to maintain absolute consistency and save a lot of time. I could simply prepare a template containing the look of the page and menus, but the page-specific navigation, such as the next page link at the bottom of the page, would have to be redone with every issue. By working as described here, considering that I usually create columns with the same number of pages, the more complete template allows me to concentrate only on the content.

There are many variations on the two examples I present here for starting with an existing page to create a new one. In the past, I have opened a page and deleted all but one section of the page as a start for a new page. In other cases, especially when I have done two similar sites for one client, I have opened the original and simply changed colors, images, and of course, content.

Caution

Always, always, and I mean *always*, save the file to a new name immediately, and I mean *immediately*, upon opening. After you are on a roll, making changes to the page, customizing and tweaking the code, the risk is extremely high that you will save the changes, overwriting the original file. I have done it, and I cannot count the number of students in my classes who have done it. Protect that original file. Make it a habit to not even click your mouse once before you have saved the file to a new name.

Exercise: Creating Dreamweaver Templates

HTML templates are wonderful timesaving gems to have in hand. However, sophisticated HTML editors, such as Dreamweaver and GoLive also offer automated template capability. An automated template enables you to make changes to the template file and have the changes reflected in every page that is associated with the template. If you are working on large sites with an editor that offers templates, you *must* learn to use this feature. Not only will you save countless hours of construction time, but also your site consistency is guaranteed and troubleshooting is very easy.

In Dreamweaver, you have two ways to create a template. You can create a template from scratch, adding editable areas and building the page as you create the template. You can also build your page and create a template from the completed page. I prefer to work out my design without worrying about the template regions, however.

In order to create a template, you must plan your page well. Each area of the page that you want to change will have to be converted to an editable area, which takes a little planning and preparation. However, as soon as you have your template prepared, you can easily create consistent pages for an entire site.

On the
CD-ROM

To complete the following exercise, copy the file, `templatetest.html` from the Chapter 25 folder on the CD-ROM included with this book to your hard drive.

To create a template in Dreamweaver, follow these steps:

1. Open `templatetest.html`. You are going to make some changes to this page and then create a new page, so you must save it with a different file name. Save it as `templatetest2.html`.

2. Choose File ➪ Save as a Template. The Save as a Template window opens. Type **templatetest** in the Save As field.

3. Open your Assets window and click the Templates icon, which is located just above the Library icon in the left toolbar. You should see the templatetest listing in the lower portion of the screen, as shown in Figure 25-5. A preview of the template appears in the upper window.

Figure 25-5: The template listing for templatetest. Note that the top window provides a preview.

You have just created your first template. However, it is not much use at this point because Dreamweaver creates a new template with the page title as the only editable region. Unless you are planning to create multiple pages that are exactly the same, you have to make some changes.

Creating editable regions in Dreamweaver templates

Follow these steps to create editable regions in Dreamweaver templates:

1. Highlight the Company Times graphic, located in the upper-left corner of the templatetest template you created in the previous exercise. Choose Modify ➪ Templates ➪ New Editable Region. The New Editable Region window opens. Type **logo** to name this region.

2. Click your mouse pointer anywhere in your document to deselect the graphic and then look at the logo area. A box that contains the label "logo" now surrounds the image. (When we create a document from this template, the image that is shown here appears, but it can be changed.)

3. You also need to be able to enter different text in the menu areas. Select all of the text in the small menu at the right of the screen. Choose Modify ⇨ Templates ⇨ New Editable Region. The New Editable Region window will open. Type **housekeeping** to name this region. Your document should resemble the document shown in Figure 25-6.

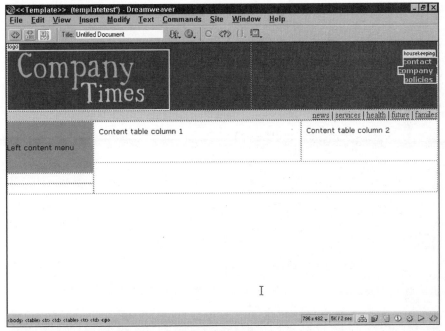

Figure 25-6: Editable regions added to a template

4. Repeat Step 3 for the main menu area, naming the editable area, **main menu**.

5. The left side also features a menu that I have left with just a title in the original. To make the entire cell an editable region, providing maximum flexibility, select the cell and create a new editable region called **side menu**.

6. Finally, the content table should obviously be an area that you can edit. To make the entire table that can hold the content editable, select the table and then choose Modify ⇨ Templates ⇨ New Editable Region and name the new region, **content**.

7. Save the new template. You can now move on to creating a page from this template in the next exercise.

Tip

If you want to see the page without the template code, choose View ⇨ Visual Aids ⇨ Invisible Elements and the template code disappears. Repeat these steps if you want to redisplay the template codes.

Creating a document with a Dreamweaver template

Now that you have a well-planned template, it is time to put it into action. Use the template you created in the previous exercise to create a new document:

1. To keep confusion to a minimum, close all documents in Dreamweaver. You must have the site containing your template active.

2. Choose New ⇨ From Template. The Select Template window opens. Select templatetest. Click Select to close.

3. A new document has been created with your template features. You should save this right away with a new name.

4. Try adding text, changing menu items, and adding content to the document you created from the template. (Changes you make on this page do not affect the template page.) Save the document.

5. Repeat Steps 3 and 4 to create a second document. Again, make some changes to this document and save the file.

You have just created two pages. If your original document was well tested before you converted it to a template, the new pages can be assumed to have the same stability for the elements that are part of the template.

A completed copy of the template file described in the previous exercises called templatetestdone.html is in the Chapter 25 folder on the CD-ROM that accompanies this book.

Working with Dreamweaver Templates

Templates provide a quick way to create new pages, but the time savings go past just creating pages. You can also edit the template and have the changes passed on to every page that is attached to that template. You also have the freedom to break the connection between the document and the template.

Editing a Dreamweaver template

The true power of a template comes to light when you edit the original file. To edit a template, you simply open the original template file and make your changes to the template. When you save the changes, you are given the option to update all the pages that have been created with, and are still attached to, the template. All of the updated pages appear with the changes you made to the template. The changes occur only on the local files (you have to upload the changed files to see changes on the Web.

Breaking the link to a Dreamweaver template

You can break the link that updates pages created with a Dreamweaver template. Breaking the link can be useful for providing you with quick page creation and a consistent look of a page without requiring that the connection to the template remain. Pages with forms or changed layouts are often candidates for breaking the connection between pages and templates.

To break the link to the template, open the document that you would like to set free from the template. Choose Modify ➪ Templates ➪ Detach from Template. That's it. Your page is now an independent operator, with no connection to the template. Of course, any changes you make to the template from this point on won't appear on this page.

> **Tip**
>
> If you are maintaining a large site that is based on templates, keeping a list of the pages that are no longer attached to the template is a good idea. Forgetting that you have broken the template link on a few pages is easy, and you may believe you are making changes to the entire site via the template, but a few will be left behind.

This chapter has provided a glimpse at some of the ways you can work once and use that work over and over. Keep your eyes open for new opportunities to share code, layouts, and menus between your sites. The quality of the work will come up at the same time as your speed in creating new pages increases. Resisting that combination is hard.

✦   ✦   ✦

Pulling It Together, and Test, Test, and Test Again

Y ou've done it. After many hours of planning, research, sketching, learning, experimenting, and building, you have a page that makes you happy. Doesn't it feel good to have the finished product? Hang on . . . not so fast. You may have your structure in place, and you may think you have the job done, but if you have not tested your page meticulously, and checked for accessibility issues, you aren't ready for the site-warming party yet.

If you compare building a Web site to building a house, the part you have yet to do to your site is the final inspection by the by-law officer. As a house is constructed, the electrical, structural, and plumbing is all checked at various stages. As you build a Web site, you are usually testing as you go, checking with other browsers and often even gathering opinions on the look. But just as a new home requires a final inspection before the building permit is marked complete and satisfactory, there are final issues with a Web site to settle.

In this chapter, I take you through the final steps necessary to ensure that your site is not only ready for company, but also will serve all of the visitors who are likely to drop by. You can't guarantee that there will be no problems when you launch your site — one or two details always seem to slip through the cracks — but you certainly can make sure that disaster does not strike just when you have announced that your doors are open.

Creating an HTML Proof

Deciding on the most appropriate place to test a page thoroughly is often hard. The testing is only valid if you have all of the elements in place on the page, especially for tables, CSS, JavaScript, DHTML, or any technique that is known to behave differently in the various browsers. However, you also want to test as soon as possible, before you spend the time adding elements that do not cause compatibility problems, such as plain text. The more you add to the page, the less you will want to make changes to the structure should a compatibility issue arise. In addition, you should be using fully tested pages only to build subsequent pages.

So, how can you test without completing the page? How can you tell if the page is balanced without having any text or images in place? You can create an HTML proof with the finished menus and page graphics in place, but using placeholder text and images for the content areas. I find that working with dummy elements enables me to focus on the structure of the page and the quality of my code before I move into page composition mode. It is too easy to get distracted by grammar, paragraph structure, image cropping, or enhancement, and lose track of the job at hand — making sure that the page works.

Print designers have used dummy text, often referred to as *Greek* text, since the printing industry began centuries ago. The text is not recognizable, so that you, or your client, are not distracted by any message. This technique is a good one to borrow from the print tradition, filling in text content areas with Greek text for testing and design approval.

On the CD-ROM   For a sample Greek text file, go to the Chapter 26 folder on the CD-ROM that accompanies this book and look for `greek.txt`.

When I am working with clients, I often find that images are the last content to arrive, or that the text content and structure of the site determines what images should be used. However, designing a page that will contain photos without using an actual photo to determine how it will look is impossible. I keep a folder with generic images of several types to use as I proof a page.

The difference is dramatic. In Figure 26-1, I have a basic page layout. Troubleshooting could be done for this page as it is, but compare the empty page to the page shown in Figure 26-2. Adding content illustrated that I needed more color on the page, which I added by adding table rows with background color. However, tables should always be fully tested. Had I tested this page before I added the dummy content and then discovered that I needed table rows or columns to complete the page, my troubleshooting would have to be repeated.

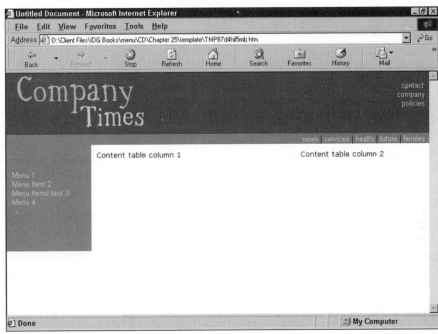

Figure 26-1: New page with all basic elements in place

Figure 26-2: Adding dummy content reveals weakness in page design and often prompts table changes. Troubleshooting is best done after the page has been tested with dummy content.

Gathering a Testing Team

Artists can be solitary souls, and Web designers are artists. However, unlike any other medium for artists, Web design cannot be done alone. When you paint, you can choose when the work is finished. Anyone who sees the canvas sees what you intended. They may not like what you painted, but they see the exact strokes you placed. Print designers must make sure that their work can be output to film or a digital press, but after the mechanical process is perfected, they can be assured that anyone who looks at their page sees the same thing.

Web designers have no such comfort. Not only is your work open to whether people enjoy it, you have no way to know exactly how each will *see* the page. Web design is, at best, a series of compromises, balancing how your code will display on many browsers and operating systems. You cannot make the decisions on which compromises you can live with unless you know how each browser, on both Macintosh and Windows platforms, displays the pages you create.

 Chapter 4 covers many browser compatibility issues.

Most of you only have one platform available for testing. I hope that you have Internet Explorer, Netscape Navigator, and Opera available for local testing. However, even if you test with every version of each common browser, your page is only tested with one operating system and one monitor. That is not enough. You must establish a testing team to help you ensure that your visitors all receive an acceptable display of your work.

Building a testing team locally

If you are heavily involved with people who work on computers regularly, you may have the personal and professional contacts to build a well-rounded team. You will need testing on the opposite platform from yours. (In other words, if you work on a PC, you must have a Mac tester on your team, and that person should have at least Netscape and Explorer available.)

I recommend that you also find people who have varied computer experience to test your work. Family members and coworkers (non-Internet based workplace) can be an excellent source for testers who are not computer or Internet experts to test your site.

No matter how you build your team, I recommend that you write down the platforms, monitor resolution, and browsers used by each person on your testing team. Thinking you have all bases covered as your testing team grows is easy, but omitting one important combination, such as Internet Explorer on a Mac platform can be disastrous.

Accessing online testing

I would not be as successful as I am today had I not become very involved with online discussion groups devoted to professional Web design. In my early days, the knowledge I gained from having my pages tested by professional designers shortened my learning curve by at least one year. To this day, I *never* release a site to a client before I have had the designers from several groups test and critique the site. My pages are tested on both platforms, with every connection from modem to DSL, on every version of every browser, including WebTV. Each page is subject to scrutiny on monitor resolutions ranging from 640 pixels wide, to the highest on the market at any time.

In addition to the comfort I get from knowing the navigation works and the content is legible in a variety of circumstances, I also have experts checking my work and providing not only trouble reports, but suggestions for correction, or just generally improving the site. Accessibility experts are usually in every group as well, and they can help you meet accessibility standards for visitors who use aids to surf the Web and to comply with increasingly strict standards required for public sector sites. The value of honest, knowledgeable critique cannot be measured.

Cross-Reference   You can read more about accessibility standards and tools in Chapter 4.

Becoming a member of a design discussion group is not difficult. The discussion groups are free, and most groups ask only for your e-mail address in order to become an instant member. I recommend that you become an active participant, however. Many people join groups and "lurk," or simply read the information that flows through the group. Although you can learn a lot by observing, you will only tap into the full power of discussion groups when you ask for help when you need it and provide help when others are a few months behind you in their learning.

You have hundreds of groups from which to choose, but I have listed a few popular groups for you.

Yahoo! Groups

There are many design related groups that reside at Yahoo! Groups. Go to `http://yahoogroups.com` and search for the aspect of Web design work you require. Group description and signup procedures are very clear. To find an active group, which usually means value is there, check the number of messages each month.

Note   eGroups was purchased by Yahoo! and has become Yahoo! Groups.

HTML Writer's Guild (HWG)

There is probably not a better one-stop source for Web development information on the Web than the HWG groups. Go to the home page and select the newsgroups that apply to the work you do. Be prepared for a high volume of messages from many of the groups. (http://hwg.org)

Note   The Critique list is the only HWG group that permits requests for a site review.

Evolt.org

Another excellent source for Web development information is Evolt.org. Click the Join tab to join. (http://lists.evolt.org)

Tip   Before you join a high traffic group, which describes most of the groups I have listed, you should be prepared to filter any group messages into a separate folder. At times, any of these groups can produce well over one hundred messages a day, and if allowed to flow into your regular mail, they can be more harm than good. Don't try to read every message. Scan headlines for the interesting topics.

Soliciting a Productive Site Review

I am making plenty of noise about testing, so I had best set you on the right path to *worthwhile* testing. Just asking your friends and family members to visit your site and tell you what they think can be good for the ego, but little else. You will never get a productive site review unless you guide the process.

To guide the process, you must first take an honest assessment of your own work. What has caused you trouble? Take inventory of the trouble spots and rather than just hoping they are fixed, draw attention to them. Your site is only as good as its weakest link. Your testers do not share your investment in your site, and even if professional, will only take a surface glance at the pages. Unless something jumps out at them as missing or wrong, you will simply hear that all is fine. But that one pixel gap you have been fighting with may well get past tester's scrutiny.

Specifically ask people to check on load time. So many in the world still use slow modem connections, so you should have someone on your testing team with a slow connection. I connect at 24K, so I am the official tester of slow pages for many groups. However, unless someone specifically asks for a load time test, I will often start the page and flip to another task. Although I can offer a superb load time test, many people miss that test by failing to ask.

Ask people to pay attention to how easy it is to get around, if the mouseovers send the signal to click here, if the teaser menu items attract attention. If you want a true test, don't ask people for specific menu questions, but instead ask them to observe the first three elements they notice when the page loads. If you have four people tell you that they first noticed the last updated entry, you may have some work to do yet.

Don't let anything that is important to your site goals be missed. You may think it is demanding to list what you would like volunteers to be doing as they review your site. Remember, they are donating their time because they want to help. Wouldn't you prefer to take part in a volunteer exercise that actually answers questions and solves problems? People in discussion groups often answer only what their expertise allows and are comfortable ignoring requests you make that are outside their skill base. They know that the next one who answers will have a different set of skills and can fill in the rest of the answers for you.

Making Final Tweaks to Perfect Your Pages

When you have tested all your pages, have built a testing route, feel very confident about the structure and function of your site, and have finally placed all the content, you may think you are finally finished. Many sites are launched at this stage, but the making of a perfect site does not stop quite yet.

When I write, I try to put 24 hours between the last word I write and the final check through. Even if I think the work is perfect when I finish, leaving it alone for at least a day gives me fresh eyes to find errors or simply better ways to word a sentence or two. Maybe one section ends too abruptly and needs one sentence to improve the flow to the next section. Little changes make a big difference in quality work.

Web design is no different. If you can leave a day or two between completing your site and doing a final review, you will have a much better product. Code tends to run together when you have been working steadily on it. The pieces that can often make a difference, such as simple spaces in your code, suddenly jump off your page after you take a rest.

Check writing and spelling

A final read through copy is very important. Web design is, by nature, a page-by-page activity. Losing the connection between content on pages is easy. In fact, before doing the final tour through your site, reviewing the original site goals is a great idea (see Chapters 2 and 3) to keep in the front of your mind as you run through the site page by page. Often, small omissions or duplication (duplicated information can be very confusing for visitors) become obvious only on a visitor-like tour of your own work. On the other hand, if it all seems to flow well and hold together, you can gain a great deal of confidence in your product, which is valuable as you plan and implement your marketing.

Check your grammar. If you have never been good with grammar, do not assume that becoming a Web designer has changed that fact. Find someone who does have a good command of correct language and have him or her always check your work. I have seen so many beautiful sites, with well-presented content, but filled with grammatical errors. Although it may not be fair, my reaction, and that of many others, is to assume that a site with incorrect grammar is not to be taken seriously or trusted. Errors in grammar are almost worse than spelling errors. An argument can be made that many spelling errors are simply typos, a much lesser crime in our judgmental minds. However, I do not advocate any carelessness with spelling either.

A Web site with spelling errors, or typos, is still a pretty quick way to present an unprofessional appearance. Most HTML editors have a spell checker built into the program. If yours does not have a spell checker, find a stand-alone checker that can check any passage of text for spelling errors. Make sure the spell check is the last thing you do on a page. I have been caught a few times doing a thorough spell check and then sneaking back to tweak a word or two in a paragraph. Almost without fail, I will include a typo with the last minute edit. I try to check my spelling just before I FTP the file to the server.

Do a final code check

Finally, get your hands dirty and skim through every line of code in your site, especially if you are a professional designer. Although it may seem redundant if all pages are performing perfectly, serious designers should be concerned that all of their work is at top level. The attention to detail allows professional designers to command high rates, and that the professional part of that title is taken seriously is important.

There is a practical reason for working with immaculate code. Rare is the page that is not changed at some point, and editing a page many months later is much easier if the base is excellent. A few minutes of clean-up leads to a professional appearance and saves time later — great reasons to add the final step.

Copyright: Is It Yours? Theirs? Anyone's?

Web development has brought the issue of copyright to common discussion like it never has been in history. To confuse issues further, the discussion can come from many different directions, from copying material from an existing page, to the copyright path between designer and client.

Isn't the Web about sharing?

The Web began with a culture of sharing information. Web developers are unbelievably generous about sharing techniques that have taken them days, even months at times, to develop. A time-honored way for new designers to learn how a look or function has been accomplished is to study the code for a page they admire.

It is also child's play to copy almost anything from the Web. Images can be saved with a click, entire pages, even sites, can be downloaded in minutes, and all code is there for the world to see and take away.

Unfortunately, this easy access has led to a common attitude that if it is on the Web, it is free for the taking. Nothing could be further from the truth. Creating a page for the Web is covered by the same legislation as written material or art. Copying and using an image from a Web site is no less a crime than scanning a photograph on a postcard and reproducing it.

Code is also included. It is not illegal to download a page, study the code, learn how the technique was accomplished, and then write your own code to implement that effect on your page. That could be compared to touring an art gallery and taking inspiration from the works you have seen. But if you cut and paste code from another developer's page without permission, and paste it into one of your pages, you have broken copyright laws. Period!

Enforcing copyright

Copyright is hard to enforce. You can usually have the offending material removed from the server if the one who copies it refuses to do so, but beyond that, little can be done. As designers, we must set high standards of ethics for our own work and try to spread the word as much as possible. There will always be those who blatantly steal another's work and claim it as their own, but many beginning designers are truly unaware that copying from the Web is not acceptable.

I have followed the efforts to protect code and images, from scripts that prevent right-clicking to produce the save menu (robs many other functions from the visitor) to special programs that wrap images in a cloaking code (too many incompatibility problems, plus extended download time). You can add a copyright notice to your work (you must find the one who steals it before action can be taken), or even have it digitally signed (fee-based service) to try and protect what is yours.

Currently, there is really not a solution to the copyright theft problem. Many designers take the same attitude I have developed, even after I had an entire site stolen, images, text, code — the entire package. If you are placing it on the Web, someone can, and quite possibly will, take it and claim it belongs to them. If you find the offense (and the Web world can be surprisingly small) always force the offender to remove the material as your contribution to education. But do not let a few morally bereft thieves sour you to the great mood of sharing that most of the Web development world still offers.

Copyright and clients

I can feel the impending doom music playing right now. I have been a professional designer for over 12 years, in print design and now in Web design, and I certainly know that what I am about to say is going against the standard belief of my industry: I think that the Web has presented graphic designers with new situations, which call for different rules.

What exactly gives you a copyright?

First, let me state emphatically that if you design something, you own the copyright to it. That is a given. You do not need to register it or apply for official copyright protection, trademark protection, or service mark protection. Under the law, your creation belongs to you until you transfer that ownership to another party.

That strong statement applies to words, images, photographs, paintings, illustrations, computer-generated graphics, Web page layout, and even code. Of course, there is always a burden of proving that you created a disputed item first. Applying for official protection through copyright or trademark protection does help if you must provide proof of ownership. I am not a lawyer and have no legal training, so I cannot draw the line for when you should apply for protection and when it would not be worthwhile.

When should you transfer copyright?

However, I do want to come out publicly with the policy that I use that is opposite to "standard" industry wisdom, which I believe has been borrowed wholesale from different times and a different medium — print. When I receive final payment for a site, I transfer full copyright for the entire site to the client. In fact — and I am getting ready to duck — if the client desires the working files from any program, I also provide those as part of the quoted price. I prepare a written copyright release, and as soon as the final check has cleared the bank, I transfer ownership of the copyright to my client. As soon as I have done that, the new owner is free to do with that material what they wish. They can sell it, manipulate it, or even ruin it at their will if they so choose.

Note   I retain copyright of any design that was presented but was not selected. I only release copyright and files for the design element in the final site.

In the print world, it makes a lot of sense for large agencies to retain copyright for the major projects that they produce. Agencies often spend hundreds of thousands of dollars preparing proofs to win a contract. There must be a way to recover that cost, and retaining copyright forces the major companies to remain with that agency for the life of the campaign. There are probably similar cases in Web work, but again, large agency operations are the ones who require this protection. Very few of us fall into that category.

For me and many other designers I know, though we do work for some larger clients, our method of operation is different. Few of us enter into "contests" for jobs, which means that we have little to no investment in a project when we begin work. Most of us demand a sizable deposit for work to begin and do not release the product until the work is paid in full. If we are working the way we should, we do not take much financial risk. My opinion is that because we have little invested in a client and considering the speed of change on the Web, sticking to old rules created for a completely different situation, does more harm than good. I don't want to hold clients hostage in order to make my living at Web design.

However, if you have reduced design price in exchange for a long hosting or maintenance contract, my beliefs may not apply. If your fair income for a project only comes with a continuing relationship with a client, then you most likely should retain copyright. However, if like most of us, you do the job at the current market rate, I think it is best to release the copyright to the client and have them come back to you for future work because they are satisfied with the work and service, not because they must.

On the other hand, if my words on releasing copyright do not sit well with you, don't worry. Many designers, especially those who have come to the Web from the high-end print world, emphatically disagree with me. They have valid points for their beliefs as well, and you should consider both arguments if you are a professional designer.

✦   ✦   ✦

Production Tricks and Fun Stuff

If you have been following along with this book chapter by chapter, congratulations! You have made it through to the end. It's been quite a ride, hasn't it? Menus are not simple little graphics or text portions of a page, but rather elements that drive any site. It only makes sense that the route to excellence would be complex and twisted when you consider the number of factors involved in creating great menus, and that every site is unique in goals, look, and delivery.

Studying and applying the techniques included in this book can help you to create great menus. This chapter is devoted to doing your work in an efficient manner, and driving home some very important principles that will take you from knowledge and competence to Web menu design excellence.

Work Patterns that Save Time

I think I can safely say that I have been blessed with a fair share of talent and ambition and a healthy dose of common sense, but unfortunately, I have been left seriously wanting for natural organization. In fact, that I was moved to write this book is mainly a result of fighting all my life for order in my work. My practical side was never content to make pretty things to express my creative side. I always wanted a *practical* use to come from my work (a necessary quality for all but the world's most talented artists if they want to make a living through their creative work). Alas, without organization and order, it is difficult to be a commercial artist.

Because order and organization do not come naturally to me, I have been acutely aware of the process that makes a commercial artistic venture work, and what fails miserably. If you are saying to yourself that this topic does not apply to you because you are not a professional, I urge you to think again. For most of my career, I have worked as a home-based team of one, so my methods are not at all corporate in tone. They can be applied by individuals in a corporate setting, but are also relevant for the hobby designer who does not want to waste time. Whether amateur or professional, everyone enjoys completing a task in an efficient way.

Note

A good number of my most successful colleagues never set out to be professional designers. They were working at other things and started designing Web sites for fun, and then for family and friends. Almost accidentally, these colleagues reached the point where they could charge for work, leaving their jobs to design full time. Never say never when you have a talent or a consuming interest. The most successful commercial designers are not necessarily the most talented artists. So, even if you are not a professional designer, please don't skip the next few pages.

Taking the first steps

Every project needs a place to start, and Web design success depends on your early steps. Efficient work as you start the project will save many hours later on. I think I have wasted more time because my content was not determined, or forwarded by the client, than for any other single reason.

Chapters 2 and 3 in this book help you to get your project organized. After you have worked through the processes described, you will have a healthy start. If at all possible, carry that on through to get the content in place. For beginners to assume that the content can come later is natural — the design and structure of the page takes a long time and must be in place before you can build pages anyway, right?

There are two faults to that thinking. First, content can change structure. Even with my experience, I recently had a simple template design job become quite complicated when the content needed to be changed. I did my homework, grilled the contacts on their needs, created a site map (which was approved), and started the design process. I would never be the one to build the pages (the client would take care of that), so content was not important, right? Except . . . well, it *was* important. As they started to gather the content for the site, exceptions to the templates we had planned started to appear. The site map was still accurate, but there were special features within the categories that they "forgot" about until they started on the content.

The result was hair pulling on my part. I really hate redoing work, and new features always open the door for questions, such as, "Would the other design have been better considering this new information?" For the client, the price rose. The initial quote I gave was based on a logical process, not repeatedly reopening completed phases of the project. Fortunately, I worked so hard with the client in the beginning to establish site structure that it held through the changes. If the structure required change, the additional cost would have been significant.

The second problem with gathering content as you go is that it makes you spend far more time at every stage. If you are creating the content, you will tend to work the content and the page at the same time, adjusting the HTML for each page after fully testing as I discuss in Chapter 26.

In general, the more content you have ready before you prepare the site, the better off you are. I am very specific about changes in my contract, to the tune of "make any and it will be you who pays," precisely because I do so many jobs in which I have no control over content gathering. If you are working with a client, make sure you have the content, or cover yourself well in your contract. If you are designing a site for yourself, I strongly advise that you have much of the content prepared before you make your final adjustments to your page structure, and definitely before you consider that the code for the page structure is tested and proven.

Caution

If you are working for any outside party and this includes organizations, such as your church or the local animal shelter, preparing a simple contract or Memorandum of Understanding (MOU) is a good idea. This applies even if not one dollar will change hands. I have heard far more nightmare stories from the creators of pro bono sites than from those who work on commercial sites when a contract is not included as part of the process. If you are reluctant to work with a formal contract in such cases, consider an MOU. For additional information, feel free to check out an article I wrote about using an MOU, as well as a sample form, at www.wise-women.org/resources/abc/mou.

Setting up a schedule and sticking to it

A simple Web site seems . . . well, simple . . . until you add up all of the components and development stages a site must go through. You have planning, proofing, construction, testing, testing, testing, and finally, the perfection stage. (The number of testing references in that list is not a typo, but a dramatic enforcement of importance.) If you are working with other people—and that includes your spouse, sister, Mom, friend, pastor—do yourself a favor and put a development schedule in writing.

In commercial Web design, you often work with many people on the same project. One little piece of knowledge I bring to my Web work from my time in the print industry is that you should always have one contact person. I don't care how simple the project or if it is a volunteer project for your local school, taking instruction from every member of a team is a mistake. I refuse to take instructions from anyone but my contact. (I will, of course, discuss details for clarification with other team members, but they must make the request for change through my contact.) That may seem heavy-handed, but if it does, I am guessing you have not worked with many teams. Trust me on this for now, and I assure you, if I ask you after you have worked with even one team, you will agree with me.

Finally, remember that you are the expert on *this* site, and always project that attitude. Clients and well-meaning acquaintances are often very quick to offer bits of information they have heard in passing. Listen, but never do more than promise to

investigate. Remember that you are ultimately responsible for the quality and function of the site you build, and you can spend literally days trying to accomplish
something that cannot be done, or that will compromise the browser compatibility,
or worse, the very stability of the site. Those who "hear" that certain functions are
possible, often do not have the skill to discern whether the source is reliable, or if
they are missing an important qualifier in the information. Doing your planning
well, creating a site map, and generally understanding where you are going is the
best defense against the so-called "easy" ideas.

Tips for Maximum Progress with Minimum Effort

You've heard the expression, *work smarter, not harder*. In Web design, this saying is
right at home. I created two Web sites for my design business within a short period
of time a couple of years ago. The first site consisted of nearly 20 pages and took
me about three weeks to complete (not working full time), and at least some time
was spent working on it every day. The completed site lasted only a few months
before I was doing a redesign. The second version of the site took me three days to
complete, and I was working on another site at the same time. I am still using that
second site, `http://wpeck.com`. The site consists of four pages and has lasted
over a year. The difference? During the intervening time, I decided there had to be
an easier way, and I worked through many of the processes I have included in this
book. By applying what I learned to creating the second site, the job took a fraction
of the time, and the results were immeasurably better.

In that case, the main difference between the development of my first site and the
second was that I identified the site goals before I started to work. I also developed
timesaving methods. The combination of planning and watching for timesaving
opportunities can shave measurable time from your work. The best part is that
most speedy techniques also improve quality.

Prepare non-HTML proofs

If you understand HTML restrictions and can design a page that translates well into
HTML without requiring that the full page is sliced and used as an image, do your
initial proofs in a graphics program. Chapter 7 discusses creating proofs, and the
time saved can be huge.

When you are working in a graphics program, you are only concerned with the layout of a page and are not tempted from your main goal by deciding what your
rollovers will look like, or experimenting with a new script. That focus not only
saves time, but also improves the quality of your layout.

You are also much more likely to make improvements that you note as you
progress. If you have only one simple change in a graphics program to do, rather

than facing redoing all of your graphics, you are more likely to say yes, that is worth the effort for that improvement, no matter how small the gain.

Transfer images to HTML if you are a beginner

Generally, I am quite active with helping new designers in the discussion groups (or at least I am when I am not writing a book). One of the most common problems I see with new designers is a failure to understand what HTML can and cannot do. If you are creating a proof in a graphics program and do not have a good grasp of layout using HTML tags, please disregard the previous tip about preparing non-HTML proofs and pay attention to this one.

For new designers, exporting your graphics and testing them with your HTML page before you go too far with each step is very important. You can create the most beautiful page, but if it cannot be converted to an HTML page, nobody will ever get to enjoy your work. Creating the final appearance takes you longer, but unless you are doing very simple pages, or are a natural Web design genius, building and testing the page a little at a time can save you time and tears in the long run.

I worked out a method that served me well when I was developing my HTML legs. I would do my design in a graphics program and then export the images that I wanted to test. However, I did not always work in an HTML full page. I would often test portions of the images with HTML isolated on a page until I had it down pat. Then I would either paste the new element into my main page, or would redo it, by using the method I had just tested.

Tip

I almost never use my initial development HTML page. No matter how much experience I gather, I am always making slight changes here and there as I create the first HTML page for a site. I tend to put a page together quickly, not worrying too much about meticulous code until I have the page working correctly. (That does not mean I can get away with bad code — it must work. I just save perfection for later.)

Most times, I then start a new page and paste the code onto the new page or redo from scratch. I don't think this ever takes me more than ten minutes to complete, and I know that none of the changes I made as I created the initial page will cause any problems. It is easier to draw a quality line with a pencil when you do it with confidence. Likewise, an HTML page is usually better when you know what you are doing and can "just do it."

Use editor site management tools

If you use an HTML editor that offers site management tools, do not do one more site until you learn how to use the automated management tools confidently. I rely on the editor to keep track of links within my documents and to warn me if I am about to do something that will break a link. All of my life I have wished for a buzzer that would go off when I am about to do something really foolish, so I can stop and think before proceeding. I have yet to find that magic for my entire life, but the site management tools can at least fill that role when I am working on a site. Figure 27-1 shows the Macromedia Dreamweaver warning that appears when a linked file has been changed.

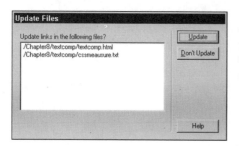

Figure 27-1: In Dreamweaver, changing the name of a file that other files are linked to brings a message and a chance to update those unseen files to the new name.

I do not do much site maintenance, so the automatic synchronization features that are included with the site management tools are usually more work than benefit for me. However, if you are maintaining several sites, I urge you to start using the full spectrum of site management. Also, if you are working with a team with all members using the same editor, synchronization features can save many frustrating errors and prevent one member from overwriting another member's work.

Tip   I have heard from several designers who are at the top of their field and true Web experts who seem to be reluctant to use on-board File Transfer Protocol (FTP) in HTML editors. I don't understand why anyone would use a stand-alone FTP program for transferring HTML pages. There are times when you want more control over how files are transferred using FTP, such as transferring CGI and other scripts. However, for most file transfers, you lose a great deal of timesaving and accuracy power when you do not use the full range of your editor's site management tools, including FTP.

Complete repetitive tasks in assembly-line style

Assembly line work is always faster. I also find that it is also more accurate. It is common that I must scan or optimize many images. Most often, the images provided by the client are from the same source and require similar adjustments. By completing all of the images at one time, you can make the changes very quickly. In fact, if you are using Adobe Photoshop, you can create actions to do many adjustments to an image with one click, if the task is the same for every image. Speed is not the only consideration. If you can do all of the images at the same time, especially if you are using automation to repeat the task, your images will be consistent, which is important to deliver the best look for a site.

You can carry this concept into your HTML editor as well. Check the manual for automation functions that can repeat the same action over and over. In some programs, you can store a set of instructions and "play" that action over anytime, and even share between sites.

Learn to use the Find and Replace feature in your editor. Most HTML editors have very powerful features that can search for a text or code string and replace it with a new one. I have saved hundreds of hours and produced more accurate results, by using automated replacements. Don't restrict this function to correcting errors. I have replaced code that actually added a new tag to every page. Simply specify a "find" code that is unique for the location in the document that you want to make changes in and "replace" it with the original code, plus the new information. This is most effective if you can replace all files in a folder or site, which most current editors can accomplish. Figure 27-2 shows a bullet and space about to be placed in front of a link.

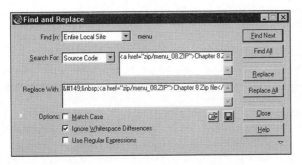

Figure 27-2: Adding a bullet and space to a link throughout a site is lightning fast with the Find and Replace feature in Dreamweaver.

Keep your site folder clean

I may be an office disaster queen, but I take no chances with my site files. When every change must be saved and then transferred to a server to take effect, I learned early that good housekeeping with your files is not only a timesaving necessity, it can also prevent insanity.

The main problem I had as a beginner was creating a mess while I did my technique testing work. As anyone in this industry knows, most skills are learned on the fly. I learned relatively quickly to set up a site completely at the start of a project, complete with folders for images and for any elements that are likely to build a large number of files. But I also always add a "test" folder. When I am wondering what would happen if I used a different mode, or am just not quite certain how I should accomplish a task, I do my work in a separate document and save it to my test folder. That one folder has made a very big difference in how tidy my site files remain, which means I can locate any file very quickly, even months after the last work I did with that project.

I also use a consistent pattern for naming files, and always use the same numbering system if I must produce proof pages for clients or to gather opinions from my discussion groups. For example, I will name my files index.html, index1.html, index2.html, or logo.html, logo1.html, logo2.html. This point is very small, but two factors happen when I use this system. First, alphabetically, logo.html and logo2.html appear together in a file listing. Also, the file naming system is so familiar to me now that the numbered system works better for my recall than sup-posedly "meaningful" file names do, especially if I am returning to the files after a delay.

Clean up your mess

I suspect the fact that I have recently brought three teens to near adulthood is starting to show. But really, really, it is for your own good.

When you are working on HTML files, it is easy to get carried away with the task and to work into the wee hours of the morning to get the page working. By the time you realize that finally, all the pieces have fallen into place, and you have a working page, you are so sick of it that you just yell out whatever your praise phrase is, and call it a wrap. Stop!

Right now is the time to clean up your code. By tomorrow, trust me, what you have done will start to fade, and you will spend a lot more time cleaning up the docu-ment. The same is true for deleting unnecessary files, on both your computer and the server. This can be a cost issue if you have a large site, as most hosts only include a limited amount of storage space. Trying to remember which files can be deleted at a later date is almost impossible, which means you must open each one to determine its value and then repeat the exercise for files on the server. Compare that to a few minutes of deleting as you realize the file is not needed — there is no contest. *Do it now* applies to Web file clean up perfectly.

Now You Can Think about the Bells and Whistles

Hey, wait a minute, Wendy. You just signed off the site. You planned and created and tested and perfected. Now is the time for bells and whistles? What gives?

I suppose this is a little late to present the idea that not all cool things that you can do on a Web page are bad. However, I wanted to cover every topic we had to cover before I brought this subject up — for a very good reason. Many a potentially excel-lent designer has been ruined by chasing after the perks, rather than creating pages that were designed to serve visitor needs.

Actually, you can add some bells and whistles to your pages earlier in the process than this mention implies. I want to warn you to be very careful about the criteria you use to add special techniques to a page. When is the last time you went to a site to play with a special effect? I'm sure you have visited sites to figure out how an effect is accomplished, but I mean to actually *see* the special effect. Most surfers go to a Web site to see the information that is contained within the site. If a special effect helps them to reach that goal, it is a positive addition. Until the structure of your site is established, it is highly unlikely that anything special will be added for any more than novelty value, and because you really want to try a technique.

Weighing the benefits of special effects

How can you tell whether a special effect advances your site? The decision should be made with careful planning and justification as with every other aspect of your site. I want to examine the process of deciding whether a pop-up window or a link that opens in a new window, is a wise way to present information.

When visitors click on a link, the page changes to contain the page indicated by the link. For most page changes on the Web, this method works well and resembles the act of turning pages in a book. When information flows from one main topic to another, plain links perform very well.

But suppose you have a topic that requires additional information for some visitors, but, if included in the page, the information would be a deterrent to a significant number of people who did not need the extra definitions. Suppose as well that each extra piece of information is only a paragraph, or really too short to create a special page with a plain link. You look for a solution to this communication problem, and you will probably soon find that the idea of a small window appears as a solution. The length of the content will lead you to that conclusion. Therefore, a small window is added to the list of requirements for your site.

But how will you present this small window? Remember that only some of your visitors will need the information, so you want to keep it out of the way for those who do not. At the same time, you want it instantly available for those who do need it, so that they can get the supplement without breaking the flow of the main page. A link is the obvious answer and added to the small window requirement, a pop-up window seems to be a reasonable solution.

Before you go to buy a book on JavaScript to create the script for this window or search for a prewritten script to include in your page (make sure you keep copyright notices in free scripts as required), stop for a moment and consider any disadvantages. There are always drawbacks to a technique, but you want to determine if the benefit outweighs the cost.

You use JavaScript to create a pop-up window. Some surfers browse with JavaScript turned off, so those people will not be able to invoke the extra information. People who are new to the Web often find new windows opening very confusing. If you are creating a site that caters to new computer users, you may want to consider bypassing a pop-up window, or creating one that is only open when the mouse is over the window, and automatically closes if it is off. Of course, the same people who would be confused by the extra windows, may become totally lost if windows just up and disappear on them. Pop-up windows are used a lot on high-pressure sales and porn sites, usually without benefit of visitor invitation, but many people hate pop-up windows on general principle.

If you think that I am working to an absolute conclusion as to whether pop-up windows are good or bad, you'll have to think again. I don't have enough information to make that decision. You must take the answers to the questions in the previous paragraph and weave them into the site goals and potential visitor desires and capability (see Chapters 2 and 3). With all aspects of the site and technique in hand, you can then make a decision. My guess is that unless you have extremely new computer users as a main visitor group, given the description of the problem, a pop-up window solution would make an excellent choice.

The yea or nay of the question is not the main value in the pop-up discussion, however. What is important is the process, asking the questions and finding the answers. There is always some compromise when you add anything to a Web page that is not pure HTML. Your job is to know the cost and assume only acceptable losses for the benefits you gain.

Exercise: Determining the Value of a Special Effect

Use the following list of questions only as a guide to help you determine whether a special effect adds or detracts from your page. For some techniques, you may have more questions to ask, and if you are creating effects for a controlled intranet, you may find some questions are irrelevant.

1. What is the special effect you are considering?

2. What is the problem that the special effect will address?

3. How does this special effect solve the problem?

4. List at least three other solutions to this problem.

5. List why the three other options are not as good a solution as the effect you are considering.

6. List any known problems that this effect can cause for browser compatibility (research if necessary).

7. Briefly describe your visitor base and their computer equipment/savvy.

8. How does your visitor capability compare to the problems the effect can cause?

9. Are there any alternate methods to solve this problem that better match visitor needs? (Refer to Questions 4 and 5.)

10. In a sentence or two, explain why the method you have chosen to solve the problem is the best.

Note You may have switched to a different plan after answering Question 9. If so, answer the questions again with the new method as the answer to Question 1.

If the result of this exercise is positive, you can move forward with your effect, knowing that you have included a function that will make your site a better experience for your visitors. When it comes right down to it, isn't that really what Web design is all about?

What You Have Learned and How It Can Be Used

When we were discussing the next project, which led to this book, I made the statement that I was surprised that this book had not already been written. Just before it was complete, when I was running behind schedule and finding the subject the hardest I have hit to cover effectively, I commented that it had not been written because all of the other authors were smarter than me. *This is a tough subject.*

Creating a menu is not a single technique. In fact, it is like stringing beads—each portion of planning, construction, and perfection are the many tiny pieces that all must be placed together in the right order. What a menu is not, is luck. Nor is it an artistic pursuit. If you can work artistic elements into a clear and concise form, you are a skilled designer. Engineers in a car plant must first make a car that will run and be safe, before the aesthetics enter the mix. You must create a menu that is clear and useful before you can indulge in the luxury of art. Too many designers work the opposite way.

The tools are all in this book. You have learned how to identify your products and customers, create a site map, and work with text. You have learned how to use text for attractive and speedy menus. You know how to prepare menus with graphics that work quickly and show up well on the page. And you have gathered some techniques to put all of the previous facets into action.

I like to refer to this book as the *Interface Book with Instructions*, but you know by now that there really is not a clear set of instructions that can be used for a menu. Too many components come from the particular site for which the menu is built. By following the steps and principles in this book, however, you at least have a map to guide you to an effective menu for every site you build. If the site is worth creating, it is worth a good menu.

Practice as much as you can and return to these chapters occasionally as you work through your future projects to make sure you are not wandering from the map. I do occasionally. If I find I am having trouble with a menu, 100 percent of the time when I stop to analyze why, it is because I have not put proper planning into place. Before you bang your head against the wall, browse through the chapters in this book to get you back on track.

Pompoms in Hand, I Send You Off to Menu Excellence

In a class, as long as the teacher is competent and cares that the students learn the material, almost every member of the class leaves the lessons with much the same knowledge. However, some always go on to take the learning to a higher level while others never break the barrier of excellence. Why?

I have spent a lot of time teaching and know that the range of student success after the class ends has nothing to do with talent or learning ability. Without fail, the students who excel with the information I provide in a class have an attitude of success. They are fiercely interested in the subject, hungry for every scrap of knowledge they can find about the topic, and beyond just doing the lessons, they are always watching, observing, and questioning why.

I came to Web design with a lot of graphic experience, but the one area that really mattered — creating menus — was as new to me as it probably is to you. When I created print material, I did not have to figure out how someone was going to get through what I produced. There are standards for print publications, and only so many ways you can create something on paper. While writing this book, I did not need to think too hard about how you would find the information. There are chapter divisions, a table of contents, and an index. You are either reading page after page, or looking subjects up with the reference tools. Not a lot for me to think about beyond the words.

But Web design adds a multidimensional and constantly moving set of options. There are no standards other than common sense to apply to Web menus. Yet nothing is more important. If I must point to one single factor that has led to the success I now enjoy in this field, I would have to point to the effort I put into learning how to create a great menu. My menus today are far simpler and way less fun than they were when I started, and I am proud of that. Ironically, I spend a great deal of time learning the fancy ways to put menus and pages together. I could have saved much learning time had I known then what I do now.

Well, you do know now what I did not know then. Every technique that I use to create a Web menu is contained in this book. Technically, that means that if you absorb what is contained on these pages, you will be creating professional level menus. And I don't say that to make you feel better. It is the truth. I am guessing that you will now start to realize how many bad menus are on the Web. Even more valuable, is that you will start to notice the good menus on the Web. Not because they flash or bop, or are breathtakingly beautiful. You will notice them because they work. In fact, you may not even notice the best until you realize that you have rolled all through the site without even thinking. A site like that is a site worth studying.

It's up to you now. Keep the learning going, perfect your CSS and optimization, and make planning for a Web site as natural as opening your Web editor or graphics program. With a little practice, menus will no longer create stress, but instead will be like a challenging, but achievable puzzle that brings great pleasure to you and each of your visitors once accomplished.

✦   ✦   ✦

What's on the CD-ROM

The CD-ROM included with this book contains all of the images, scripts, and sample files required to complete the exercises discussed in the text of this book, as well as a PDF version of the book for easy viewing on your computer screen with the Adobe Acrobat Reader. The CD-ROM also contains trial versions of the many terrific software programs often used when creating a Web site, including evaluation software from Adobe Systems, JASC Software, Macromedia, and Harrow Productions.

System Requirements

Make sure that your computer meets the minimum system requirements listed in this section. If your computer doesn't match up to most of these requirements, you may have a problem using the contents of the CD-ROM.

For Windows 9x, Windows 2000, Windows NT4 (with SP 4 or later), Windows Me, or Windows XP:

- ✦ PC with a Pentium processor running at 120 Mhz or faster
- ✦ At least 32 MB of total RAM installed on your computer; for best performance, we recommend at least 64 MB
- ✦ A CD-ROM drive

For Macintosh:

- ✦ Mac OS computer with a 68040 or faster processor running OS 7.6 or later
- ✦ At least 32 MB of total RAM installed on your computer; for best performance, we recommend at least 64 MB

Using the CD-ROM with Windows

To install the items from the CD-ROM to your hard drive, follow these steps:

1. Insert the CD into your computer's CD-ROM drive.

2. A window appears with the following options: Install, Explore, eBook, Links, and Exit.

> **Install:** Gives you the option to install the supplied software and/or the author-created samples on the CD-ROM
>
> **Explore:** Allows you to view the contents of the CD-ROM in its directory structure
>
> **eBook:** Allows you to view an electronic version of the book
>
> **Links:** Opens a hyperlinked page of Web sites
>
> **Exit:** Closes the autorun window

If you do not have autorun enabled or if the autorun window does not appear, follow the steps that follow to access the CD-ROM.

1. Click Start ⇨ Run.

2. In the dialog box that appears, type *d*:**setup.exe**, where *d* is the letter of your CD-ROM drive. Doing so opens the autorun window described above.

3. Choose the Install, Explore, eBook, Links, or Exit option from the menu. (See Step 2 in the preceding list for a description of these options.)

Using the CD-ROM with the Mac OS

To install the items from the CD-ROM to your hard drive, follow these steps:

1. Insert the CD into your CD-ROM drive.

2. Double-click the icon for the CD-ROM after it appears on the desktop.

3. Most programs come with installers. Simply open the program's folder on the CD-ROM and double-click the Install or Installer icon.

Note

To install some programs, just drag the program's folder from the CD-ROM window and drop it on your hard drive icon.

What's on the CD-ROM

The following sections provide a summary of the software and other materials you'll find on the CD-ROM.

Exercise files

Often, image files and/or text files are required to complete the exercises discussed in the chapters of this book. Watch for the On the CD-ROM icon throughout the book for notes that tell you which files are required and where to place these files on your hard drive. The exercise files are arranged in folders that correspond to the chapter in which the exercise appears. To install the exercise files, simply copy the appropriate folder that corresponds to the chapter in which the exercise appears to your computer's hard drive. You will also find samples of completed exercises in many folders. Again, watch for the On the CD-ROM icon for completed samples.

 Note   If you have any questions about this book or simply want to follow along with an FAQ created from letters from other readers, you can visit the *Web Menus with Beauty and Brains* resource page at http://www.beauty-and-brains.com.

Template files

In addition to the templates included with the exercises in the book, you will find additional templates for pages containing menus on the CD-ROM. The templates each have their own folder within the Templates folder. Copy the entire folder to your computer and follow the instructions and notes in the Readme file included with each template.

Software programs

Many software programs are required to create a Web site. For example, you must create the images you require in graphics program, such as the programs included in demo format on the CD-ROM included with this book. You must also have an Internet browser, such as Microsoft Internet Explorer or Netscape Navigator to test your pages. This CD-ROM contains a handful of demo versions of useful programs you can use to create your Web pages. To install the demo programs, double-click the install icon located in the software's folder and follow the on-screen prompts.

 Note   When creating Web pages, it's always a good idea to have as many Internet browsers as possible available at your disposal to test and view your work. If you do not already have a copy of Microsoft Internet Explorer and/or Netscape Navigator, these browsers are available for download. Go to www.microsoft.com to download IE 6 and http://home.netscape.com/computing/download/ to download Navigator.

Shareware programs are fully functional, trial versions of copyrighted programs. If you like particular programs, register with their authors for a nominal fee and receive licenses, enhanced versions, and technical support. *Freeware programs* are copyrighted games, applications, and utilities that are free for personal use. Unlike shareware, these programs do not require a fee or provide technical support. *GNU software* is governed by its own license, which is included inside the folder of the GNU product. See the GNU license for more details.

Trial, demo, or evaluation versions are usually limited by time or functionality (such as being unable to save projects). Some trial versions are very sensitive to system date changes. If you alter your computer's date, the programs will time out and will no longer be functional.

Adobe Acrobat Reader

Freeware. The full version of the Adobe Acrobat Reader 5 is included on the CD-ROM, which enables you to view and print PDF (portable document format) files. For more information, visit Adobe at `www.adobe.com/products/acrobat/readstep.html`.

Adobe GoLive

Adobe GoLive is a professional-level HTML editor that has been designed to integrate with other Adobe products, such as Photoshop. A 30-day trial version is included on the CD-ROM. For more information visit Adobe at `www.adobe.com/products/golive/main.html`.

Adobe Photoshop

A trial version of Photoshop 6, the most popular graphics editor among professional designers, is included on the CD-ROM. This powerful program offers image editing and special effects and includes ImageReady 3, a program dedicated to producing images for the Web. Photoshop integrates seamlessly with Adobe GoLive. Note that the tryout version does not enable you to save, export, or print artwork. Adobe will not provide any technical support for the Adobe Photoshop 6.0 tryout. For more information visit Adobe at `www.adobe.com/products/photoshop/main.html`.

Macromedia Dreamweaver

Macromedia Dreamweaver is one of the top HTML editors on the market today and used by many professional designers. Dreamweaver is designed to work easily with other Macromedia products, such as Fireworks and Flash. A trial version is located on the CD-ROM. For more information, visit Macromedia at `www.macromedia.com/software/dreamweaver`.

Macromedia Fireworks

A 30-day, fully functional trial version of Macromedia's specialized Web graphic creation program, Fireworks 4, is available on the CD-ROM. This program integrates seamlessly with Dreamweaver and is powerful and easy to learn. For more information, visit Macromedia at www.macromedia.com/software/fireworks.

Macromedia Flash

Macromedia Flash 5 is another Macromedia product designed for Web development. Try your hand at creating movies for the Web with this full-featured, 30-day trial. For more information, visit Macromedia at www.macromedia.com/software/flash.

JASC Paint Shop Pro

For Windows only. Enjoy a 30-day evaluation version of JASC Paint Shop Pro 7, a powerful, yet easy-to-learn program. This version's price makes it a popular choice for many designers, including professional Web developers. For more information, visit www.jasc.com/products/psp.

Harrow Productions' SWiSH

For Windows only. SWiSH, from Harrow Productions, lets you create complex animations with text, images, and graphics. A 15-day trial version is included on the CD-ROM. For more information, visit www.swishzone.com.

PDF version of the book

Web Menus with Beauty and Brains is available in PDF format on the CD-ROM for easy viewing from your computer screen.

Troubleshooting

If you have difficulty installing or using any of the materials on the companion CD-ROM, try the following solutions:

- ✦ **Turn off any anti-virus software that you may have running.** Installers sometimes mimic virus activity and can make your computer incorrectly believe that a virus is infecting it. (Be sure to turn the anti-virus software back on later.)
- ✦ **Close all running programs.** The more programs you're running, the less memory is available to other programs. Installers also typically update files and programs; if you keep other programs running, installation may not work properly.

✦ **Reference the ReadMe:** Please refer to the ReadMe file located at the root of the CD-ROM for the latest product information at the time of publication.

If you still have trouble with the CD-ROM, please call the Hungry Minds Customer Care phone number: (800) 762-2974. Outside the United States, call 1 (317) 572-3994. You can also contact Hungry Minds Customer Service by e-mail at techsupdum@ hungryminds.com. Hungry Minds will provide technical support only for installation and other general quality control items; for technical support on the applications themselves, consult the program's vendor or author.

✦   ✦   ✦

Index

Hungry Minds, Inc.
End-User License Agreement

4. Restrictions on Use of Individual Programs. You must follow the individual requirements and restrictions detailed for each individual program in the appendix of this Book. These limitations are also contained in the individual license agreements recorded on the Software Media. These limitations may include a requirement that after using the program for a specified period of time, the user must pay a registration fee or discontinue use. By opening the Software packet(s), you will be agreeing to abide by the licenses and restrictions for these individual programs that are detailed in the appendix and on the Software Media. None of the material on this Software Media or listed in this Book may ever be redistributed, in original or modified form, for commercial purposes.

5. Limited Warranty.

   (a) HMI warrants that the Software and Software Media are free from defects in materials and workmanship under normal use for a period of sixty (60) days from the date of purchase of this Book. If HMI receives notification within the warranty period of defects in materials or workmanship, HMI will replace the defective Software Media.

   (b) HMI AND THE AUTHOR OF THE BOOK DISCLAIM ALL OTHER WARRANTIES, EXPRESS OR IMPLIED, INCLUDING WITHOUT LIMITATION IMPLIED WARRANTIES OF MERCHANTABILITY AND FITNESS FOR A PARTICULAR PURPOSE, WITH RESPECT TO THE SOFTWARE, THE PROGRAMS, THE SOURCE CODE CONTAINED THEREIN, AND/OR THE TECHNIQUES DESCRIBED IN THIS BOOK. HMI DOES NOT WARRANT THAT THE FUNCTIONS CONTAINED IN THE SOFTWARE WILL MEET YOUR REQUIREMENTS OR THAT THE OPERATION OF THE SOFTWARE WILL BE ERROR FREE.

   (c) This limited warranty gives you specific legal rights, and you may have other rights that vary from jurisdiction to jurisdiction.

6. Remedies.

   (a) HMI's entire liability and your exclusive remedy for defects in materials and workmanship shall be limited to replacement of the Software Media, which may be returned to HMI with a copy of your receipt at the following address: Software Media Fulfillment Department, Attn.: *Web Menus with Beauty and Brains*, Hungry Minds, Inc., 10475 Crosspoint Blvd., Indianapolis, IN 46256, or call 1-800-762-2974. Please allow four to six weeks for delivery. This Limited Warranty is void if failure of the Software Media has resulted from accident, abuse, or misapplication. Any replacement Software Media will be warranted for the remainder of the original warranty period or thirty (30) days, whichever is longer.

(b) In no event shall HMI or the author be liable for any damages whatsoever (including without limitation damages for loss of business profits, business interruption, loss of business information, or any other pecuniary loss) arising from the use of or inability to use the Book or the Software, even if HMI has been advised of the possibility of such damages.

(c) Because some jurisdictions do not allow the exclusion or limitation of liability for consequential or incidental damages, the above limitation or exclusion may not apply to you.

7. **U.S. Government Restricted Rights.** Use, duplication, or disclosure of the Software for or on behalf of the United States of America, its agencies and/or instrumentalities (the "U.S. Government") is subject to restrictions as stated in paragraph (c)(1)(ii) of the Rights in Technical Data and Computer Software clause of DFARS 252.227-7013, or subparagraphs (c) (1) and (2) of the Commercial Computer Software - Restricted Rights clause at FAR 52.227-19, and in similar clauses in the NASA FAR supplement, as applicable.

8. **General.** This Agreement constitutes the entire understanding of the parties and revokes and supersedes all prior agreements, oral or written, between them and may not be modified or amended except in a writing signed by both parties hereto that specifically refers to this Agreement. This Agreement shall take precedence over any other documents that may be in conflict herewith. If any one or more provisions contained in this Agreement are held by any court or tribunal to be invalid, illegal, or otherwise unenforceable, each and every other provision shall remain in full force and effect.